7.15

W9-CDT-956

WITHDRAWN

MOB COP

MOB COP

MY LIFE OF CRIME IN THE
CHICAGO POLICE DEPARTMENT

FRED PASCENTE
WITH SAM REAVES

CHICAGO
REVIEW
PRESS

Copyright © 2015 by Fred Pascente and Sam Reaves
All rights reserved
Published by Chicago Review Press Incorporated
814 North Franklin Street
Chicago, Illinois 60610
ISBN 978-1-61373-134-5

Library of Congress Cataloging-in-Publication Data
Pascente, Fred, 1942–2014.
  Mob cop : my life of crime in the Chicago Police Department / Fred Pascente,
Sam Reaves.
       pages cm
 Summary: "The tell-all memoir of a Chicago police officer and mafia associate
who played both sides of the law"— Provided by publisher.
 Includes bibliographical references.
 ISBN 978-1-61373-134-5 (hardback)
 1. Pascente, Fred, 1942–2014. 2. Chicago (Ill.). Police Department—Corrupt
practices. 3. Police—Illinois—Chicago—Biography. 4. Police corruption—
Illinois—Chicago. 5. Organized crime—Illinois—Chicago. I. Reaves, Sam,
1954– II. Title.

 HV7911.P366A3 2015
 364.1092—dc23
 [B]

                              2015002298

Interior design: PerfecType, Nashville, TN

Printed in the United States of America
5 4 3 2 1

To my father, who would not approve of this at all.
And I apologize, because I know you're in heaven.

CONTENTS

THERE YOU GO

The calls came at three in the morning sometimes, the bleating of the phone tearing Fred Pascente out of a deep sleep. Those were the hard ones, the ones that got him out of his bed in a bungalow on a quiet street in Melrose Park, Illinois, a blue-collar town on the western fringe of Chicago. The hardest were the ones that took him out into the dead of a bitter winter night, a harsh wind in his face and hundreds of miles ahead of him.

Other times the calls interrupted dinner or deep-sixed plans for an evening on the town with May, his wife. They took him away from family celebrations and card games; they cut short shopping trips and movie outings. When the calls came it was drop-everything time, and the cell phone was always on.

When the calls came, it meant somebody somewhere needed something and needed it now. Fred Pascente climbed into his well-traveled Chevy Silverado and drove. Sometimes the first stop was O'Hare or Midway to meet a flight; he had Homeland Security clearance for *access to secure parts of both airports. Often it was a hospital: Loyola Medical Center in Maywood, just down the road from his house, or one of the cluster of institutions in the Illinois Medical District, a massive hospital complex on Chicago's Near West Side that looms over the old Italian neighborhood on Taylor Street.*

Occasionally there was time to grab a cup of coffee or a sandwich; often there was no time to do anything but jump on the expressway and get there, fast. And sometimes it was hurry up and wait, stand around and banter with the security guard while a team of doctors packed up something that would save a patient's life in Minneapolis or St. Louis.

The security guards liked him. Fred was good at the banter, the jokes and the jibes and the bullshit—he'd been doing it all his life. Fred Pascente still moved like the athlete he'd been in his youth, a big man and still robust, curly black hair gone mostly gray and face filled out, carrying the weight from a lifetime of good Italian cooking but carrying it well. He liked to laugh and to make other people laugh; make him wait by the door with the security guard and in two minutes he'd make a new friend.

Fred Pascente was an independent hauler of emergency freight. Working mainly for a courier company based in Rosemont, Illinois, hard by O'Hare, he was on call from nine at night to six in the morning, six or sometimes seven days a week, to deliver medicines, freshly harvested organs, whatever needed to get from Chicago to somewhere else, usually in the Midwest but sometimes as far away as New Jersey. He delivered vital parts to a Lear jet stranded on the tarmac in Cincinnati and isotopes for surgery to a hospital in Madison, Wisconsin.

He got paid per job plus mileage and expenses; he made a good check. He needed it. At seventy-two Fred Pascente was still a 1099er, hustling to make the nut. His kids were grown, but there was a wife to support, a mortgage to pay, and repairs to make, grandkids to buy presents for, friends to buy drinks for. And there was no pension and never would be.

THERE YOU GO

The pension was supposed to come after a twenty-six-year career as a Chicago police officer, but it went up in smoke when a pension board ruled that a man who did the things Fred did doesn't deserve to retire on the taxpayer dime. If you asked Fred what those things were, he'd tell you. Fred wouldn't give you excuses. What he did, he did, and that's why he was out there on the road at seventy-two years old instead of in a beachside condo in Florida or a house on the edge of a golf course in Vegas.

Las Vegas was another thing that had gone up in smoke; Fred spent a lot of time in Vegas over the years, but that was all over. The people that run Nevada have certain standards to maintain, and some years ago they were persuaded that Fred Pascente failed to meet them. Nevada officials keep something called the Black Book. You won't find a copy at the library, but you can see it online. Its official name is the Excluded Person List of the Nevada State Gaming Control Board, and you can find it on the GCB's website. If you went to the Excluded Persons page and scrolled down a few rows, you'd see Fred Pascente's photo there. This is the list of people who are banned for life from entering any casino in the State of Nevada. They would commit a felony by doing so, and a casino that fails to report the presence of a listed individual on its premises will be sanctioned.

Out of all the wiseguys, card counters, and slot cheats in the country, the Black Book currently lists just over thirty people, making it a very exclusive club—more exclusive than the United States Senate, as Fred liked to point out. Past honorees, now deceased, include names a lot better known than Fred's: Giancana, Caifano, Spilotro. Pride isn't exactly the word for what Fred felt about his listing, but in the circles he moved in for much of his life, it was a mark of distinction.

It wasn't the only one in Fred's life. There were also the police department commendations: for breaking up a rape in progress or nabbing a prolific North Side burglar. There was the write-up in Gay Life *magazine for collaring a predator who had been drugging and* robbing gay men in Chicago and other cities across the country. Those awards tend to complicate a person's attitude toward Fred Pascente just a little. We like to think that the line is sharp and clear between good guys and bad guys, white hats and black hats, cops and crooks. Fred's career says otherwise.

"He's a scumbag," said a veteran Chicago law enforcement figure, a longtime organized crime foe with no sympathy for wiseguys. "He's a nice guy," said another retired copper, equally straight but perhaps a little more willing to separate professional from personal criteria. Comments posted on Second City Cop, a blog on Chicago police affairs, were split: "Fred was a good detective with a dogged determination to lock up bad guys," read one comment. Another responded: "If we looked at those arrest reports of yore I'm sure the bad guys were just fellow hoods taking away business from the guys Freddie was looking out for." Ambivalence reigned in Fred's career: in the game of cops and robbers he was both a cop and a robber.

The ambivalence is a crucial part of Fred's story. From its earliest days, Chicago was the kind of town where you couldn't always tell the cops from the crooks. If people can't quite make up their minds about Fred Pascente, it's because Chicago couldn't ever quite make up its mind about the mob.

Fred Pascente's story tracks the waning years of the greatest criminal empire in American history. Fred had a role in that empire, and if it wasn't a starring role it was an instructive one. Not everybody in the mob can be a boss, and not everybody needs to be a killer. The business of organized crime, like any other, requires role players and specialists and guys who are willing to put in the hours. You could say Fred was a specialist. One thing the mob can always use is a discreet copper or two.

But Fred's story tracks more than developments in criminology and sociology. It's a story about good and bad people and the good and bad choices one person can make. It's a tale of moral failure, bad judgment, callousness, and greed. But there's also loyalty, generosity, *and frequent outbreaks of goodwill. Fred's ethical system had holes in it you could drive a truckload of stolen whiskey through, but if you didn't hit the hole, you'd have a fight on your hands. It's easy to disapprove of Fred, but it's hard not to like him. Getting to know Fred Pascente means learning that people are complicated, even if the Ten Commandments are simple.*

If passing judgment on Fred Pascente is easy, understanding him is a little tougher. To make a start, you could do worse than just listen to him as he rolls across the vast flat heartland, lights passing in the dark, talking about things that happened a long time ago in a very different Chicago.

∽

The Feast of St. Rocco was big. It was a weeklong festival. St. Rocco's statue would come around through the streets, and your dad would pick you up and you'd put money on it. The band would come around—they were always out of tune, but they would be marching. We loved it.

The feast was a moneymaker for the church. The people that wanted to put up concession stands had to pay, so much to the priest. The guy who put the roast beef sandwiches together, he had to pay. The pizza guy, the hot dogs, the stand to play cards or toss rings, the rides that come from the carnival, they had to pay. And they couldn't overcharge. The priest would tell them, "This is what you charge these people."

Father Broccolo was a greaseball. When I say greaseball, that's not to be offensive—it just means he was from the Old Country. He was a handsome man, with a full head of black hair. He was a nicely built guy. He would sing at parties, and he thought he was Dean Martin, and who knows if he didn't try to hit on any of the women. Everyone loved him.

The priest would organize grease pole races. Louie DeMarco and his son were carpenters and handymen. They took two wooden poles and sanded them till they were almost white. And then they would set them up on an incline and grease them. And we would race to see who could climb up the poles the fastest.

Everybody that served a Mass, the altar boys, they were in the races if they wanted to be. But if you were flunking a grade, you were out. You had to have high marks in school to do this. Me and my friend Sammy Gambino would win most of the races. Sammy would race this guy, I'd race that guy; we'd do five races, and then they'd switch. We'd finish covered in grease. The clothes we threw away. I couldn't get that smell off for months. My mother would scrub, but it got in there.

My uncle Sam gave me the trick. He says, "I'll give you the shoes. They're gonna be too big, but we'll put paper in there, we'll make 'em fit." He had these shoes that were pointed. You could kill a cockroach in the corner. And those would stick, grab hold. "And your nails. From now, you don't trim your nails."

Guys would bet on the races. "All right, who do you want? I'll take that skinny guy." This was among the guys who wanted to bet—the church didn't sanction it. And if you wanted to get into the betting circle, they had to know you. But they bet. Twenty, fifty, a hundred bucks on this guy.

Father Broccolo promised all the racers that after the feast broke up he would give us all five dollars each and a spaghetti dinner. So after the feast broke up we went and asked him for the money. He says, with that greaseball accent, "Now, boys. You boys did a good job for the parish, for the church. And this izza sad, but I gotta tell you, I can't-a give you the five dollars."

And I'm dying. I'm waiting for this five dollars.

"But we'll make it up next year."

Well, next year I ain't gonna be in this. And where are you gonna make it up?

"We gonna have the spaghetti and the sausage and the meatball dinner, it'll be nice fun, but we have many poor people . . ."

Who the hell is poorer than us?

"Oh, please-a forgive . . . I love you boys."

Love you boys? What about the five dollars?

To me, he was a con man. He stiffed us. We're talking about maybe a hundred bucks. What's that to him? He made a lot of money. You don't stiff the kids. Stiff anybody, but don't stiff the kids. I was bitter.

So then we're going around, complaining, making noise, and who comes over but Johnny Bananas. This was John DeBiase, my grandmother's cousin. He was the boss of our neighborhood. He gave them all their jobs, the Outfit guys. They all worked for him.

Bananas comes over, he says, "What's wrong with you guys?"

I says, "That m—"

"Don't talk that way about the priest. What's wrong with you?"

"He didn't give us the money he promised."

"How much money?"

"Five dollars, each guy."

"Leave the priest alone. I'll take care of you guys." So he gets Bosco. Bosco was his heavy guy, his runner. He says, "Bosco." He takes three fifties, he says, "Go getta this changed, all five-dollar bills." Gave him three fifties. I'll never forget it. He took care of it.

And the priest was embarrassed. But he should have given it to us. And who gives it to us? These criminals gave us the money. And there you go.

2

PARADISE

In 1830 Chicago was a muddy nowhere of a frontier outpost in a swamp on the shore of a vast lake. At a time when the river towns of Cincinnati and St. Louis were thriving metropolises, Chicago had a population of about three hundred rogues and villains, not counting a few demoralized Indians.

The railroads changed all that. A scant thirty years later, the time it takes a man to lose his illusions and gain a paunch, Chicago hosted the convention that chose Abraham Lincoln as the Republican candidate for president. By that time it had metastasized into a city of about a hundred thousand. The rogues and villains had been joined by the land speculators and their hangers-on in one of the greatest boomtown explosions in history.

A city growing at that rate does not grow rationally or under any kind of administrative order. Things get done in a haphazard and ad hoc way, with many palms greased and no corner left uncut. The rogues and villains tend to rise to the top. And boomtowns are *thriving markets for vice: Chicago's saloons, gambling dens, and brothels were legendary.*

Next came the Civil War, with the usual economic benefits for a city fortunate enough to lie far from the battlefields. Chicago prospered from the carnage. A few years later an apocalyptic fire wiped out the heart of the city, providing a clean slate for infrastructure upgrades and the biggest building boom yet. The political infrastructure for the necessary sweetheart deals and breakneck speculation was already in place.

As the nation lurched toward big-power status, Chicago's gravitational pull on fortune seekers, refugees, and cheap labor increased. Immigrants fleeing the feudal society of southern Italy, with its patron-client relations, tight kinship bonds, and mistrust of remote authority, found Chicago's political culture oddly familiar. The ward heeler with his favors to dispense was somebody they had seen before.

The Italians settled in the "river wards" on the fringes of the central city, replacing the Irish, Germans, and Swedes who were moving up the economic ladder. On Taylor Street and Grand Avenue on the Near West Side and along Twenty-Sixth Street to the south, they created something approximating the village culture they had left behind: insular, closely knit neighborhoods held together by family ties and a common origin. Those neighborhoods came to be known collectively as "the Patch," shorthand for the tough Italian districts where the writ of law did not always run.

The rule of law was never strong in Chicago, and the Italians had little experience of it in their past. They adapted to their surroundings and began, like all immigrant communities, to assimilate. Poor, Catholic, and clannish, they were not encouraged in the process. A minority of them inevitably prospered in the less legitimate sectors of the economy. By the time Prohibition made an outlaw of anybody from a wine-drinking culture and exponentially multiplied the returns on ruthlessness, the elements were in place for the establishment of the most enduring and politically best-connected crime syndicate in American history.

In Chicago they call it the Outfit.

❧

I was born to Rocco and Edna Pascente in 1942. My mom and dad were born here, but their parents were born in the Old Country. They were from a region called Basilicata, which is south of Naples. It's a mountain region near the Gulf of Salerno.

There were lots of Italians in Chicago at that time. Each neighborhood had its own parish. There was St. Callistus, there was Mother Cabrini, all Italian. Ours was the Most Precious Blood, on Congress Parkway where the expressway is now, and Western Avenue. We all went to Catholic schools. Immigrants were still coming. In our neighborhood, the Gismondos were from the Old Country. They were nice kids—we used to play with them. The brothers were Alfio, Italo, Mario . . . and Pete. We always used to say, "Pete, how did you get in this family?"

My dad was an educated guy. He went to Marshall High School, which back then was a great school, and he had a couple of years of college. He was an intelligent guy, an influential guy, a sharp dresser. My father was an accountant. He was a bank examiner who worked for the Auditor of Public Accounts. That was a big thing then, especially for our neighborhood. They called my dad "the Mayor." He did books for everybody—did their taxes, took them to the Bureau of Vital Statistics, got their licenses. He did everything for people.

My mom loved her kids more than anything. This was a saint. She also took care of her mother and father, who lived in our house. My grandfather worked on the railroad, which wasn't far from the neighborhood. He used to ride the streetcar to work. My grandfather was not educated, but he was smart. And cool—slow, calculating, I never heard him swear. He always sat at the table in the kitchen, his chair, and he had a hat on, one of those old fedoras, drinking wine and smoking his Parodis.

Let me tell you how good my grandmother was. There was a Mexican family that lived across the street, the only Mexican family in a neighborhood of Italians and some Irish. The husband went to jail; I never knew why. But my grandmother would make dinner for them every night. The wife was too proud to go collect aid, but my grandmother took them in.

My father had six brothers. My father's brothers were not book smart like him, but they were successful. My favorite was Uncle Sam. He lived with my other grandmother only a block away. He was divorced, which was a no-no. But he had a heart of gold. He was a handsome guy, with black hair. He would flirt and flatter all the women, especially the good-looking ones. He'd tell stories, and he was funny. I would be excited to see him, listen to his war stories—Uncle Sam had been in the Pacific during World War II. He was always in trouble. He gambled, he played the horses. He'd come by the house and my father would give him money and holler at him.

Uncle Sam was a joker. One time my grandfather who lived with us was waiting for some wine. He had a friend who made wine at his house. The way my grandfather described it, nobody made it like him. He would brag to my uncle Sam, with that accent, "Goombah Luke, he's make the best wine in the whole world. There ain't a better wine on Hurt." Not "Earth," "Hurt." So he's waiting for weeks for this wine. And that's all he talked about: "The wine, the wine . . ."

Sam wanted to get my grandfather. But he wouldn't do it without consulting with my dad, because my father was the head guy

II

in the family. So Sam tells my father, "I'm gonna get him. Goombah Luke dropped the wine off by me. I got it stashed in the garage." And he tells him what he wants to do.

My dad was a joker, too. So he says, "OK, but if it gets serious, I'm not taking the rap."

So my grandfather's shopping with my gram and my mother. And my father and Sam get to work. In place of the wine, they fill some bottles with grape juice.

My grandfather comes home. Sam says, "Goombah Luke dropped the wine off."

"Oh, the wine is here! The wine, the wine is here!"

My uncle says, "I'll get it." He goes to the garage. And my grandfather was watching. He couldn't wait. My uncle comes walking out on the path from the garage with the bottles, and then he just dropped them, both of them at once. They broke all over.

My grandfather is crying. "You . . ."

I said, "Tell him! Please, tell him!" If you saw his face when he broke the wine . . . I'm laughing and crying at the same time.

&

My father was not a tough guy. He was in a bowling league. Now, I want to see the mobster that bowls. They'll use a bowling ball on a guy's head, but they're not bowlers. Still, the Outfit guys in the neighborhood respected my dad—they all came to him for favors from the ward committeeman or just to do their income taxes. Joe Pettit, the Caifano brothers . . . My dad loved the Caifano family. They were really good to him, and he was good to them. They all loved my father.

&

PARADISE

The Caifano brothers were Taylor Street boys who had come up out of the old 42 Gang, a band of juvenile delinquents that had run riot in the Patch in the 1920s and '30s. The 42ers were so precocious that an entire cohort was recruited into the Outfit and by the 1950s they had risen to leadership positions. Notable alumni of the 42 Gang included Sam Giancana, Milwaukee Phil Alderisio, and the Caifanos: Rocco, Leonard, and Marshall.

Rocco, or "Rocky," was the eldest and perhaps the wisest; he managed not to leave much of a mark as a criminal. The same cannot be said of his younger brothers. Leonard "Fat Lenny" Caifano's career was cut short in 1951, when he was shot dead by the bodyguard of a South Side "policy king" during the Outfit takeover, masterminded by Sam Giancana, of the area's black-run gambling racket. Marshall, a feared killer, would survive to become the Outfit's principal overseer in Las Vegas.

⌒

When guys came over I would stay close, because they'd see me hanging around—they'd throw me money. One time I overheard my dad talking with Rocky Caifano, Marshall's older brother. My dad was real close with Rocky. Marshall was the big guy, who made a name for himself in the Outfit. But Rocky was the fire. He was the toughest of all of them. I'm listening, and my dad's telling Rocky, "Rock, you're smarter than all them guys. I told your brother, I'm telling you. Don't mess with the black people. Stay with your own. Don't mess with them."

Marshall Caifano was with Sam Giancana. Giancana was trying to muscle in on a black guy named Teddy Roe, because Giancana knew he and his guys were making big money with the policy racket. All they did was play the numbers, like the lottery. They'd take a penny bet, a nickel bet. But they were making lots of money. So Giancana tried to wrap up the blacks. He took Fat Leonard Caifano with him, because Leonard was a shooter, and they tried to kidnap Teddy Roe. And Fat Lenny got killed by Roe's bodyguard. The guy that killed him was a policeman, on the payroll working for Teddy Roe.

My father knew: don't mess with them. If they had listened to him, Lenny wouldn't have got killed.

⁓

I also knew Joe Pettit through my dad. Joe was tight with the 42 Gang guys—that's the neighborhood he was from. And he was a big bookmaker, a well-liked guy. My dad got him out of trouble once. There was a place on the West Side, the Paradise Ballroom. It was at Crawford, which is now Pulaski, and Madison. This was the place to go. It had dancing and the best bands. You didn't want to miss that place, because this was where you met the girls, this was where it happened. Well, Joe and his brother Larry and Marshall and Rocky Caifano, they had a fight. A bad fight. The owners were nobody to mess with, either, and they barred these guys out. They can't go there anymore. It's all over.

They came crying by my dad. I was in the house. "Rocco, please. You gotta get us back in there."

My dad says, "What the heck? You guys threw the joint up for grabs."

"Rocco, please. You gotta get us back in there. Can't you help us out? This is the place to go."

My dad was almost crying, to beg these guys to leave him alone. But he liked them. Finally he says, "OK, let me go talk to a guy."

He went to a guy by the name of Sam "Teets" Battaglia, an old 42 guy. Our neighbor Chuckie Nicoletti took him. My dad tells Battaglia, "Sam, for me. I need the favor. These guys are good boys to me."

And he got them in. He came back, he says to Joe Pettit, "That's the end of it. Behave yourselves."

And Joe never forgot. He told me once, "Here's what they thought of your father: 'Rocco was not a tough man, but the tough did not fuck with Rocco.'"

~

They didn't fuck with him, but that didn't mean they always saw eye-to-eye. My father always talked about one election that happened when I was little, in 1944. It showed him how these guys played hardball.

My father was a Republican. He worked for Bill Parrillo, the former head of the Illinois Commerce Commission and the Republican Party committeeman for our ward, the Twenty-Fifth. Parrillo was a legitimate, straight-shooting guy. He had a dairy company, Meadowmoor Dairy, which was huge. My father did the books for them.

Parrillo wouldn't go along and play ball with nobody. The Outfit couldn't control him, because he had too much money—he didn't need these Outfit guys. So they wanted Parrillo out. They wanted their guy, named Andy Flando, as ward committeeman. Flando you could play ball with.

To keep Parrillo from winning, Outfit guys went to their own neighborhoods and made sure that all the precinct workers did what they wanted. Some got beatings; others were threatened. The Outfit knew all the precinct guys. They targeted a dozen of them, key guys. And my father was one of the targets. They leaned on him, told him to stay away from the polls. But the voters kept coming in, voting big anyway, because he'd already been promoting them for weeks. So Parrillo won my dad's precincts, at least. But Flando won the seat.

And when Parrillo got voted out, he lost control of a lot of jobs to Flando. So a lot of people switched over to the Democrats, because they controlled everything else in the ward. They weren't bad guys—they just went with the strength. They tried to get my father to go with them, but my father was too loyal to Parrillo. He wouldn't switch.

⌇

William Parrillo may have been a legitimate guy, but he owed much of his success to a client of his legal practice back in the 1930s, a hustling entrepreneur by the name of Al Capone. Meadowmoor Dairy was actually a Capone front operation designed to undercut the city's reigning milk cartel and get cheaper Wisconsin milk into the city. The milk drivers' union cried foul and resorted to the standard union tactics of bombing and slugging to hamstring the new competitor, but that was playing to Capone's strong suit; he had his own pet branch of the Teamsters to deliver Meadowmoor's milk. In the ensuing milk wars, both sides claimed to be protecting the public against "racketeers," while Depression-stricken housewives merely rooted for affordable milk.

As a reward for representing Meadowmoor in the legal battles that finally did in the opposing cartel, William Parrillo was granted ownership of the dairy by a grateful Capone.

As for Andrew Flando, the Chicago Tribune, *in a February 8, 1952, article on mob involvement in ward politics, described him as "an intimate of the Accardo mansion" and reported that he had been installed and later deposed as Republican committeeman of the Twenty-Fifth Ward by Tony Accardo himself, "the No. 2 boss of the Mafia in Chicago."*

⌇

PARADISE

With my dad I would go to Little Jack's out on the West Side at Madison and Kedzie. Little Jack's was the best Jewish deli in the world. I don't care about New York, Little Jack's was the best. They had the best cheesecake anywhere. One time in Little Jack's Mike Gargano was sitting with my father. Mike Gargano was the toughest guy you ever met. I was six, seven years old, and I was eating my cheesecake, loving it. A guy sat down nearby, a stranger. He was a scary guy with a scar on his face. And I stopped eating my cheesecake and shrank back, hiding behind my dad.

Gargano says, "Yo. What's wrong, Fred?"

"I don't want him to see me, that scary guy over there."

And I'll never forget it, this was a lesson. Gargano says, "Freddy"—making sure the guy heard it—"don't worry about the guy with the scars. Worry about the guy that give him the scars."

My father loved those guys, but he always told us kids to stay away from them. My uncle Sam would argue with him about it. When my dad warned us to stay away from Chuck Nicoletti, Sam told him, "This is a neighborhood guy—he's not going to bother the kids."

I liked the bad guys more than the good guys.

༄

Chicago of the 1940s versus today? It was night and day. To me it was paradise. No air conditioning, no television. At night the visitors were on the front porch, talking and laughing. My grandmother would send us to the watermelon stand for pieces of watermelon. There was no big monster supermarket. Every corner had a grocery store. We'd go all over—the barbershop, the florist, the glass man. The neighborhood was full of shops, and you knew all the owners.

We didn't have a lot of money; we didn't have expensive pleasures. A big score was going to see Buckingham Fountain. We'd
go to the drive-in with whoever had a car, we'd pile in. It didn't
matter who went with who, it was just for fun, to watch the movie.
The lake was beautiful. To go down there was heaven. Grand Avenue beach was like an oasis. My father would buy up a catch of
smelts from a fisherman. We'd bring the smelts home, my grandmother would cook them. And she'd make a *cicoria* salad, which is
dandelion leaves, and we'd have pop. That was a treat.

At Halloween we'd come home with bags full of stuff. We
didn't go buy costumes. We made our own. We took the cork out
of a Pepsi-Cola cap and burned it, to make our own makeup. We'd
rip a shirt, we covered our faces up. Who's a monster, who's this?
Cheap.

I mentioned one of our neighbors was Chuck Nicoletti. Chuckie
was a dapper guy, handsome. And he gave a quarter to all the kids.
You know what a quarter was in those days? I can't tell you how
many trips I made. I changed my costume, and he'd look at me . . .
After the fourth time he says, "You were here already."

I says, "No, that was my brother."

"Well how'd you know it was your brother that was here? It
was you."

He was an Outfit guy, Milwaukee Phil Alderisio's partner. We
didn't know it when we were kids, but they were a hit squad.
They were feared. But we didn't know any of that.

༄

*Alderisio and Nicoletti were a team, like Abbott and Costello, Mar-
tin and Lewis, Rowan and Martin. But nobody laughed. In the 1950s
and '60s, Milwaukee Phil Alderisio and Chuck Nicoletti were the
Outfit's executioners.*

"That was the front-office team," says Chicago Crime Commission executive vice president Arthur Bilek, who tracked them as an investigator for the state's attorney's office at the time. "There were other hit men for crew bosses, but these guys were the heavy team." Sources vary and attributions are shaky, but both were certainly well into double figures in the business of sanctioned Outfit hits.

And business it was. Professionals don't fire wildly into crowds or loose off shots from moving vehicles. They stalk their victims with patience and make careful arrangements for Judases to plant kisses on their cheeks. They don't leave prints. They never get caught with the gun, and they never brag.

Professionals have the tools: in 1962 Alderisio and Nicoletti were arrested while staking out a victim in a specially modified Ford sedan. Registered to a fictitious name with an address that proved to be a vacant lot, the car featured switches under the dashboard to turn off the taillights and to open a hidden compartment with brackets for storing firearms. In the absence of a statute prohibiting such modifications, Alderisio and Nicoletti were released without charges.

Alderisio had wavy gray hair and eyebrows still fiercely black, a cleft chin with five o'clock shadow, a rough blue-collar look despite the fine suits he sported. Nicoletti was the handsome one, with square-jawed leading-man looks. A 1968 Chicago police mug shot shows him smiling urbanely into the camera; he could be a successful middle-aged executive in a corporate prospectus.

He smiled because he knew nobody was going to send him to prison; in Outfit hits convictions were next to nonexistent. Intimidated witnesses, paid-off cops, and bought judges made for a congenial work environment. For Alderisio and Nicoletti, killing was just a business technique.

What does it take to produce a man for whom shotgunning another man to death means no more than signing a promissory note or hiring a new secretary? Ignored in the glamorization of organized crime is the extent of the misery, abuse, and despair necessary to turn a boy into a stone killer. In 1929 twelve-year-old Charles Nicoletti killed his father to stop him from beating his mother in a drunken rage. It was ruled a justifiable homicide—the first, last, and only one of Nicoletti's career.

~

We played ball in the streets. One morning I hit a baseball right through Chuck Nicoletti's window. We panicked; we got ready for the worst. Instead Chuck came down—I remember he was unshaven, and he had his pajama bottoms and slippers on—and he goes, "Why don't you guys go to the park?" Real soft.

"But we live over here."

"Yeah, but the park is nice." He says, "Come on. I got an idea. All of yous jump in the car." He had a brand-new Packard. We get in the car—who's sitting on the floor, who's on the seat.

"Man, this is cool. Look at this car!"

He put on the radio: "I got a radio."

"Oh, all right!"

He pulls up by the store, he buys us two new softballs and two new bats. He says, "Here, I'm gonna drive you by the park." He drives us to the park. "Play here."

He's gone. I says, "Tomorrow, we'll do it again, he's gonna give us some more bats and balls."

When my father found out about it, he was like, "Why'd you go by that guy?" He put his foot down. No more playing in the street.

3

TROUBLE IN PARADISE

We lived just a couple of blocks north of Taylor Street, at Lexington and Western. Our neighborhood was pretty much blue-collar, hardworking people. In these neighborhoods, any problem, the police were very seldom called. Everything would be squared away in an informal chat. If a guy broke into a house, they'd settle it. But that was rare—burglary almost never happened by us. People drank, they had their vices. But there was no junk, no dope. That was forbidden.

꧂

More than half of all Americans now live in the suburbs. Most residents of Yonkers or Bloomfield Hills or Park Ridge or Glendale are two generations removed from the world of the old ethnic urban neigh-borhood, with its homogeneity, density, and insularity. Twenty-first-century Americans don't live on the street. They live in a network of dedicated spaces—homes, schools, shopping malls—connected by the automobile. The street is a way to get from one environment to another instead of an environment in its own right. The neighborhood is a real estate agent's label.

Before the suburban migration, the neighborhood was a village. It had borders and nerve centers and a heart. It had history and tradi-tions; it had heroes and villains and cranks. It was a refuge and a redoubt.

If the neighborhood was a refuge, it was due less to formal insti-tutions than to a sort of tribal solidarity that is millennia old. The urban environment was chaotic, throwing diverse groups together in competition for economic resources and, particularly in Chicago, failing to provide consistent, impartial enforcement of the law. The resulting evolution of informally enforced territoriality produced what sociologists call "defended neighborhoods," in which young males on street corners or cruising in cars provided eyes, ears, and when neces-sary muscle against outsiders.

Inevitably, the muscle found other uses. Criminal enterprises spotted people with the talents they needed and recruited them. A symbiotic relationship evolved between the neighborhood and its criminals, the community grateful for safe streets and conceding a certain legitimacy to the criminals in return. Some considered it a good bargain; some didn't.

༄

One time a little girl was raped in our neighborhood. She was just visiting, and she was in the wrong place at the wrong time. The police were all over. And they said in their description that the guy was Hispanic. So some guys went out like a hunting party and caught a Puerto Rican. This was the first Hispanic they came across, walking in the neighborhood. And they killed him. They hung him from a garage and left him. This guy that got killed wasn't even the guy that did it. Maniacs. That's the way the neighborhood was. The police never did solve it.

I was walking to church one day. I served Mass as an altar boy, and I would walk through the alley. I see a guy lying there. His head was blown off. You couldn't see any features, nothing. They must have got him at close range with a shotgun. Gone.

That's a traumatic thing for a kid. I ran, I told my mother. My mother took me in and locked the door. I'm a kid, but I remember thinking, "What is she locking the door for? It's over with. The guy's gone."

❧

On December 21, 1948, the Chicago Tribune, *under the headline* HUS-BAND SLAIN, *reported the death of Anthony Pellegrino, thirty-three, "an ex-convict and minor hoodlum with a police record dating back to 1931." The article reported that Pellegrino had done three years in federal prison for selling narcotics and that federal agents had been "keeping an eye on him" recently, suspecting he might be involved in "olive oil black market operations." The article was accompanied by a photo of the victim's wife and daughter and quoted the wife as saying she and her husband had taken their daughter to a movie on the night of his death. Pellegrino had gone out near midnight to buy cigarettes and had never come back. The article gave the location where the body was found as "an alley at 2416 Lexington Street."*

❧

You grow up fast. You're not an intelligent guy bookwise, but you're smart. You learn. Living in the neighborhood was challenging. You had to fight your way and if you didn't you were looked down on. I'd have a fight with some guy, the others would be watching. Afterwards I'd put my arm around him, we'd walk over there, pals again. I was as tough as they came. Always sticking up for my younger brother and cousins. My older brother could handle himself.

Everybody knew everybody. The policemen were on foot. They'd walk Western Avenue, the main drag. And the beat cop knew everybody on that block. I remember his name was Jack. He was a big Irishman. One time when I was seven years old, he caught me turning the fire hydrant on. On a hot day we'd have twenty, thirty kids at the fire hydrant. We knew how to stuff up the sewer. You made a flood, you had your own lake. And the police would come. This time, everybody fled, he got me.

Well, I'm pinched. I'm shaking. He took me home; he knew exactly where to take me. And my mother answered that door, and she grabbed me. "I got him, Officer. Do you need him anymore?"

"No, he's in good hands. I'm sure you'll tell your husband." He knew what to do.

I was scared. She says, "You stay in your room. You ain't leaving this house. When your father gets you . . ."

Now my father came home from work. He always dressed in a suit, he had the fedora on, and he's walking past the neighbors. And before he got to the house he knew the story: "The police took your son home."

Well, he didn't know which one. The first guy he gets is my brother Billy. Billy's nine. He's two years older than me. And my dad grabs him. Now I'm up in the house, because my mother's punishing me. I'm on the second floor, and I hear the screaming.

Billy's saying, "No, I didn't, Dad."

He says, "If you didn't, who did?"

"I don't know."

"You don't know?" *Boom*, he hits him.

Billy knew. He never said a word. These guys today, all you got to do is scare them, and they'll beef. Men. This was a kid. He was a man at nine years old. Growing up in the neighborhood you learned at a very young age not to snitch or tell on your pals. We didn't like guys who were rats. You don't tell on another guy.

People in the neighborhood feared Outfit guys, because in the past they preyed on them. That went back to the Black Hand guys in the early days, who muscled all the Italians just off the boat: "This is the deal. You go to work, you gotta bring it in." Then the Young Turks came up and put them out of there. Al Capone just wanted that bootlegging business. And he thrived on it. But then he didn't have the brains to step it up.

The new guys were supposed to be more intelligent. And they let up on the stranglehold on the Italians, for the most part. In our neighborhood, people loved Johnny DeBiase. Johnny just took care of the bookmaking. And that was the strength of the Outfit. There were no whorehouses in our neighborhood. There were book joints, there were dice games. And Johnny oversaw that, and he got his fair share, and he brought his end to the boss. That was Paul "the Waiter" Ricca at that time.

Johnny used to tell my dad that it was his neighborhood and he didn't want anything to change. "If I can help, I help. This is a good neighborhood. Everybody knows everybody. No one's gonna get hurt." And he was right. He kept an eye on his fiefdom, or whatever you want to call it. He'd walk through that neighborhood, and he would stop and talk to people—the Leonis, the

Fioritos, anybody. They'd have coffee for him, they'd maybe have an Italian biscuit, or a bagel, or something. He took care of people.

⤳

Chicago organized crime histories trace the evolution of the five traditional Outfit neighborhoods: Taylor Street, Grand Avenue, Twenty-Sixth Street, the North Side, and Chicago Heights. Each had its marks of distinction: Taylor Street had the 42 Gang graduates, Giancana and his crew. Grand Avenue produced boss Paul Ricca's second in command, Tony Accardo. Twenty-Sixth Street lies just south of Chicago's oldest Chinese community, and its Outfit branch inevitably became the Chinatown crew. The Near North Side had the principal nightlife districts. Chicago Heights was an early center of Italian immigration in the south suburbs and became a bootlegging hot spot during Prohibition.

The location of the neighborhoods determined the specialties for which the crews became known: Twenty-Sixth Street had the freight depots and became known for truck hijacking; the North Side crew handled the vice rackets in the nightlife districts. Grand Avenue nurtured burglars. Chicago Heights was where a car thief could find a reliable chop shop. All the crews were involved in gambling.

Cities are never static, and centers of Outfit activity have shifted and mutated over the years. As Italian Americans joined the migration to the suburbs after the Second World War, Outfit activity went with them. Taylor Street and Grand Avenue largely relocated to the western suburbs of Elmwood Park and Melrose Park, with the more prosperous, including a number of Outfit bosses, establishing themselves in the tonier communities of Oak Park and River Forest. Taylor Street was gutted in the late 1950s by the construction of the Eisenhower Expressway and the Chicago campus of the University of Illinois, and today it is a stretch of a few blocks with some good restaurants and the label LITTLE ITALY hung on it by the tourism promoters. The North Side crew dissipated as the Rush Street nightclub scene declined; Chicago Heights now has almost as many black residents as white.

Today some observers say there are three Outfit crews: North, South, and West, their activities extending to the far exurbs; others say there are five territories, the borders defined by Chicago's expressways radiating out from the Loop. All agree that the traditional structure is gone.

A long-serving Chicago police officer who grew up on the Near West Side remembers the way it used to be: "The minute you go out the door you see these guys that control everything. I'm standing on Ohio and Leavitt one night, with a whole bunch of guys. And Joe Lombardo—I had no idea who he was—walked up: 'Corner's closed.'

"Everybody: 'Yes, sir,' and left.

"And I go, 'Who is this guy?'

"They said, 'Shut up, shut up, don't say nothing. It's Joe Lombardo.' He was the king of the neighborhood."

4

THE MACHINE

The Twenty-Fifth Ward, where we lived, was part of what the first Mayor Daley later called the West Side Bloc. They were all Italian neighborhoods—people from the same part of Italy settled together. Pre–World War II, if you were from Bari, you better be with the other Barese. After the war, that was less important.

In the early 1950s, the alderman of the Twenty-Fifth was Vito Marzullo. He had made his money from funeral homes before he became the alderman. Vito was direct from the Old Country. He had that strong accent. We used to go and play gin with him. His main guy was a guy by the name of George Barbuscia, who was a close friend of my father's. When we would go over there George would say, "Let him win. Let the alderman win. Whatever you lose, I'll take care of you."

"We gotta let him win?"

"Let him win. He loves it when he wins."

So we let him win.

Marzullo's son Willie, who was friendly with my uncle Sam, was a big gambler. My father got him out of a lot of trouble. He owed the bookmakers big money. So my father got him on the payment plan, and he got it reduced. He said to the bookmakers, "You can't bother him, this is the alderman's son. What's wrong with you?" He knew how to tell these guys. He could tell them and get away with it.

~

In Chicago the Machine can make you and it can break you. It made Edward Kelly mayor in 1933 when Anton Cermak took a bullet for FDR down in Miami (though malicious tongues said the mayor rather than the president was the real target all along). Cermak had built the Machine, and Kelly kept it running through the Depression and the war with his mastery of graft and patronage and the help of federal money steered to Chicago by FDR, who was keenly aware of the Machine's electoral usefulness. Kelly ran things until 1947, when the Machine broke him; it needed to throw the reformers a bone, and Kelly had irked the Irish power base by extending patronage to blacks and integrating public housing.

In his place the Machine made Martin H. Kennelly. Kennelly was honest enough to pass muster with the reformers but, it was hoped, realistic enough to know the rules. Unfortunately he showed an annoying independent streak, undertaking to reduce patronage and professionalize various city departments. When he took on Streets and Sanitation, traditionally the province of the Italians, the Machine broke him, too.

In 1955 the Central Committee of the Cook County Democratic Party slated County Clerk Richard Joseph Daley instead of Kennelly as the party's mayoral candidate. Kennelly, refusing to go quietly,

insisted on running in the Democratic primary. Daley had the sup-
port of African Americans, whom Kennelly had angered by going
after the policy rackets in black neighborhoods while leaving white
gambling interests alone. And he had the support of the Italians who
saw in Daley the man who would let them quietly go about extending
their control of the rackets.

Daley dispatched Martin Kennelly in the Democratic primary in
February and on April 5, 1955, he went up against Democrat turned
Republican Robert Merriam, a youthful, reform-minded alderman
who appealed to voters across party lines and warned that Daley
represented the old, entrenched ways of doing things.

ᔥ

The Outfit guys were with Daley, and they wanted to make sure
everything was in place for him. They targeted the key precinct
workers again. My dad was a Republican and he took care of like
five precincts, so he got scooped up. Not to hurt him, just to keep
him away from the polls.

He had one main precinct where we lived, which was right
around the corner from home. On Election Day my dad had to
be there every hour, every minute, to greet all the voters. The
polls opened up at 6 AM. My father walked there at five o'clock
to get ready.

The first we knew was when somebody from the polling station came to the house looking for my father. He wasn't there when
the polls opened. And that was not like him. The people were coming out anyway, because he'd already been promoting the vote for
weeks, but he wasn't there.

So now we knew something was up. Where's he at? Gramps
and Gran, along with my mother, paced the floors, pacing, pacing,
pacing. I was twelve years old, but a nineteen-year-old version of

twelve. I knew something big was going on. So Gramps went to see George Barbuscia. He told George to get ahold of Rocky or Marshall, either of the Caifano brothers.

Marshall and his guys came and they put two and two together. They knew what was going on. My father and several others had been kidnapped in order to keep them from the polls. Marshall and Chuckie Nicoletti went to the people who counted, and they got him released. And they were pissed, because the kidnappers roughed my dad up.

First somebody had gone to talk to him, thinking they could scare him into staying away. He went anyway. And they grabbed him. They scooped him right off the street. I'm surprised he didn't have a heart attack then. They had my dad and the others held up somewhere, we never found out where.

When my dad came home, he was ashen. He was brokenhearted, he was sick. My father wasn't a hardball guy. He never thought it would happen to him. But it did. He never told us where he had been kept. We were just happy to get him back.

I never found out who the actual guy was, the guy that ordered the kidnapping. My strong suspicion is that it was Angelo LaPietra and the Twenty-Sixth Street crew, because LaPietra was from Daley's ward. Once Daley was in, they'd get more city jobs than anybody. So LaPietra could have said, "Hey. We want Daley in, and everybody follows in. And then we're gonna get what we want."

The election was a win for Daley, which started the longest dynasty for any Chicago mayor to that point in history. But Daley double-crossed everybody. They were supposed to have the gambling, they were supposed to have this, don't touch this, don't touch that. Daley went south on everything.

ᔐ

One Sunday I was outside in the street, playing ball. A neighbor, Mary Orlando, came running over and said, "You gotta come home, now."

"Now? I want to play."

"You gotta come home." I went home, and there's my mother. One look at her face was all I needed. "Your father had a heart attack."

We had a clinic for the neighborhood, run by Dr. Bellucci. He was on Flournoy Street and Western, right on the corner. Nice guy. But what could he do? They brought my dad in there, and Dr. Bellucci got an ambulance, and they took him to Presbyterian Hospital on Congress. And he died shortly after. If it was today, he probably would have lived.

My house was full of people. I remember my little brother Dicky said, "Does this mean we're orphans, Ma?" Danny DeStefano handled the funeral, because he was a family member, a cousin. I can't tell you how many people were there. I counted 103 cars. I never saw so many grown-up men crying. His brothers—that was natural. His family—that's natural. But Mike Gargano, crying? Rocky the florist, the Pettit boys? Rocky Caifano, he couldn't get off of the casket. These guys were crying. I never saw so many men cry.

My dad would have been a big guy. Everybody that knew him told me that. The election was in April and he died in June. So I can't help believing that that killed him.

I was bitter and mad and sick that my father died. My dad was my guy. The chances are, if my father had lived, I wouldn't have become a criminal. Because he was a stern guy, and we listened to him. We respected him. We feared him. If he was around, he would never have stood for the stuff we did. We'd have been in huge trouble. And so we missed the boat.

He was gone, we run amok.

5

GRAND AVENUE

After my father died, my mother was left with three young boys and an infant daughter. My mom was just distraught, broken up. Now she couldn't afford the house. And my father was all ready to buy a big house in Melrose Park when he died. They were just building the Winston Park area, and he was going to buy there. She always said, "You guys got cheated when he died."

But we went on. I cried, but I just went on. I went to work at the hot dog stand across the street, making seventy-five cents an hour peeling potatoes. For my mother, because she needed help. I worked, I never stopped. I was a man at thirteen. And my mother was worried more about me than anybody.

We were loose kids. We were a handful for my poor mom. With no father figure, we were devils, roughnecks, and she couldn't handle us.

I pulled my first score on Western Avenue. My dad's gone. I'm like thirteen years old, I'm with my guys. And they come running. "Hey, there's a lot of money in this guy's car."

I says, "A lot of money, what do you mean?" The Schiavone restaurant, on Flournoy and Western, the delivery guy had his car parked there. And for some reason, he left his change bank in the car.

"Yeah, the door's open." They knew I had more nerve than all of them.

I said, "Well, let's go." I went right over there. They stayed back. I look around, I grab. I grabbed rolls of quarters, whatever change there was. That was it. And I treated everyone.

～

My mother needed a strong man, and that was my uncle Nick. He was my grandmother's brother, Nick LaCalamita, who was a grocer. My mom got rid of the house, and we moved to my uncle's building at Ohio and Hoyne, just off Grand Avenue, about a mile north of the old neighborhood.

My uncle had a seven-unit apartment building with a grocery store on the first floor. We took one flat, and he gave my mother, out of the goodness of his heart, part of his store, which we turned into a sandwich shop, like a small restaurant. She probably only had four tables. And it thrived—she had good food, my grand-mother and she worked there, we worked there as kids, and all the guys used to come hang out there. She'd make spaghetti for you. She always had sauce. And she had at her disposal the grocery store. So if she didn't have something in stock, she'd go get a box from the store. Anything the guys wanted, she made.

Uncle Nick and his son kept an eye on us as best they could. My uncle was a rough guy, so he could handle us. He taught me a lot about life. He was also a butcher, and I used to help him kill and clean chickens, deliver groceries. I delivered milk, I delivered papers. I did it all for my mother.

The new neighborhood was familiar to me, because I had worked for my uncle before my dad died. I liked that neighborhood better, because of the guys, the sports we played. I had friends in the old neighborhood, but this was better. The people were great. Everybody knew everybody's business. Everybody knew, "Ah, that guy's a fruit. This guy, he's a cheapskate—he's got a ton of money, but he's cheap." How did they know? They did. Everybody would look out for one another.

You choose your friends, and I wound up with a good selection, because my mother's store was the meeting place and guys would come in there. Anyone who was anyone hung in the restaurant. I didn't have any enemies in that neighborhood. I got along with all of them. My cousin Mike Swiatek was as bad a guy as they come. He was about six years older than me and my guys. He was half Polish. His mother was Mary Caffarello, and she married Joe Swiatek. *Madonn'*, when I met this guy . . . motorcycles, fast cars.

Frankie Furio and his father lived in our building. His mother had died, and it was just him and his father. We were a couple of years apart, and we palled around. My mother's alone, she's working. Frankie's father was in the same predicament—he lost his wife. So after a few years they made what they called a *masciata*, an arrangement, and they married. So we got Frankie as a brother. She didn't adopt him officially; he came as a stepbrother. But it was great, because we were friends prior to that.

A guy named Jerry Krueger became my best friend. I knew him from when I was six or seven years old, when I was delivering the groceries. I would deliver to his house on Ohio Street. He and I did everything together.

‿͜͡

I met Tony Spilotro when I was about thirteen. He was just a neighborhood kid. Sometimes you like a guy, sometimes you don't. Even the guys you don't like, the reasons why you don't like them are not serious. You don't like them because you're jealous, probably. This guy's got a better pair of pants, he's more handsome than you. And then it's over. That's small stuff.

With Tony, it's hard for men to say, but it was instant love. My sister has since pointed out, "You know, Tony loved you. He adored you." And there were reasons. Like me, he had no father: his father died when he was young and left him with his mother. He had brothers, I had brothers. He was a young, rough-and-tumble kid. He was nobody to mess with, I was nobody to mess with.

I met Tony in the park. He wasn't a baseball player, but I was. We were playing line ball. That's a kind of baseball you can play in the streets or in the park. We used to play with a sixteen-inch softball. You had a pitcher, a catcher, and one player who played "off the wall." And you were very close, maybe fifty feet. There were a lot of broken fingers in this game. You had to be fast, agile, and a great baseball player to do this.

Guys used to play this game for money, sometimes big money. Steve the Greek lost his car to Joe Lombardo betting on a line ball game. That was a few years later, in 1964—I know the year, because he'd just bought it, it was a coral-colored Pontiac.

But the day I met Tony Spilotro, we were at Mitchell School playground. I was playing with this kid who was a burglar, Joe D'Argento. Big guy. I was good sized, but not as big as Joe. Tony was watching. In line ball you get one strike. So I was throwing the ball at Joe's bat, because if I hit his bat, he's out. My friend Jimmy Andriacchi was there, and Jimmy was telling Joe, "Hey, Joe, watch your bat, he's gonna hit your bat."

"Fuck him."

Well, I hit his bat. And the ump said, "You're out."

"I'm out? What do you mean I'm out? You . . ." He started swearing.

Tony was laughing. He loved that. Because we were playing for money, a couple of bucks.

The next time Joe D. came up to bat, he swung and let the bat go, and I was right there. He tried to hit me in the head with the bat. I ducked it. I said, "You . . ." I went after him, I beat his head in.

He said, "I'll kill you."

Tony said, "You ain't killing nobody. You're a nitwit. This guy got the best of you, so fuck you."

That was when I was about thirteen. And from there Tony and I did a lot of stuff together. Tony was my guy. I never had a fight with him.

⸙

Buried deep in the archives at the Chicago Crime Commission is a letter typed on flimsy green paper with many Xed-out corrections. There is no record of why or when it was collected. It is a reminiscence of Tony Spilotro from a classmate at Steinmetz High School in the early 1950s. It describes Spilotro's "exceptionally violent temper and unruly behavior" and "unpredictable displays of cruelty" and calls him "a constant center of turbulence and trouble." The letter recounts how Spilotro fought with other students, "waylaying" them in locker rooms or after school; it describes how he stole other students' projects and erased their names on written work to submit it as his own.

The letter also mentions Spilotro's frequent "moodiness and depression" and his statement that he didn't care if he lived or died. The writer observes that Spilotro obviously needed help; apparently he never got it.

Criminals keep an eye out for young talent just like baseball teams. The Outfit doesn't keep scouting reports on file, but police records show Tony Spilotro's first arrest, for shoplifting, in 1955, when he was seventeen. Shoplifting doesn't get you to the big leagues, but evidently Spilotro had the grade-A malevolence that marks the top prospect. The early 1960s would find him working for Sam DeStefano, a West Side loan shark with a special reputation for viciousness. By the late '60s Tony Spilotro was being mentioned in newspaper reports as a "rising young hood," a major figure in the high-interest "juice loan" racket.

His star would continue to rise. Along with the ruthlessness he had soulful good looks, swagger, and charisma. Before he succumbed to the prime occupational hazard of mob life in 1986, Spilotro had become a gangster celebrity, a face on the evening news and a name in newspaper columns.

Attached to the letter in the CCC files is a blowup of a corner of a class photograph from a Steinmetz High School yearbook. It shows a recognizable but very young Tony Spilotro, frowning at the camera, looking not so much tough as moody and depressed, already lost.

ᔐ

When I moved to Grand Avenue, that was it. I could see these guys moving, doing things. Who's got a new car, who's got new shoes, and who's going here, who's going there. I says, this is the way to go. How's my mother gonna control me? She couldn't. My uncle Nick tried his best, but we ain't his kids. They would say things and I'd go, "Oh, yes . . ." and then I'd go off on my own.

Greed. I wanted money. They're not gonna give it to me.

You look up to the Outfit guys. They were like judges: they kept order, they handed out justice, and in a much more efficient way. If somebody does something wrong to your business and you want to go after the person that inflicted the losses on you, you gotta go through the court system. You gotta file a suit, and that takes years. But with these guys, there was none of that. My cousin Mikey Swiatek and this guy Tommy had a fight in our shop. Destroyed it. Tommy put Mikey right through the door. Old Johnny Bananas got Joe Lombardo, Lombardo grabs Tommy and my cousin: "Fix the door, fix the tables, it's gonna cost you X amount. And get it done now." I tell you, you can't believe how fast they got it done. Now you look at it, you say, "Wow."

I already learned that you couldn't trust the priest. He screwed us. So what side am I gonna take? Not the priest's.

⌇

There was a championship title fight here in Chicago, at Chicago Stadium. It was Carmen Basilio versus Sugar Ray Robinson. And we got the head usher—his name is Lester Modesti—from our neighborhood. So he lets us in, sends us up. We went all the way up into the second balcony, standing room. All my guys: Tony Spilotro, Krueger, and a friend of mine named Junior Bisceglie.

Now you see all the celebrities. At the time, whoever the big celebrity was, they announced him, and they come into the ring and say hello to everybody. Just a bow. "Frank Sinatra!" And he was in the front row. He had his hat on.

Tony says, "We're gonna nail that fuckin' hat."

"OK." We're watching the fight. So now it's getting toward the end, and we gotta make our way down. Everyone's standing. So we're wheeling through there, and we're right by him. You could see him there, he's got that gray straw hat. And he's sitting next to Leo Durocher, that was his good buddy, and Leo's wife, Laraine Day, and there were a couple of other guys.

And I'm *this* close, and he's enjoying the fight, and I go for him. And he goes, "Yo!" And the hat falls, my hand goes in his pocket, I come up with his handkerchief. I ran, I was fast. And we go to the neighborhood. From Madison Street to Grand Avenue ain't that far. Couldn't get the hat, since it fell off. But I got the handkerchief. I wish I had it today. Tony took it from me. It was an orange handkerchief, and it had "FS" on it. Beautiful.

6

THE BADLANDS

The Grand Avenue area was called "the Badlands," because they were all crooks there. Every crew in the Patch used to come by my mother's restaurant. Everyone showed up sometime during the day or night—the crème de la crème of the crooks. Guys would hang out, eat, scheme, listen to music. And that meant the police came by there, too. Bill Hanhardt was a rough-and-tumble cop. Everybody was afraid of him. He was born in St. Michael parish, around North Avenue and Sedgwick Street. That was an old Italian neighborhood. His father, Ed, was an old bookmaker, a wonderful guy. And his mother was Sicilian. He knew kinky guys; he roughed and toughed it with these guys. This guy was a tough man in his own right.

Well, Hanhardt gets aware of my mother's place and he comes to roust these guys. Some snitch must have told him this was the hangout. Tony Spilotro was there with his guys. Some of the guys that he hung with were Joe Hansen, a real maniac; my stepbrother,

Frankie Furio; and a guy named Bob Sprodak. Sprodak went missing and nobody knows what ever happened to him. These guys were big.

Hanhardt would know that they were there, and he'd grab them. He was a burglary sergeant. He knew every burglar there was. If he knew a score was made, a load of furs or something, he'd rustle somebody up. He'd be in his car and he'd find, say, Steve the Greek: "I'm taking you in for a new picture, new prints." And the guy would duke him, meaning pay him, just because he didn't want to be hassled. Especially weekends—he'd catch them when they were dressed up. Because you're fucked for the whole weekend; you're in jail. It was worth three hundred dollars, which was a lot of money. Anytime he grabbed any of these guys, they always came up with the cash.

But more important, they were all afraid of him. He was rough, and he'd blast you. There was no nonsense with Hanhardt. He fought Joe Hansen in the interview room in the old Area Six station, at Grace and Damen. Hansen says, "You ain't so tough without the badge."

Hanhardt says, "Here's the badge, here's the gun." Takes them off, puts them on the table. Beat the fuck out of him. Joe Hansen was a rough guy, but he had no chance with Hanhardt. Hanhardt was tough.

One time Hanhardt grabbed me and Nucci Lombardo, Joe's younger brother. I'm working for my mother at the sandwich shop. Hanhardt walks in with his big bulldogs. All the guys are there—Tony, my cousin Mikey . . . Everybody's a bad guy except me and Nucci.

So Hanhardt's going, "How you doing, how you doing?" He's just looking around. He says to me, "What's your name?"

I know his reputation. And if you see him, them eyes go right through you. I said, "Freddy Pascente."

"What do you do?"

"This is my mother's store. I work here."

He looks at Nucci. "Who are you?"

"Andrew Lombardo."

"What do you do?"

"I work for the city."

"You two. Outside."

Everybody's looking. "What the fuck, did he make a mistake? He's got all these guys, he took the only legit guys." And later I asked him about that. I said, "Why did you grab us?"

He said, "Because I knew everybody. I wanted to know who the new faces were." So he took all the information, and he let us go. That was Hanhardt.

They like their cops tough in Chicago. Frank Pape was the toast of the town from the 1930s through the '60s; he boasted of sending three hundred criminals to prison and five to the electric chair. But his signature move was the shootout. Pape is best remembered for killing nine men in the line of duty. He dropped them with the .38 Police Positive he carried in his specially reinforced trouser pocket; he perforated them with a Thompson submachine gun; on one occasion he drilled a wanted man with a deer rifle from a second-story window. He never suffered a scratch and never underwent the indignity of a suspension, though one of his exploits did move the Supreme Court to rule that the federal government could bring civil rights cases against local police officers. He died at ninety-one, lionized in a New York Times *obituary and a biography titled* The Toughest Cop in America.

When William Hanhardt joined the department in 1953, the Frank Pape model was still SOP for the Chicago Police Department. Before Monroe v. Pape, *before* Miranda, *police work was a trade more than a profession—and a rough one at that. "The police were the police," says a retired cop who knew both Pape and Hanhardt. "Their word was law and you did what they wanted you to, and you didn't fuck with them."*

Hanhardt made detective in 1955 and started racking up arrests and headlines. In those days informants were the most useful tool in a detective's kit, and Hanhardt had the most and the best. A scan of old arrest reports filed by him and his partner John Hinchy turns up countless phrases like "We had information that . . ."; "An anonymous tip . . ."; "Rec'd in anymous [sic] letter . . ."; "Based on info we rec'd . . ." Hanhardt had grown up on the streets, and he knew how to work them. He understood the ecology.

In 1963 his extensive network of informants made him a natural choice to lead the new Criminal Intelligence Unit, which specifically targeted career criminals. Working with his own handpicked detectives and with considerable autonomy, Hanhardt produced a steady stream of busts from among Chicago's large population of cartage thieves, hijackers, and heist men.

After the busts, Hanhardt brought the full range of tactics to bear, including the occasional head bounced off the wall. A copper who worked with him recalls, "In Area Five Hanhardt used to have a seat next to his desk, and behind the seat there was always a hole in the wall. The plaster guys would be up there once a week." Once Hanhardt dropped in while a burglary suspect was being questioned, asked the arrestee his name, and was answered by an obscenity. "Hanhardt picks up the big old-time arrest book, bam. *Knocks him on the floor. He goes, 'I'm Hanhardt. You'll never forget it.' This is why guys loved him. He was a legend."*

The legend grew with headline-grabbing exploits like Hanhardt's ambush of a particularly vicious home invasion gang in 1962, when, acting on a tip, he was lying in wait for the thugs when they broke into the house they had targeted. Wielding a submachine gun, Hanhardt killed one of the burglars and wounded another. The next day's Tribune *showed a photo of Hanhardt brandishing the tommy gun.*

⌇

We were afraid of Joe Lombardo. He was seven years older than us, a kinky guy. We all knew who he was. Johnny Bananas didn't let anybody put the arm on people, but there were guys that tried it. Lombardo went by the old rules. He used to grab the cleaners, he used to grab the Gonnella bakery, he used to grab even the guy that sharpened the knives. And he had tried to put the arm on my mother. A little person like my mother, what the hell kind of a thing is that? And it didn't stand. Good guys in his racket wouldn't stand for it. And that upset him.

So now one day we're hanging in front of Bert's Tavern on Leavitt and Grand, all kids, sixteen, fifteen, eight, nine. Lombardo drives by with this woman in the car. And one of the guys hollers, "You fuckin' jag-off!"

Well, he backs up, and he says, "Which one of you assholes said that?" And no one would own up, because they're afraid, understandably.

Me, I was reckless, and I said, "I did it." Just not to let us all look bad.

Well, he gave me a beating, which he should never, never, do. You're a big guy—you don't hit a kid. I don't care, I could take a beating. That's the way he wanted to be, all right. Anyway, I took it. And then afterwards I hit the kid who had yelled and then I went to my mother's store to clean up.

"What the heck happened to you?"

"Nothing, I caught a shellackin'." I didn't say who. I didn't say another word about it.

A few days later I was working at the restaurant. I was waiting on tables; all the guys were in there. Tony was there, Mikey was there, they were all there. Now, Lombardo comes in, and he sticks his finger in my face and says, "You didn't say that to me." He's trying to make a half-ass apology.

I says, "OK, what'd you beat me up for?"

Now Mikey's mad. "You beat him up? How'd you hit a little kid?" My cousin says, "Come on outside. Let's go, we'll talk." They went outside, they went at it. And Lombardo didn't get the best of Mikey. *Badda-bing*, he gave it to him. Mikey told him while he was laying on the ground, "You're twenty-two years old. How could you hit a sixteen-year-old?"

I went outside, picked Joe up, and brought him inside the restaurant to clean him up. My mother was making the sign of the cross.

Mikey could have gotten in a lot of trouble for that. It was only knowing Tony that saved him.

૭

For a guy who claimed to dislike the spotlight, Joe Lombardo did a lousy job of staying out of it. The papers started calling him "the Clown" early on, maybe because of his habit of mugging for mug shots. One published in 1964 shows him with a gaping yawn, the wide-open mouth and the hair hanging in his eyes making it worthless for identification. Another from the mid-1970s shows him in modish mock-Beatles haircut, wire-rimmed glasses, and a fashionably wide tie, flashing a broad grin, amused by the spectacle of a Chicago law enforcement agency going through the motions of booking a man of his stature. In a third he is refusing to look at the camera, contemplating weighty matters somewhere high on the wall behind the photographer.

THE BADLANDS

Walking out of federal court in 1982, he played peekaboo with reporters, holding the morning edition of the Sun-Times *up to cover his face, with a rectangular hole cut in it for him to see through. In 1992 he placed a classified ad in the* Tribune, *coyly denying any involvement in organized crime and requesting that "if anyone hears my name used in connection with any criminal activity, please notify the FBI, local police, and my parole officer, Ron Kumke."*

The clowning had a purpose: it made the public forget the real nature of the business. When your nickname is the Clown, you don't scare people. They know you're a rogue, but they don't mind a few rogues in their city; rogues give the place character. The Outfit always had a good public relations slant: the business of organized crime is to regulate the vice the public demands; the laws are hypocritical and the crimes are victimless. As for the violence, it is necessary to keep famously unruly men in line. But it is selective, discreet, and rule-governed. The only people at risk are guys in the business.

Danny Seifert was a blue-collar guy from the western suburbs. He had never finished high school, but he had energy and initiative. In 1974 he was running his second company, a plastics manufacturing firm in Bensenville, Illinois, an undistinguished suburb just west of O'Hare Airport. He had a wife and two young sons and was making a comfortable living. He had made only one mistake: he let a bookie named Irwin "Irv" Weiner invest in his first company, a fiberglass molding firm. Weiner in turn had sold his interest to a group of investors that included Joe Lombardo.

Being in business with Outfit guys as partners is like swimming with sharks. Sooner or later they're going to get hungry. Seifert liked the affable, fun-loving Lombardo, who became a family friend, but he didn't like what Joe and his pals did to the company. When Seifert realized that dirty money from the rackets was getting a wash in his company accounts, he sold out and started fresh.

Then the FBI came calling. Danny Seifert reluctantly agreed to testify against Joe Lombardo in a federal fraud case. He moved his family and concentrated on running his new business. One morning in September 1974, Danny Seifert brought his wife and his four-year-old son to work with him. Two masked men burst into the office, shoved Seifert's wife and son into a bathroom, and then pistol-whipped Seifert, chased him across the parking lot, and finally shotgunned him to death, leaving his body for his wife and little boy to find.

Seifert's wife told police she had recognized the voice and gait of the man who had shoved her into the bathroom: the man her kids had come to consider almost an uncle, Joe Lombardo.

⌒

We used to play baseball every Saturday at Mitchell playground, walking distance from my house. Joe Lombardo was the organizer for the baseball. We all played, and we played for money. So I'm out on Friday, I'm working. It's eight o'clock in the morning—I just got home at five-thirty. I'm asleep, I feel somebody shaking me, waking me up. I look up, who's over my head? Lombardo. Here's me: *Holy . . . What the fuck is he doing here?*

"Come on, let's go! We're playing baseball."

So he left, I get my mother. I says, "Ma, what do you let this guy in the house for?"

"It's only him." If he knocks on the door, she says, "Come on in, Joe."

I told her, "Don't let him in the house."

7

TOUGH GUYS

I started high school at St. Ignatius, at Roosevelt Road and Blue Island, in 1956. I was in the class of '60. That was my father's wish. He had sent my brother Billy there. It was tough to get into that school—St. Ignatius was the top school academically in the entire state. Judges, US attorneys, the state's biggest pols, practicing attorneys, brokers, they all went to this school. But I got in.

It was all Irish. There were very few Italians. I went to school with Michael Madigan, who is now the Speaker of the Illinois House of Representatives. I threw Mike Madigan's books off the bus. I didn't do it to be a bully, I just challenged him and he took me on. He was a little guy, a scrapper. Then we were buddies. That's the way it was.

When I went to St. Ignatius, my best friend Krueger went to Wells High School, which a lot of the guys did, because that was the neighborhood high school. One time when I was sixteen and Krueger was maybe two years older, we went to a dance. The dance was a big thing on Friday night. Dressed up, sixteen years old. At the time, I was working the elevator part-time at the Continental Bank downtown.

There were lots of girls at the dance, and that night I got the best girl there. Krueger was hot: "You . . . How did you get this girl?"

She liked me. Her name was Dolores, a pretty girl. While we were dancing, she said, "Well, what do you do?"

I said, bragging, "Well, I own a string of roast beef stands all over the city."

Krueger was rolling his eyes. "Yeah . . ."

All of a sudden a girl came running from across the dance floor, toward me. "I know you!" In front of all my guys and the girl, she said, "You're Freddy, the elevator boy!"

Well, it was all over. Krueger said, "Yeah, and you own them beef stands."

&

I was a good student. And I played football for two years. I started at quarterback my sophomore year. But I had to quit school, because I could see my mother couldn't make ends meet. Looking back, we probably could have gotten through, but at the time it didn't seem like that to me. I said, "Ah, the hell with it."

My mother was sick about it. But my older brother, Billy, wasn't finished—he wanted me in school. So he said, "All right, you don't want to stay in St. Ignatius, I got the coach at St. Mel." St. Mel was farther west, off Washington Boulevard. "He wants you. He'll make arrangements, they'll get you in there for zero tuition, because of your ability with the football." Billy tried his best, but I turned it down. I was stupid. I quit after my second year.

A guy named Slugger Padula had a tavern on Grand Avenue. I was friends with his son, Terry. Slugger was a big political guy, but he was also just a wonderful guy. He'd help anybody. He had a connection with the Central Wisconsin trucking company. Everybody worked there, because of Slugger. He got me a job on the docks. The rules weren't as stringent as they are today. "So what if he's not eighteen? He can lift that."

⸎

Now it's 1959. I'm seventeen years old, a tough guy, and I'm hanging with a good bunch: Tony, Krueger, Junior Bisceglie, Frankie Furio. Louie Tenuta. Vince Ruggierio, who we called Poopsie. Poopsie was a wealthy kid. His father had a snack shop in city hall on the tenth floor. How's that for clout? Sold cigarettes, pop, candy, everything; made sandwiches. He made a fortune. And Poopsie was a good-hearted guy. He was never a kinky guy. But he hung with us.

We had a great time. There were always sports. And there were dice games, card games. One time we were playing *brisco* in the gas station near our house. We had made our own card table; we had a light rigged up. And we looked up and saw one of our friends, a guy named Freddy, in the middle of the street, and there was a black guy with a knife. And they were squaring off to fight.

"What the . . ." I went running over there, and on the run I hit this guy, *badda-bing*. One punch, he was out. His leg was shaking, but he was out.

He was trying to steal Freddy's car, and Freddy caught him, but he pulled out the switchblade. We picked him up, we put him on the grass, went back to playing cards. Somebody called the police and they took him away.

⸎

We feuded with other neighborhoods. The Grand Avenue guys versus the Taylor Street kids. The big Outfit guys were prominent in that rivalry. On Grand Avenue we had Tony Accardo, who was called Joe Batters or just JB. So a kid would say, "Fuck you guys. We got JB." Taylor Street had Mooney—that was Sam Giancana's nickname. And Twenty-Sixth Street, Chinatown, they had Angelo LaPietra and his brother Jimmy. Another neighborhood would have this guy or that guy. Elmwood Park, they were considered spoiled brats. They had Jackie Cerone and Joe Gags—Joe Gagliano.

There were five or six different groups. They all answered to Tony Accardo and Paul "the Waiter" Ricca. Those two held everything together. And they took a piece of what everyone else made. If you're the boss of this crew in Elmwood Park, your tax was probably fifty thousand dollars a month. So those top guys made their money. And they didn't care where the crews got the money.

They did it with bookmaking, they did it with whorehouses, card games. And they taxed the burglars. They'd say to a burglary crew, "You come up with this amount, or you bring us the goods, let us look at them, we'll sell it." So they made their money, all illegally. Accardo didn't care what else you did—but if you messed with drugs, he'd kill you.

They also controlled the unions. That's where their jobs would be, the bosses' sons and their nephews. They would get the jobs, the nice jobs, not us. They would keep them for themselves. Tony Accardo had the projectors' union. No theater could have an automatic system. You had to have the projectionist. That paid big money. Those were great jobs.

◡◠

Tony Accardo had the projectionists' union and a lot more. On the basis of assets controlled and length of tenure he was probably the most powerful organized crime figure in US history. Accardo oversaw the Outfit at the height of its power, in the 1940s and 1950s, and retained elder statesman status until his death in 1992. He boasted of never spending a night in jail, and while evidence has surfaced of at least one overnight stay after a roust, he certainly avoided incarceration on all the major charges brought against him.

Coming up on Grand Avenue in the 1920s, Accardo did heavy work for Al Capone, earning his nickname "Joe Batters" by using a baseball bat to deliver an unsatisfactory performance review to a couple of employees. In the early 1940s he was mentored by Paul Ricca as "the Waiter" consolidated his control. When Ricca was sitting in federal prison from 1943 to 1947, Accardo regularly visited him under an assumed name, taking instructions and clout back to Chicago. The Outfit does not announce management changes at press conferences, but it appears that Ricca handed off executive control to Accardo at some point in the 1950s.

In 1960 a specially appointed federal prosecutor named Richard Ogilvie, later to become Cook County sheriff, managed to convict Accardo on charges of income tax evasion. The case rested on Accardo's fictional job as a salesman for Premium Beer Sales Inc., which provided him with an explanation for what income he was willing to admit to. Ogilvie managed the conviction despite the untimely and spectacular demise of one of his key witnesses, Joseph Bronge, a Melrose Park beer distributor. Bronge was shot six times by two assailants wearing burnt-cork blackface who stalked him along a Melrose Park alley and up a gangway, laughing and cursing his refusal to die, in full view of numerous witnesses gathered for the annual Feast of Our Lady of Mount Carmel. A witness was found who was just courageous enough to identify the shooters—Milwaukee Phil Alderisio and Obbie Frabotta—before suffering an abrupt loss of memory that prevented an indictment.

Accardo's conviction was reversed on appeal in 1962, on the grounds that the jury had not been sheltered from prejudicial newspaper coverage "highly damaging to his character and reputation."

Tiring of the grind, Accardo made several attempts to designate a successor, starting with Sam Giancana in the late 1950s, but he had poor results with his picks. He ended up calling the shots from the shadows while yearning for the luxury of true retirement. Paul Ricca, meanwhile, dedicated the rest of his life to fending off federal attempts to deport him while living comfortably off the proceeds of a successful career in crime.

〰

My friend Jimmy Andriacchi's older brother Dominick had a lot of trucks on the city payroll. And we used to drive his trucks. He gave us five dollars an hour. We were kids—we had no chauffeur's licenses. But he didn't care. We got stopped, he knew the mayor. So we worked for him. It was a nice living.

Every Saturday Dominick would take me, Krueger, Junior, and Frankie, my stepbrother, and we'd go clean Paul "the Waiter" Ricca's house. The house was in River Forest, on Bonnie Brae. Beautiful house. We'd rake the leaves, we'd clean the house. And Dominick would say, "Don't take no money from this man. You work for me, you understand?"

We go there, we're sweeping, Ricca would walk around. You'd think he was a plumber or something, this old guy. He never looked like he was a mob guy. This was the boss. He'd come around: "Hello, boys." He had an accent. "You gonna eat? I got some *sopressata*, I got prosciutto, the best." And we'd eat. He said, "Did Dominick take care of you guys?"

The guys said, "Yeah, sure."
Here's me: "He never give us a fuckin' dime."
"What?" So he paid us.
And these guys are going, "Are you crazy?"
I said, "Fuck him. This guy's worth nine zillion dollars."

Meanwhile, the guys I hung with were making scores. We used to steal tires. We'd get ten dollars a tire, with the rim and everything. So if you pop the trunk, get the spare tire, too, that's fifty dollars. That's a lot of money then. One time I'm with a buddy of mine, I had a Cadillac. I open it up, I get a flat tire. My friend's on the other side, he opens up, he's screaming. A bag of money. Six hundred dollars.

We were always doing it. We were on the prowl, every day. One time we went into a shop on Harlem Avenue in Elmwood Park. It had the most beautiful clothes. It was one of maybe two or three places that carried these Italian knit shirts. They were Gino Paoli, very expensive, high-line. And this place had stacks of them. So we go in there. I'm with Junior and Frankie. We're just gonna grab the Gino Paolis. So we go in, the guy is waiting on somebody, *whoosh!* We grab a stack, we run out. We got fifty shirts. That's huge. Throw them in the car, we're gone.

Well, we got rid of them, *that* fast. That's how hot of an item it was. Now we're rolling. We got money, we're by my mother. Who pulls up? Tony and his guys. They walk in. Tony goes, "Come here." Nobody else, just me. I jump right up, I wasn't afraid. I says, "Yeah, what's up?"

"Did you rob that fuckin' guy in Elmwood Park?"

I'm not gonna deny it. I would never lie to this guy. I says, "How the fuck do you know?"

"You were recognized."

"Holy Christ."

He says, "That's my guy." The owner was paying Tony every week for protection. That's how it was. You kicked in for protection, nobody fucked with you. That's how guys like Tony made a lot of their money.

I says, "Aw, fuck, Tone. If I'd known . . . The shirts are gone. What, do you want me to go get them?"

He says, "No, don't worry about that. But I'm telling you, tell your fuckin' *bandidos* to stay away. That's my guy."

He took care of it. He must have told the guy, "Listen. Whatever happened, they're gone." The guy isn't gonna argue with him.

∽

There was a currency exchange at Chicago and Grand. And next door to it was an empty store. So Tony, Frankie, and my cousin Mikey went in on the weekend, into the empty store, and it was like a work of art. Michelangelo couldn't do it—they got into the common wall, and they chipped away, down to the slats. They took the slats out. Finally, it was down to the plasterboard. That was all that was separating them from the currency exchange. They couldn't go in there and open the safe; they weren't equipped. But when the Brink's guy came in, the security stayed outside. Junior Bisceglie was outside, watching the Brink's truck. Only one Brink's guy and the currency exchange woman were in the store. Well, they broke through and they heisted it. They took all the money. It was perfect. Right through the wall. Can you imagine what those two in the currency exchange were thinking? A guy coming through the wall.

All of it in order to make the nut—make a living. After a score the guys would cut up the money at my mom's shop. They just robbed a joint, now they got the money all over the table. Grandma would sneak behind the counter and write out a label and tape it to a big jar. The label said St. Joseph Charity. She would bring it to the table where the split was. "Come on, you lousy things. Give some to St. Joseph." St. Joseph was her.

Every week we were coming in with loads of shirts, loads of clothing, and we'd sell them through the restaurant. Every apartment in the building was filled by a family member—we would set up racks, and they would sell the clothes right off the rack. My cousin and his wife would sell the stuff right in the house and then give us the money. You'd go there and get whatever you want. People would order stuff.

I could not show my poor mother the money. "Where you getting money like this?" I would hide it. I would have five-thousand-dollar bundles, and I would hide them all over the place. Here, there. She never caught it. But she never needed money. "Here, Ma." I wanted to do everything for her.

When I started going with these guys, the money was unbelievable. Every week there was something. We were living high. We went to Las Vegas, we went to the racetrack. It was easy come, easy go.

Tony was a lot smarter. Tony stashed it all, and he bought a house for his mother. He told me, "What's wrong with you? You're blowing your money. Let me keep your money for you."

"No, I'll take care of my own money." Stupid. If I had thought about it, I'd be a millionaire today. Tony was pretty smart with that stuff.

One day when I was broke, I was going to a wedding—the suit was in the closet. I took that suit out, and I was trying it on, looking in the mirror, and I felt in a pocket and went, "What the hell is this?" A bundle. Five thousand dollars, a bundle that I had hidden and forgotten about. I was happy.

The Blackhawks won the Stanley Cup in '61, and we had season passes. We had like ten seats in the front, and you could squeeze three or four little kids in there, too, because of all the room there was. Our pal Lester Modesti, the head usher, would let us sneak in the kids. One time one of our guys said, "I want to bring my friend, Big Leo." Leo was a jeweler, and he was wearing a beautiful ring. I was eyeing the ring—it was over four carats.

Leo was cheering for the Hawks, like us. They scored, he threw his hands in the air, and his ring flew off. "My ring! My ring!" So everyone was on the floor looking for it, and who came up with it? My little nephew. He started to hold it up, saying, "I—" That's all he said. I grabbed him and clapped a hand over his mouth and pocketed the ring.

I took the ring to a jeweler Mikey knew down on Wabash Avenue and got fifteen hundred bucks for it. I made sure Leo got his insurance. And I slipped a hundred bucks to my nephew. I told him, "Now, aren't you better off with Uncle Freddy? You would have got maybe five dollars from Leo. This way, I got the ring, and I gave you a hundred to put in the bank."

8

CONNECTED

Sam DeStefano took on the young Tony Spilotro as a collector in his juice loan operation in the early 1960s. DeStefano maintained a higher profile than the garden-variety loan shark, establishing a reputation for extravagant violence and psychotic behavior. The stories are many and often impossible to substantiate; rumors credited "Mad Sam" with a preference for the ice pick as a tool of persuasion.

Leo Foreman was a bail bondsman who dabbled in real estate and insurance; he was also on Sam's staff in the loan racket. The word on the street was that Foreman crossed Sam by holding out on him and then throwing him out of his office when Sam came to confront him. Whatever the case, Leo Foreman turned up in a car trunk in his underwear on November 19, 1963, dead of multiple gunshot wounds and bearing numerous injuries inflicted with a sharp instrument.

Nearly a decade later, three men would be charged with his murder: Sam DeStefano, his brother Mario—and Tony Spilotro.

In the early '60s, Tony Spilotro got recruited and became one of the youngest made guys in history. Tony was made at the age of twenty-two or twenty-three years old. That just doesn't happen. When you're made, that means nobody can hurt you; if they do, there's retribution. To do anything to a made guy, you have to get the OK from every boss.

When you're made, there's no ceremony. Your sponsor just says, "I'm Milwaukee Phil, I'm making this guy." The only guys he has to go to are your crew. If one guy objects, the sponsor says "Why? Let's hear the trial right now." And then he goes to see the boss: "We're making Tony Spilotro." And Tony was made. That's how it's done. There's no ceremony, no burning of the hand, forget about it. That may have happened in the old Mustache Pete days, in the '30s, but not anymore.

Tony was one of three partners that worked under Milwaukee Phil. The other two were Joe Lombardo and Frank Schweihs, "the German." Schweihs was not a made guy. And he couldn't be, because he wasn't full-blown Italian. You had to be a hundred percent Italian in those days, and Schweihs was half. But they took him anyway, because of his ability to do things.

What these guys did was, they were the hit squad, the goon squad. Not everybody in the Outfit is a killer. There are certain guys. But the guys that have the most killers are the bosses, and Milwaukee Phil's were the best in that field. Everybody had to go to them for that kind of thing. Now, I may sound like I'm condoning it. Far from it. But I'm trying to convey where this crew got their power, their status. And there's always a reason when people get killed. If you owe money, they ain't killing you. They're gonna protect you, hold you, make you healthy, make sure you got a job, so you can pay that money back. Now, if you're gonna put somebody in jail, hurt somebody, whatever, that's how you get killed.

These guys also had the book, a big book. That was Matt Raimondi—he was the top bookmaker at the time. Tony and Lombardo were partners in all their ventures, though Tony had to answer to Joe. Joe was promoted by Milwaukee Phil after Johnny Bananas died. Joe Lombardo had many guys. He recruited all the kids from our neighborhood. Tony had half a dozen guys, and they were all bad guys, badasses like Joe Hansen and Paulie Schiro. But ultimately they all worked for Phil, who was in line to be the top boss. So he became the guy with the premier hit squad: Milwaukee Phil.

ॐ

When I got to be about eighteen, I went to work for a place called Jet Air Freight, at the airport. I was a truck driver. My cousin was a union boss, Teamsters 705. His name was Tony Marzano. He got me in over there. But he didn't know what I was planning. When you went into the airport, you had Jet Air Freight, Emery Air Freight, everybody. You went in there, there was no security checking you. Each individual airline had its own security. They said, "We're watching out." But they didn't.

I watched, under the guidance of Tony Spilotro. I spotted some mink pelts, coming in from Minnesota. Another airline had watch movements, coming from Switzerland on Swissair. And then records were coming in. This was before tapes and CDs—these were long-play, $33\frac{1}{3}$ records. They'd come thirty in a box. Those were the newest thing.

I learned all this stuff. I told Tony. He said, "That's a fortune."

I put my cousin Mikey and another guy on the truck. They put hats on, with the buttons on them, they looked like the real deal. The pelts and the watch movements were kept in a secure area—supposedly secure. You could see it behind this screen mesh. Mikey and his partner went in there with their clipboards, like they're doing a pickup: "Yeah, OK, I got that, Moe." You got a clipboard, you get away with murder. That's how simple it was.

Badda-bing, they got the pelts. A lot of money. *Boom*, the watch movements. We got them. Now, the records would come in from Terre Haute, Indiana, the distribution center for Columbia Records. They'd come in with a trailer. And they always took the same route.

Tony's guys stopped the truck. They didn't hurt the guy—nobody ever got hurt. They told him, "Step out of the truck." He did, and they took the whole forty-foot trailer load of records. The driver had to walk so they had enough time to get away. There were no cell phones, no phones on this road. They took the truck, put it in a drop where they had a legitimate truck. They would unload, and then they would leave the first truck on the street and drive to where it was safe and sell the stuff. They never got caught.

My stepbrother, Frankie, he had a guy in the music business. He had spots all over, music stores, and Frankie would bring it all to him. He'd get fifty cents a record. We made thousands and thousands with these records. The guy who sold the pelts and the watch movements was a neighborhood guy who had connections all over the country. They would come and take them out of town, the watch movements and the pelts.

Some thieves sold stuff directly, but a lot of them would take it to a fence. They didn't want to be bothered selling it themselves. They wanted the money right away. And in our neighborhood we had two guys who were big fences, one named Nick and one named Augie. These two guys would buy everything. There was a network. There were so many thieves. Everybody was looking to sell something. You'd go by this one guy's house, he had rows and rows of clothes hung up. You'd think it was Wieboldt's.

Nick used to sell everything to a guy who was a wholesaler in Melrose Park. This guy was really big—he was in business for years and years and years. He would go to these railroad yards and buy loads and tell his customers it was hot. He had hot stuff in there, too, and he would mix everything up. He would get a thief and he would tell him, "I want nylons, I want diapers, I want razor blades, I want suits, shirts, underwear." Stuff like that sells—people would flock to his store. You could go in there and get any suit you want. "Go back there, your forty-fours are over there." You could get everything there. He had luggage, he had clothes. Everything in life.

If you sell it all to the fence, you only get 20 percent, 25 percent. But it's right there, cash transaction. And that's the best way to go, take the 20 percent. It's a hundred-thousand-dollar load, you're getting twenty thousand. Now he in turn sells it, pieces it out for a third to a half more, depending on what the merchandise is. That's retail.

Now this beautiful place is built, on Mannheim Road, the Sahara Inn. It was a motel, a club—they had gambling there. The owner was a guy by the name of Manny Skar. He was the Outfit's front man, a rough-and-tumble guy. The place was actually owned by Milwaukee Phil, Teets Battaglia, Mooney Giancana, Fifi Buccieri, that whole crew. All these guys had a piece of it. Of course, a bundle went up to Accardo, because they had to pay him—he was the boss. Tony Spilotro was the overseer of the joint. Not on paper—nobody knew. He couldn't even be seen in the joint. But he was protecting Milwaukee Phil's interest. So when the place opened, Tony came to me and said, "I want you to do me a favor."

I'd do anything for Tony. "Sure, Tone. What do you need?"

"The opening act is Bobby Darin. And there's a junk dealer that's fuckin' with him. Bobby Darin is not a junkie, but he's naive, he's weak. He ain't gonna mess with this guy. And the guy's trying to muscle him. I'm supposed to protect him, but I can't be in there. Freddy, I want you to do it. Get yourself a few guys and take care of it. Just give the guy a shellacking. Don't worry about the cops. I don't care if the chief of police of Schiller Park is there, nothing's gonna happen to you guys."

Well, when you get that kind of word, *madonn'*, you can do anything.

I get Frankie, Junior Bisceglie, and another friend from the neighborhood. We go out to the Sahara and go into the restaurant. And there's Bobby Darin—can't miss him. So we're sitting in another booth, and here's the guy that comes in and sits by him. And that was it. Junior grabs Bobby Darin and says, "Get out of here." Bobby Darin didn't know what was going on.

My friend got the guy with a sugar bowl, and he was gone. Right in the head, he was leaking all over. People were screaming.

We squared that one away.

〰

"Manny Skar's Sahara Inn," aka the Sahara Motel, on Mannheim Road was the crowning achievement of Manny Skar's career as an Outfit "beard," or front man. Unlike the run-of-the-mill airport motel, the Sahara hosted a gourmet restaurant with strolling violinists, a cocktail lounge with live music, and the Gigi Club, a flashy newcomer on the nightclub scene. There was also gambling, but since that was illegal it was not featured in the prospectus or the media

coverage. An item in the June 16, 1962, Billboard *touted the Sahara as "a posh, elegant and dazzling structure" and, noting Bobby Darin's opening headline act, predicted that the Gigi Club would spawn "a nightclub revival." The item noted that "reliable sources" were proclaiming that Mannheim Road would "soon become another Las Vegas-type strip."*

Sadly, Mannheim Road, a heavily traveled commercial artery running down Chicago's western flank past O'Hare Airport, never quite took off as a destination of choice for nightlife aficionados. And Manny Skar's reign as a nightclub impresario was truncated all too soon by a federal indictment on tax charges.

Skar's career illustrates classic Outfit tactics for leveraging other people's money. Skar had dabbled in burglary and mail fraud before becoming a partner in several construction companies funded by shady savings and loans that poured investor money into construction projects at inflated prices and escaped regulatory sanctions by judicious use of clout. After presiding over several of these projects to everyone's satisfaction, Skar was tabbed for the leading role in the Sahara production.

Skar got the gullible owner of an S&L in suburban Riverside to put up the money, and the game was on. Outfit-controlled construction firms inflated costs, Skar diverted money to his private accounts and thence to the Outfit, and more than a million dollars' worth of building materials were stolen in the course of construction. The Sahara opened on June 6, 1962, to great media and law enforcement interest, news photographers jostling with representatives of multiple agencies in the lobby as celebrities disembarked from limousines.

When massive theft from one construction company was exposed, the compliant S&L found its backbone and foreclosed on the Sahara; while the lawyers bickered, Skar stopped paying bills and the Outfit guys got busy stripping assets, the type of business they did best. Skar was bought out by the S&L in an amazingly generous deal, leaving hundreds of thousands in unpaid bills. He went before a grand jury and failed to produce the records it subpoenaed; he was cited for contempt. When on top of this the feds came calling with grumbles about Skar's tax returns, the stage was set. Rumors began to float that Skar was considering cutting a deal—the worst thing that can happen to a man who has broken bread with the Outfit. The other shoe would finally fall on September 11, 1965, in the form of four .38 slugs in the parking court of Skar's Lake Shore Drive high-rise, ending Skar's two years as a walking dead man.

According to testimony by federal witness Nick Calabrese in the 2007 Family Secrets trial, the killers were Joe Lombardo and Tony Spilotro.

〜

Tony had a friend named Moe. He was a good guy but a gambler. Oh, this guy. He gambled like you never seen. Tony got him out of more trouble . . . Moe owned a chain of restaurants in Chicago. He must have had a dozen of them. They were small, mostly breakfast joints, but they were open through the night. Moe also had a club on Mannheim Road, right by the Sahara. We used to go in there if you couldn't get into the Sahara. So one night we're there and he had a duet act in there, a black couple. Harold Ward, a good singer, and the girl was named Pat Bowie. Good singers, good show.

I'm with Frankie Furio, a bunch of guys. And Al Sarno was there. Al Sarno was a guy that worked for Joe Gags and Willie Messina on the Elmwood Park crew. And he's trying to mess with the girl, Pat Bowie. "Come on over here, baby. I could buy this joint." Stuff like that.

Moe, the owner, is saying. "Why is this guy bothering this girl? She's afraid, she can't even do her show."

66

I says, "I know him, Moe. Let me talk to him." So I says, "Al, could I talk to you?"

"Yeah."

"You see the guy over there? This girl is his wife."

"Is he complaining, that nigger motherfucker?"

"This is the way you act?" I says. "If you ask me to talk to you, I talk to you like a civilized person. This is a dear friend of mine, this is his joint."

He says, "Who the fuck? A Jew and a fuckin' . . ."

That was it. The show was on. *Boom!* I hit him. Blood starts coming. And that was it. I beat his fuckin' head in. Moe was going, "Whoa . . ."

I called Tony right away. "Let me tell you something, buddy. You're gonna have to go to work."

"What happened?"

I told him. He says, "You hit that fuckin' Sarno?"

"Hit him? I spouted him. He looked like a geyser."

"Who were you with?"

"Furio."

"Anybody else?"

"No. It was me and him."

"Meet me by the hot dog stand." He had a piece of a hot dog stand, Parse's Hot Dogs. I go over there and I tell him what happened.

He says, "Ah, fuck him. Don't worry about them guys." He went, he saw somebody, that was the end of it.

⁓

Slugger Padula, who got me my old job with the Central Wisconsin trucking company, used to sit in his tavern looking at the racing form. Never picked his head up from the form. But he knew anybody that would come in. "How you doing, Fred, how are you? Terry ain't here, he's working."

One day, Tony and me, we walk in, he's in the same position. "How you doin', fellas? Go make your own drinks."

Tony had a pop, he gave me a pop. Two hillbillies are in the corner. They were probably truck drivers—they stopped, they wanted to have a drink, they never thought they'd run into a fuckin' maniac like Tony. And they were playing some hillbilly song on the jukebox, a country song. "*Da-da, bump-bump . . .*" whatever the song was. They got a jukebox full of Dean Martin, Frank Sinatra. But they kept playing this one song.

Here's Tony: "Hey, fellas. Can't you play another song?"

"It's my fuckin' money. I'll do whatever I want with the money."

Slugger says, "Don't fool around, you guys." He's reading the form.

So now the guy gets up, he goes to the jukebox, he puts his nickel in, and he plays the song.

Tony says, "This motherfucker . . ."

Slugger says, "Don't fool around, Tony."

Tony goes to the car, comes back with a .45. Here's me: "What the . . ."

So the hillbilly gets up and again he plays, "*Da-da, bump-bump . . .*"

Tony gets up and kills the jukebox. *Boom, boom!* Shoots it. Smoke is coming out, broken glass. The two hillbillies run out.

Here's Slugger: "You know you gotta pay for that, Tony." Never took his head up from the racing form.

꒰꒱

One day Tony came to my mother's store. He says to me, "You're gonna make a thousand dollars tonight."

"A thousand dollars! Man, OK, I'm in."

He says, "We're going to the ball game. We're gonna go watch the Sox. This is all Lefty's deal." Tony was pals with Frank "Lefty" Rosenthal—that's the guy Robert De Niro's character in *Casino* was based on. Lefty had gotten the other team drunk the night before—he had them all wiped out. They were in hot tubs all night long, with girls, at Lefty's expense. Tony says, "They ain't gonna play ball. They can't. It's impossible. They're wiped out."

So we go to the game. The visitors scored four runs in the first inning. Tony was hot—he had a vein in his head that came out when he was mad. "You fuckin' Jew . . ." That's the way he would talk. He loved Lefty, but he was swearing at him. "Let's get out of here."

So we went, Lefty dropped me off. I'm home—where's my thousand bucks? Then the newscast says, "The power was out at Comiskey Park. The generators were out. The game is canceled."

And I thought, "You son of a . . ." I knew it. I knew it was Tony.

I see him the next day; he comes by my mom's. I wasn't going to ask—I knew the rules, you don't ask anybody anything. I says, "Did you see what happened over there?"

"Yeah, what a terrible thing." He did it with that look on his face, like he knew all about it.

"You got 'em, you son of a bitch."

He got them. He went there with a crew and they cut the power. They cut the backup generators, everything. Everything went.

He didn't win, but he didn't lose.

9

RUSH STREET NIGHTS

Times Square, the Sunset Strip, Bourbon Street . . . Once upon a time you could mention Rush Street in the same breath and nobody would laugh. When people still went to nightclubs, when Chicago was the oasis in the desert for celebrities on the long train ride from New York to Los Angeles, when jazz was hip and comedy could get you arrested, Rush Street was hot.

Cabaret has gone the way of vaudeville, but once it was what you did for a great night out. Every decent hotel had a club with a dance band, and there were venues everywhere for headliners and sidemen, crooners and comics. Those venues made up a lush neon nightscape, a nocturnal ecology that supported species as diverse as hatcheck girls *and hookers, carhops and gossip columnists. Rush Street had critical mass.*

The street itself isn't much as Chicago streets go, starting at the river behind the Wrigley Building and petering out a mere mile north after kinking left at Chicago Avenue and veering over to merge with State Street. The north bank of the river was where Chicago's first vice district was, way back when, but by the time Rush Street had its moment this was a high-rent district, with Michigan Avenue and the Gold Coast to the east and the Loop skyscrapers just south of the river disgorging fat cats into taxis at cocktail hour.

The kinked part of Rush Street was where all the fun was: Mister Kelly's, the Chez Paree, the Tradewinds. There were famous joints every few feet. Lenny Bruce got himself arrested at the Gate of Horn for saying things that wouldn't rate a bleep on Comedy Central today. Ramsey Lewis was a kid fresh out of DePaul, a local boy making good, when he started playing at the Cloister Inn. The list of musicians and comics who played Mister Kelly's is a hall of fame, from Ellington to Vaughan, Allen to Sahl.

It couldn't last, of course; television and rock 'n' roll killed cabaret in the '60s, and the handwriting was on the wall. Vice had never been absent from Rush Street, but now it started to come to the fore. Strip joints and clip joints popped up as the old famous venues went away. Jazz clubs became topless bars; Club 19 boasted an ALL GIRL REVUE and Six East offered TOPLESS HAREM GIRLS. Mister Kelly's never bounced back from a fire. The hotels became SROs and the upscale restaurants plunged down-market. By the early 1980s Rush Street was a prime hooker stroll and a great place to score cocaine.

Like Times Square, Rush Street has been cleaned up and has shown some bounce-back. Walk around Rush Street today and you'll see the same mix of chain store outlets and trend-chasing restaurants you'd find in any reasonably preserved entertainment district

*in the country. There is still nightlife here. Division Street is prime
singles bar territory; a couple of blocks south the joints cater to an
older, more prosperous crowd. Where Mister Kelly's stood, now there
is Gibsons, a power-dining steakhouse for people who don't worry
about their cholesterol, their liver, or the size of the check. The pleas-
ant little tree-shaded plaza that it dominates, where Rush Street runs
into State and ends, is known as the Viagra Triangle.*

〰

I'm nineteen, and I don't want to drive the truck anymore. Tony's
saying, "You're gonna go to jail. There's too many scores." And
I'm afraid. All the fights I had, I was never afraid of getting hurt.
I wasn't afraid of nothing. But I didn't want to go to jail. So that's
the end of it.

I couldn't go to work at a regular job; I didn't want to do that. So
Tony says, "Go downtown—go see Pete Speren." Pete Speren was a
Greek bookmaker who used to pay Tony. Tony says, "You just tell
him you're my best friend and I told you to come down there."

I go see Pete. He had the Walton Club on the corner of Walton
and Rush. Now, I'm not twenty-one. But I don't volunteer that
information. I tell him, "Tony told me to come here. I want a job."

He says, "Well, what do you want to do?"

"I think tend bar."

"OK, come on. Let's go." We leave his joint and go to another
one called Bourbon Street, which was right down the street, on
Rush between Walton and Oak. Here's the owner, Ken Eto, who
they called Joe the Jap. Joe the Jap was a bookmaker. He had the
entire Puerto Rican community under his wing. He used to have
a game called *bolita*. That's a numbers game that's played in the
Puerto Rican community. How the hell he had the Puerto Ricans
I don't know, but he did have them. And he made nothing but

money, and he kicked in to the North Side crew. Really a good-hearted guy. And one of the best pool players you'll ever see. He was a shark, this guy. He stands up—what a gentleman he was—and he says, "You want to tend bar, huh? You ever tend bar?"

"No."

"I'll send you to school. You go to school on Wabash."

Just like that. There was no fooling around. "Whatever you say, Joe."

I went to bartending school, paid for the whole thing. It was a short class, maybe three days. I didn't learn anything. I learned everything when I got behind the bar. I learned from an Irish fellow. I'm gonna call him Clancy. This Clancy was a good bettor, a street guy. He taught me a lot. He put me to work, broke me in. I was making $150 a day.

One thing I didn't go for: Clancy didn't want black guys in there. You could get away with things like that back then. Black guys come in, he gave them their drink. When they finished the drink, he took the glasses, right in front of them, and he broke them. He threw them away and he says, "What do you want?" That was a message to the black guy that he ain't gonna use that glass again. And that was the way he told them.

I says, "Holy Christ. Do I have to do that?"

"No, you don't have to do that. This is my personal thing." Clancy was a hateful guy.

Jimmy Allegretti, one of the local Outfit crew, used to come in there. He was a huge tipper, a crazy drinker. He wanted the whisky here, the water here, the ice here, lined up in a row on the bar. Clancy just said, "Give him whatever he wants."

"Sure. Hello, Mr. Allegretti."

"How you doing, buddy?" Always a twenty-dollar tip.

Hookers loved me. The hookers would come in, they'd be sitting there, waiting. We were supposed to get rid of hookers. Not me. I loved it, because they took care of you. A girl would be in there for a few minutes, I'd give her a glass of pop, never booze. The guy she was meeting would come in, and she'd say, "Could I have my check?" She'd tell the guy, "Hey, take care of my tab here." Well, I had a tab all ready for him—twenty-six dollars, that goes in the cup. She'd look at the guy: "Aren't you gonna tip him?" And here comes another fin. And then she'd come back, she'd give me my end, twenty bucks. How's that?

Joe the Jap told me, "Don't you steal nothing. You listen to Clancy."

"OK."

So Clancy says, "Here's the way you do it. Don't ever steal out of the register. But certain customers, when the conventions come, you know who they are. Get them. Do whatever you want with them."

I had a vest, a tie, a name tag with my name. And in the vest I had a lighter in one pocket and a dollar bill in the other one. Now, the convention guys would come in, they had their badge: Clyde McFarkle from Iowa, whatever the name was. The joint would be three deep, standing, loaded. "Three beers," a guy in the back would say.

"OK." Every drink was a dollar fifty at Bourbon Street. So when he handed you the money over the guys, it'd be a twenty. So you would take the twenty, and you'd drop it in the sink. He couldn't see it, and automatically the dollar would come out of your vest. You'd wave it at him and say, "Yo, it's four-fifty."

"Well, I gave you . . . Oh, I'm sorry." He'd give you another twenty. I had more twenties floating in the water . . . You couldn't do it with guys that didn't have the badge, because they'd catch on. I think they all caught it, but they didn't argue. It was that fast. The twenty's gone—it's in the water. We were drying the money afterwards.

And the Jap was great. He loved me. I used to drive him nuts with Jap jokes. He had three or four joints down there. He had the Tony Paris Show Lounge on Walton, he had Bourbon Street, he had a strip club. He had all the joints. I'd fill in at Tony Paris, wherever, but I liked Bourbon Street. Bourbon had the classy people, the better tippers.

This bartender at Tony Paris, a guy named Ronnie, was stealing. Now, the Jap's bosses were Caesar DiVarco and Big Joe Arnold, and they worked for Ross Prio, who was the top guy down there. But the heavy-duty stuff, the rough stuff, Tony Spilotro was the guy. Guys had to go to Tony when they had a problem. So the Jap wanted to deal with Ronnie, he saw Tony. Now, Tony comes to me and says, "You know what? You guys do it. You'll really get in good with the Jap. This Ronnie's a shit-in-the-pants guy. Don't hurt him, just rough him up."

So me and Junior and another guy from the neighborhood, we get Ronnie: "Ronnie, come on, the Jap wants you to unload some booze." In this parking lot on Rush Street behind the Banquet on a Bun, that's where we take him. Ronnie opens the trunk, and *bad-dam*, *boom*, Junior hits him. A woman's screaming from the apartments upstairs. "What's going on?"

Our friend hollers, "We're playing ring-a-levio!" That's a game we played in the street.

"You jag-off." I was laughing.

And poor Ronnie . . . But he didn't get hurt. I says, "Ronnie, don't come around, quit the fuckin' job, that's the end." Joe never saw the guy again.

⌒

"Guaglio." I hate that name to this day. It means "little boy," that's what the interpretation is. If it's said correctly, and by the right

person, it's an affectionate thing. You might call your son, "Hey, *guaglio*."

I'm in the Bourbon Street, I'm tending bar. I'm watching a beautiful redheaded woman. And she's with this Jewish guy. Nice looking guy, spending money. I give them their drinks, I got my vest, got my name on it. So he wants a refill, he wants to order again. He calls me, loud, and he says, "Hey, *guaglio*." In other words, "Hey, you fuckin' greaseball." Well, that ain't affectionate. My grandfather could call me that all day. Not this guy.

So I go up to him, I says, "Listen." I point, I says, "This is my fuckin' name. It ain't *guaglio*. Okay?" I walked away.

Clancy says, "What the heck?"

"He called me fuckin' *guaglio*."

"What is that?" And I explained. He says, "Listen. I'll take care of it, you don't wait on this guy."

So the guy asks for another drink, and now Clancy is taking the order. The guy asks him about me: "Hey, what the hell's wrong with that guy?"

Clancy says, "Ah, he's a little touchy." And in doing the drink, behind the bar, Clancy throws a little something in the drink. And he winks at me, and he gives him the drink.

Let me tell you something. I never saw anything work so fast. He took the drink and he started squirming. "Where's the bathroom?"

Here's me: "It's over there, *guaglio*." And he didn't make it.

I learned afterwards it was called croton oil. They use it at the horse track. It's an animal laxative, when the horse ain't feeling good. Let me tell you, if you give a person a lot, you kill the guy.

〜

Bill Hanhardt was a big customer on Rush Street. At that time he was a sergeant out of old Area Six, at Grace and Damen, and he had that area. A lot of those Outfit guys from the North Side were from his neighborhood. He knew them all.

I was always with Krueger and Junior, constantly. We'd run into Hanhardt: "Hello, sir. How you doin'?" We never had to pay a check when we were with him. I was a young kid, but Hanhardt liked me, because he had fun with me. Once he took me to Mike Fish's, a great restaurant, high line. We saw Tony Zale there, the champion boxer. He's with a woman, I send him a drink, he comes over and talks to us. He was my idol, Tony Zale.

We would go by a place called the Stork Lounge. It was on Walton, down the street from the Playboy Club. The joint was owned by a guy named Ralph Scaccia. A good, funny guy. We used to have a lot of fun with him. All the Playboy bunnies used to hang in the Stork Lounge. When they weren't working, that was the place to go. The bunnies were the hottest things there were. And the guys would introduce me to them, and one thing led to another. Me and Krueger, who I got a job for with the Jap, we had an apartment, a hotel room at the Maryland Hotel on Rush Street. We kept it for the girls. And we got it for zero. Why? Because Krueger was laying the woman who was the manager. Krueger had a way with women. Between the two of us, we had every bunny in the city.

Ralph Scaccia says, "I don't know how the fuck you wind up with these girls."

I says, "I'm gonna tell you how. We give them a lot of fun. They like to laugh. You gotta be funny with these girls. You can't go, 'Yeah, I'm a big torpedo,' you can't just give 'em money. It don't work. They make enough money over there. They don't need your money. They want to have fun."

They had card games right on Rush Street. There was a place where they played, on Wabash and Delaware, a social club. We used to walk there. They would play gin, hearts, *klabiash*, Greek rummy. They had all kinds of players in there. It was mostly bartenders and club people, the industry people. Guys would come in, and they would charge by the hour. There's no money on the table—they're playing on the points. And they had the cops, my God. It ain't like today. They had all the cops.

I was a checker player; I'd play checkers for money. I'd play Ping-Pong for money—if you weren't a Chinaman, you didn't have a chance with me. Then I'd play *brisco* and Italian blackjack. It's called *sette e mezzo*, that's seven and a half in Italian. There are no eights, nines, or tens, a picture card stands for a half, except for the king of diamonds. The king of diamonds you could use for anything. You play it like blackjack, closest to seven and a half. If you get seven and a half, it's blackjack.

After the game, I'd go home. I didn't want my mother to know. I had to keep it from her. My mother, what a saint.

10

YOU'RE IN THE ARMY NOW

n 1966 the Vietnam War was heating up and I was just waiting to get a draft notice, like a lot of my friends. But my friend Krueger had a guy who worked for Litsinger Ford on Washington Boulevard who could do the job of getting you out of the army through some connection he had, for five hundred dollars. Krueger got out; he gave him the five hundred. Me, it never worked, I don't know why. So I got stuck. I had to go.

The funny part was, Krueger took along a guy named Tommy Tomillo, who later became a big racehorse trainer. The guy looks at Tomillo and says, "I don't need to take your money. I'm gonna tell you how you do it. I want you to eat like there's no tomorrow. Till you can't take anymore. At a certain weight, you're gonna beat it.

They won't take you." And sure enough, he got very fat. And he got out because of being overweight. I ran into him one day—he was fat again—and he said, "I shoulda went into the fuckin' army. Look what this Krueger did to me."

I was in the army two years. I went to Fort Knox, Kentucky, for basic training, met some nice guys. That was the big joke in the neighborhood: Fred Pascente at Fort Knox, ha ha. I had a good time. I got along with everybody, I made the rank, private first class. I was a good shot with the M14. I was a sharpshooter. Basic training at Fort Knox, advanced training at Fort Sill in Oklahoma for the MOS. That's your military occupational specialty, what your job is gonna be. Mine was artillery. And then I came home for a month, because my next spot was Fort Ord, California, where they have a Vietnam village set up, the conditions you're gonna run into over there. The climate and everything, snakes and rats, this is it. Next stop is Vietnam. I mean, you're going, all set.

So I come home, I'm home for thirty days, and for some reason I have to report to Fort Sheridan, just north of Chicago. *Boom*, I run into a guy named Bobby Tagliola, from the neighborhood. He's there, he's finishing up. He says, "What are you doing here?"

"Bobby, I'm getting ready to go to Fort Ord."

"Then you're going over to the big place. You want to go there?"

"Fuck no."

"Come on with me."

We walk in, we see the sergeant major of the Fifth Army, an Italian guy. He ran the whole Fifth Army, because the commanding general was never there. He was always going on parades, so the sergeant major ran the show. He says, "You want to go to Vietnam?"

"No."

"Well, I'm gonna get you assigned here. Is that OK?"

OK? I didn't want to tell him what I would do for him. And he did it right over the telex machine. *Tap, tap-tap.* That's how quick it was. He says, "I'm gonna get you ninety dollars a month more, because you're gonna live at home."

Ninety more? I'd take ninety less to live at home.

He says, "You got no KP, you got no guard duty, you got . . ."

So what could I do for him? He told me he loved the hockey games. Well, by this point I had twenty-six season passes to the Blackhawks. All our guys went. So I said, "How's four tickets, front row?"

Well, now I could do anything.

They sent me down to Fifty-Fifth and Lake Shore on the South Side. Part of the Fifth Army was there, because they were in transition. They were moving everything to Fort Sheridan. But there was still a little office there, and they had some apartments there for the officers, and they made me an MP. I had a guard post during the day, and I would be relieved, and I'd come home. I worked for a civilian, I was off on the weekends. It was unbelievable.

If I hadn't run into Tagliola, I would have been in Vietnam.

⌇

I'm on leave from the army, in 1966 or so. I get a call from Junior: a friend of ours got beat up. This was a neighborhood guy who later moved out to a town northwest of Chicago. This guy was a card player, a shrewd gambler. He played poker with some guys—not street guys; these were greenhorns—and every week he'd beat them silly. With the money he won from them, he opened his own business, and he was doing terrific. I loved the guy.

"Who did it?" I said.

"These guys he was playing cards with."

"Let's go."

We didn't recruit any heavy guys. We had to work with who we had available. Two guys I knew were game, but they weren't fighters. One of them, his sister could beat him up. I told him, "Get a couple of guns." He got three guns. And we jumped in the car and shot out there.

Our friend was home from the hospital. He had a lot of stitches, his head was bandaged, he had a broken arm—he was in bad shape. He told us what happened. These guys he was playing with thought he was cheating because he won all the time. Finally they went ballistic and gave him a beating that put him in the hospital. This guy could handle himself, but not with six guys. Muhammad Ali's going to have a problem with six guys.

So we went over to our friend's place and laid for the guys. We knew word would get around that we were there. We had Junior, who was tough, our friend, who was tough but laid up, and my two guys, who were not particularly tough. I had one gun in one pocket, one in another, one of my guys had the other gun.

After we had been there a little while, a car came screeching into the parking lot. Two guys jumped out. Our friend said, "There they are. These two guys."

The others wanted to run out there and get started. I was the coolest one. I told the other guys, "Listen. These guys ain't coming to fight with two guys. If they were coming to fight, they'd have eight guys. They got guns. When we walk up to them, if they go in their pants, go in their pocket, just hit the ground. I'll take care of the rest."

So we walked out. And sure enough, one of them went into his pocket, and *boom!* He started shooting.

The others hit the ground. Me, I was like Wyatt Earp at the O.K. Corral, shooting with a gun in each hand. And they ran. They jumped in the car and took off. I chased them as they were fleeing, and I sprayed the whole side of the car, real close. All the windows. I ran out of bullets, grabbed the third gun from the guys, and emptied it. They took off.

Thank God I didn't hit anybody. I was a young kid, I was reckless.

Next thing we knew, they turned themselves in to the police. They were scared. Our friend knew the chief, so we went over to the station and had a little talk with him.

The chief says, "Where's the gun?"

"We didn't have no guns."

"Well, they said you had—"

"No. We don't have no guns."

Our friend said, "Chief, it's a personal thing. I don't want to press charges. Let me in the cell with these guys, alone." He wanted to fight them both.

The cops said, "Get the fuck out of here."

And that was the end of that. Our friend never saw them again.

⌇

Milwaukee Phil's guys came to see me. Joe Lombardo said, "Listen. You gotta do us a favor. Our boss, his son is going to Vietnam. He's here now. Could you square him away?"

I didn't know Milwaukee Phil. He didn't mean anything to me. But Spilotro, I'd shine his shoes. I did it for Tony. I said, "I will positively go ask."

So I went right to the sergeant major. Now, this was after he'd gone to a couple of hockey games. I said, "I got a request."

"What is it?"

"Well, now I don't want you in trouble. The guy who you're doing it for is a mobster, a big, big guy. His son, Dominic, he's here right now. The old man wants him out of Vietnam."

The sergeant major says, "Let me see what I can do." And *badda-boom*, he got it done. Dominic got stationed there, living off the post.

Now you tell me, how big of a favor is that, to get a kid out of Vietnam? Money can't buy that. Tony and Schweihs, the German, they didn't forget. Schweihs used to see me and say, "Hey, the soldier." The guys would say, "Huh? You know that guy? That's a scary guy."

"I know him."

～

He's scary even in the photographs. There's no clowning, no feigned boredom, no effort to look unconcerned. The extant mug shots of Frank Schweihs show a man who is royally pissed off to be detained. He juts his chin at the camera, heavy-lidded and taut-lipped, letting you know how lucky you are that he is temporarily unable to lay his hands on a weapon. If anything he got scarier with age, turning from a stocky black-haired bruiser into a nasty old man with a mean streak a mile wide. From his wheelchair at his arraignment on federal charges in 2008, dying of cancer, he snarled across a courtroom at a prosecutor who had been staring at him: "Do I look like a fag to you?"

Francis John Schweihs was from the southern Patch, Twenty-Ninth and Wallace in Chicago's Bridgeport neighborhood. He would be called "the German" his whole life, but his mother was Italian. He started as a thief; his first arrest was for burglary in 1949. Stealth was not his forte: in 1952 he was captured by police after a cinematic high-speed car chase, complete with an exchange of gunfire, after a disrupted restaurant robbery in Elmwood Park. By the late 1950s he was known as a prolific hijack man and cartage thief.

But other talents emerged. In 1962 an eighteen-year-old Cicero beauty named Eugenia Pappas was found dead in the Chicago River in the industrial wastelands just west of Bridgeport with a bullet through her heart. She had been Frank Schweihs's girlfriend, much to her family's dismay, and when last seen had been driving his car. The car turned up at an auction a month later, stripped and washed clean. Schweihs was sought for questioning; he turned himself in to a Cook County Sheriff's Police investigator named Richard Cain, of whom more will be said later. Despite the fact that it was properly a case for the Chicago Police Department, Cain was allowed to question Schweihs and release him without charges.

Within a decade Schweihs had become a top Outfit hit man. Witnesses' accounts often noted the shooter's slight limp: Schweihs had sustained a gunshot wound to the leg in a brisk encounter with police in 1956. The leg didn't slow him much; he was known to law enforcement as a "police fighter," not an easy arrest. He once bolted down the back stairs while being booked by sheriff's deputies and had to be restrained by all hands on deck. Somehow he never went to jail for long.

Like many Chicagoans, he hated the harsh winters and began spending them in Florida. His police record shows the corresponding geographic diversification, with multiple arrests in the Sunshine State for burglary. But it was the killing that made his reputation. Appropriately putting a seal on a generational shift, Schweihs was a prime suspect in the killing of Milwaukee Phil's hit squad partner, Chuck Nicoletti, in 1977. By then even his professional colleagues were afraid of him.

Fear is capital in the organized crime business, and with the reputation came the clout: Schweihs became the top overseer of the pornography racket in Chicago, collecting the Outfit's street tax from adult bookstores and theaters. Prompt payment was encouraged by the deaths of two theater owners by unnatural causes.

⌇

I'll tell you when I knew Tony was something to be reckoned with. I was with Joey Glimco, who was the Outfit's union boss, Chuckie Nicoletti, Joe Lombardo. We're sitting in Milwaukee Phil's house. Nice house, in North Riverside. After I got his son out of going to Vietnam I was welcome there—I could walk in. So Phil's bragging, because Tony had told him, "This guy, Fred, he's a tough guy. He'll fight anybody. He'll fight Muhammad Ali. He'll lose, but he'll fight him. He don't care."

So Phil says to me, "You think you're a tough guy, huh?" Now, these guys are all listening like he was the king of Siam. He says, "I had a fight with three guys one time. And I had the best of them, and the one threw a bottle of pneumonia in my face, and that was the end of it. They got the best of me."

And I start laughing. "What?"

He says, "Yeah, pneumonia."

I says, "It's *ammonia*." And Lombardo's waving his arms, trying to tell me, "Don't do that!"

I says, "What the fuck? It's ammonia."

So here's Phil: "What's the difference?"

Anyway, they're talking about different guys in the Outfit. And Phil says, "Listen to me, guys." Just like that, I mean matter-of-factly. "Whoever's got that Tony, the little guy, is the boss."

~

Milwaukee Phil had a girl. A beautiful, beautiful girl. She was related to Al Meo, the owner of Meo's Norwood House Restaurant. When I tell you she was beautiful, I mean she had everything. Class. She was Milwaukee Phil's girl, and nobody knew it.

I knew, because after I did the favor for him, he had me drive her to Hot Springs, Arkansas. What a spot that was. This was better than Las Vegas. They had these baths, the hot springs. There were resort hotels. They had horses, if you want to go horseback riding, if you want to go on hayrides, if you want outdoor activity. And the action was like Las Vegas. You had gambling. Dealing, slots, crap games. Another floor, you got these baths, mineral baths, massages. Then they had lounges and entertainment. And then, the final floor, hookers. Whatever you want.

There was a guy there named Roberts. He was the biggest bookmaker in that whole region. Bookmakers in Chicago dealt with him. He had the horses and he bet sports, so they would lay off to him. And they couldn't mess with him; he worked for Carlos Marcello, the New Orleans mob boss. A southern gentleman, Roberts. He'd shake your hand. He would say, in his gentlemanly way, "The governor, he loves this place. But unfortunately, he can't partake." Roberts gave me a horse; he told me to bet this horse to win. I put down twenty, and it won by eleven lengths. I made $120.

We were in a hotel, at Phil's expense. I had carte blanche. This was my first encounter with Cristal champagne. Luxury like I had never seen. Phil called; he was supposed to come down, but he couldn't make it. "Stay an extra day."

I said, "Yeah, absolutely."

∽

Hot Springs, Arkansas, was a has-been by the time Bill Clinton's election to the White House briefly tweaked national interest in his boyhood home, but in an earlier age the spa town on the western slope of the Ouachita Mountains had had all the notoriety and magnetism that Las Vegas has today. The geothermal water supplying the city's dozens of springs was exploited from its earliest days, with a post– Civil War building boom producing a Gilded Age resort destination with all the latest conveniences. The moneyed classes coming to take the waters had ample leisure time, and horse racing and associated pursuits quickly followed them there. By the turn of the twentieth century two rival families, the Flynns and the Dorans, were shooting it out for control of the vice trade. And starting in the 1880s, teams in the newly professionalized sport of baseball made Hot Springs their preferred spring training site until another booming warm weather resort area, Florida, lured them away in the 1920s.

The town's modern era arrived with a New York bootlegger named Owney Madden in 1935; chased out of Manhattan, he settled in Hot Springs and found it to his liking. He built the Hotel Arkansas with its casino and made the town into a popular vacation spot for gangsters, drawing Chicago and New York hoods. Madden presided over the town's golden age of vice, which featured numerous casinos, racetracks, and brothels, all operating under the benign eye of a securely purchased local government and law enforcement establishment.

The golden age ended with a reforming city administration in the 1940s, but vice bounced back with the election of Orval Faubus as Arkansas governor in 1954. Faubus, best known for calling out the Arkansas National Guard to prevent the admission of black students to Little Rock Central High School, proved to be more tolerant of gambling than of integration. Under his administration Hot Springs regained much of its verve and continued to provide the guilty pleasures for another decade. The town was finally shut down by another New York carpetbagger, governor Winthrop Rockefeller, who sent in the state police in 1967 to roust the mobsters and shutter the casinos. Locals complain that the town hasn't been the same since.

∽

So now we had time on our hands. While we were driving down there, the girl had started to hit on me. Now she rubbed my leg and said, "Freddy, I like you."

"I like you, too."

"No, I mean I *really* like you."

If you saw this woman, *madonn'*. But this was Milwaukee Phil's girl. Man, I was scared. I said to myself, "Are you crazy? You'll be horse feed. There's a million women out there. What do you need this girl for?"

I told her, "I like you, too. But I ain't crazy."

Thank God she didn't take it further. She didn't say another word.

II

FAMILY FEUDS

Frankie Furio became a made guy with the Calabrese crew. That was Frank Calabrese, who had his own juice operation under the Chinatown crew. And this put us on the outs with him, because he shouldn't have gone with those guys. He should have stuck with Tony. But he didn't. They gave him a good deal and he went. He was my stepbrother, as kids we were friends, but Frankie went bad on us. My cousin Mikey wouldn't talk to him, to the day Frankie died. And I didn't know the reason at the time. They kept it from me. Mikey, my brother Billy, Tony—they knew. Those were the only three guys.

This happened when I was in the service. It stemmed from an arrest. Frankie and Billy got pinched together over a hijacking. They had a load of Gillette razor blades. Billy was the truck driver. Billy pulls in the alley where Frankie lived with a trailer and they're unloading, in the alley. Well, a citizen calls the police.

The police were smart, they called the FBI. The FBI came running up the stairs and broke the door in, they got 'em dead-bang. That was it.

Frankie got convicted, went to jail. Frankie had a bad sheet, a background, heists and this and that. Billy didn't; he pled guilty and got probation. He got a break. That's the way it used to work. If you had no background, they'd give you one chance. It wasn't like today: you go away, first time.

So Frankie wanted Billy to help pay, kick in money for the lawyer and everything. He didn't have no money. That's their beef. And he went to meet Billy. They're at a gas station on Harlem Avenue. Tony was there on behalf of Furio, because Furio worked for him. So he was at his side. And Mikey was there, and he took Billy's side.

Billy's a rough-and-tumble guy; so's Frankie. So he's threatening Billy, he gets into something, they start in, now they go at it. I mean, these are two brothers, they're going at it. Mikey and Tony were standing by. Billy was giving it to him. Well, Frankie pulls out a gun, and he hits him in the head with the gun. *Boom!* He split him. And Billy starts squirting. And he backs up, and Frankie hits him again. Hurt him pretty good. And Mikey was hot. He went after him. "You motherf—" Mikey grabs him, but Tony tells Mikey to stay out of it. Now, Tony's a made guy. What he says, goes.

I never heard about it. But when I come home on leave, then I start sensing something. I saw Billy hurt like this, I said, "What happened?"

"Ah, I got a beef with some fuckin' shines."

I knew something was wrong here. But nobody tells me a thing. I don't know nothing about it. So when I find out, I blow my top. I'm pissed because Frankie had the gun. So I went to the most important guy: I went to Tony. Those two fight, you're gonna get three stories. Tony, even though he favored Frankie, I'm gonna get the true story. I said, "What's the deal?"

Tony says, "I couldn't believe he hit his brother with a gun. I was upset, but what am I gonna do? That's my guy. I'm here just to make sure that things went smooth, and they didn't."

"But he pulled a gun, Tone. What am I supposed to do?"

"Forget about it," he says. "You either forget about it or you go kill him."

I says, "Kill him! What the hell is this?"

"Well, then, drop it. It's done, over with."

"If I was there, I'd have killed him."

"That's why I didn't tell you. We made a pact, all of us. To let it be."

And they kept it. Mikey never told me. Mikey shied away from Frankie. And Tony broke up with Frankie, so Frankie went with Calabrese. But Tony says his concern was me.

I would have shot him. I'm not kidding you. I mean, he hits him with a gun? I don't care if Billy was wrong. Which, I would probably say in the fight and what got it to that point, he probably was.

～

I don't know what accounts for the differences between brothers. They always ask that. The same blood, father, the same blood, mother. I don't know. I got a little of Billy, but I'm not as bad. And my little brother, Dicky—if I see Dicky arguing with somebody, the other guy's wrong, because this guy, he's as nice as could be.

Billy was the worst of all. Billy and his crew made Jack Cerone's house in Elmwood Park. Jack Cerone was the Elmwood Park boss. They called him Jackie the Lackey, because he had been

Tony Accardo's driver. But he became the boss of Elmwood Park, and he was one of the three or four top guys. He sat at the table with Giancana, Accardo, Buccieri. I mean, these were big guys. And Cerone was one of them.

What happened was, Billy, his friend Johnny Santucci, and a third guy made the house. If you go down Thatcher, off of North, you'll see those houses. That's where Cerone lived. It was a beautiful house. And it was against the forest preserve; Billy and his guys liked the cover. You go there at night, you drop the car off, and you walk. Anyway, they got him. They knew that the place was empty, and they made it. And they got cash, jewelry, furs, and guns.

Billy says he didn't know it was Cerone's house. But Billy lies. Today I don't know. Number one, they violated the rule: you cannot steal in Elmwood Park. No matter who. You can't bother them guys. And he did. Well, now, when Billy gets wind of it, thank God he didn't get rid of everything. They kept it, and he comes to me. He says, "You helped Milwaukee Phil. You're gonna have to help me."

But I wouldn't go see Phil until I went through the chain. So I went to Tony. I says, "Tony, I got big troubles."

"*We* got big troubles." That's the way he handled it. He says, "Well, what is it?" And I told him. "That jag-off." He was so fuckin' mad.

"What am I gonna do?"

"Did they know what they were doing?"

If Billy told me he knew, I would have told Tony. Because he wants the truth, and he'll work on it. I says, "Tony, I don't know. But you know him, he's a reckless guy."

"Yeah. I'm gonna go see Phil."

I says, "You want me to go with you? He owes me."

"No, no, no. This is nothing to do with you."

Phil was higher than Cerone. Cerone was the chief of the Elm-wood Park crew. Can't mess with him. But Phil didn't have a zone. Like I said, everybody had to go to him. So Phil says Billy's gonna have to bring all the stuff back. "The guns, and there's a manifest, there's a book." Cerone had a log, a notebook that was important. Billy didn't get rid of nothing. He was smart enough not to. Didn't sell a thing.

They didn't squawk. Billy had to turn everything back, and Cerone read him the riot act. "You punk mother . . ." He kept on telling him how lucky he was.

Billy told me, "I thought this guy was gonna stab me."

But Cerone got everything back.

⁌

Guy Mendola was from the neighborhood. He was a good guy. And he was good to us. If he had a score, he would lean it toward us. Back in 1964 he got killed, shot outside his house while he was out on bail after a bank job he did with some other guys. Nobody was ever charged. Now, when I'm in the army, I find out why. I got it from Gerry Carusiello, who we called Dinger. He was born and raised in Melrose Park. His father was a well-known guy. They loved him. His brother was a Melrose Park policeman. He was a good guy, tough as they come.

This is the way Dinger gave it to me.

The bank job was set up by a guy from our neighborhood named Pat Schang, along with Frank DeLegge Jr. and Frank Sr.—the two DeLegge boys, father and son. Mendola was in on it; so was Joe D'Argento, the guy who threw a bat at me when we were kids. The bank was in Franklin Park. Joe D. told me they had an inside person, a woman. The plan was, the Brink's driver, he comes in and the money is ready for him. It's all counted out, and it's in this holding spot, in a room that's locked. It could be there for anywhere from five minutes to a half hour. And he'd come in and pick it up.

Well, they got there first. And they had it timed pretty good—they're in there and out in minutes. When they leave, they're gonna drive to Melrose Park, which is the next suburb over from Franklin Park, where they got the stash spot. And on the way they have to go across some train tracks, and they know when the train is coming, so in case they get a chase, they're gonna beat the train but the pursuit will get blocked. They got it timed.

So they get the money, and they get away, and everything goes smooth. They stash the car, and the gloves and the masks and the money, everything. Good score. They go their separate ways to let things cool off.

When they went back, the money was gone. Everything else was there, but the money was gone. And the next thing you know, they all get arrested, except Guy Mendola.

They get out on bail. DeLegge, the son, says, "There's a snitch. We gotta go talk to the boss." The Outfit boss in that territory was one of the old 42 Gang guys. He says, "Well, boys, we're gonna give you a lie box." And they bring in this Richard Cain to give everyone a lie detector test. Cain was big—he was the undersheriff under Richard Ogilvie. But he also worked for Mooney, Sam Giancana. And Ogilvie was a legitimate guy, a former US attorney. How he wound up with this Cain, I don't know.

Cain sent a guy to give them all the lie box. And the next thing, Guy Mendola gets killed. And the word goes around: "He was a snitch."

Guy Mendola was no snitch. Pat Schang turned out to be a snitch. Joe D'Argento turned out to be a snitch. Mendola wasn't. I know Bill Roemer, the FBI's top organized crime guy, says he was, in one of his books, but the book was bullshit. Tony didn't believe it. I talked with Tony about it. I said, "How in the fuck could Mendola get killed?"

Tony was upset to no end. He said, "That guy didn't do this." Tony was sharp. He put it all together: DeLegge and the boss, the old 42 Gang guy, they were close. Tony figured DeLegge took the money and partnered up with the boss, and all the other guys got stiffed. Pat Schang and Joe D. bought it hook, line, and sinker and got screwed. But then they got arrested, and the boss and DeLegge needed a scapegoat. They figured, Mendola, he's got nobody. He's the fall guy.

Guys know what happened. And you know they're gonna be bitter. I wanted those guys, bad. But Tony told me to forget about it. There was no way I could mess with an Outfit boss. So I never did anything. They all fell by the wayside. DeLegge's dead. His father's dead. The others went to prison. Even Cain went to prison eventually, for sending his guy to give the lie box test. He did three years and got out.

But Guy Mendola was still dead.

〜

You can't fool all of the people all of the time, but Richard Cain seems to have come close. Among the people he fooled were Richard Ogilvie and William Roemer. Ogilvie was a US attorney in the 1950s, Cook County sheriff in the '60s, and the governor of Illinois in the '70s; his reputation for probity has never been shaken. An enduring mystery of Chicago politics is why the spotless Ogilvie consented to hire Richard Cain as head of his Special Investigations Unit when he was elected sheriff in 1962. It was no secret that Cain, during his stint with the Chicago Police Department, had been described as Sam Giancana's bagman. His ties to Giancana went back to Taylor Street, where Cain had spent his teenage years with his divorced mother. The long-lived story that Cain was Giancana's illegitimate son has been debunked, but there is little doubt than Cain joined the police department at Giancana's urging. A crime boss can always use another cop or two.

Cain's police career could accurately be described as checkered. An enthusiastic operative on the vice squad, he was suspended for killing a hustler in an alley behind the Greyhound station in the Chicago Loop; the shooting was found to be justified, but the killing had a bad smell that never lifted.

Ogilvie's confidence in Cain evidently dated from 1960, when Cain was lent to the US attorney's office to do legwork on the prosecution of Tony Accardo. Ogilvie was impressed with the information Cain produced, apparently not suspecting that it was carefully vetted by the Outfit. Accardo's conviction on tax charges was overturned on appeal.

In 1962, after the hyperactive Cain had spent two years in Mexico on mysterious errands, newly elected Sheriff Ogilvie hired him despite numerous warnings and put him in charge of vice investigations. An extravaganza of gambling raids followed, resulting in few convictions. Mostly the targets were independent operations that had not ponied up the Outfit street tax. Ogilvie finally fired Cain in 1964 after a staged raid was exposed.

Arthur Bilek, who headed the sheriff's police under Ogilvie and repeatedly warned him of Cain's underworld ties, once questioned Cain about his two-year exile from Chicago. Cain claimed to have been hired by the secret police in Mexico to train them in subversive techniques and the use of the polygraph. Bilek judges that to be at least partially truthful. Cain also claimed to have helped the CIA train the Bay of Pigs invasion force; Bilek thinks that "highly unlikely." The longer Bilek listened, the more Cain's claims tested his credulity: Cain said he had been parachuted into Yugoslavia to help train anti-Communist partisans. Bilek's judgment was that Cain was a talented fabulist. "He didn't speak any Slavic languages. And he knew nothing about counterinsurgency and even less about warfare."

Bilek is apparently of a more skeptical disposition than Roemer, who was the FBI's point man on organized crime in Chicago in the 1960s and '70s. After arresting Cain on charges related to the polygraphing of the Franklin Park robbers, Roemer developed him as an informant. They became close friends, and Roemer later wrote that Cain was "a made guy who became a double agent and worked for us."

In the late '60s and early '70s, Cain took FBI money and fed Roemer stories while working to extend his control over Outfit gambling operations. There was talk that Cain was positioning himself for a shot at the top spot in the Outfit. Strangely, the information Roemer paid for never seemed to allow the FBI to deliver a crushing blow.

There continue to be two schools of thought about who Cain was really working for, and it is fascinating to speculate about who would have benefited more if the head of the Outfit had been a confidant of the FBI's top organized crime man. Sadly, it never came to pass.

12

THIS IS A POLICEMAN?

I got out of the army in 1968 and went right on the police department. I was in the commander's office at Fort Sheridan. On the
wall there was a sign: JOIN THE POLICE DEPARTMENT OF A MAJOR
CITY, GET A NINETY-DAY EARLY OUT. I said, "I'm gonna look into this."

I was no policeman. But you hear things from guys you know:
"It's the best job there is. You got a fuckin' license to steal. You can
do what you want. Benefits, you never have to worry about insurance. Pension, you put your twenty in and that's it."

People that knew me couldn't believe it. Milwaukee Phil says,
"All right, now get out of my fuckin' house." He was joking. He
says, "Good for you. That might turn out good for you." That was
it. Tony says, "Not bad. That's a good thing."

My brothers, they were going, "What the— Are you crazy? You're gonna be a cop?" My mother was so happy. My younger brother, Dicky, was a cop before me. He came on with my friend Sammy Gambino. I came on after the army. And I'm glad I did it. It was a good job. A lot of benefits, met a lot of good people.

I got the application, took the test. I had no clout. I didn't need the clout; I was a good student. I passed the test legitimately. And at that time, they gave you five points towards your score if you were military, which was huge. My next step was the physical; I passed—no dope, no nothing. Now it was the strength test, the run test. I was in really good shape, coming out of the army. I did a mile in six and a half minutes. Then we had to do X amount of pull-ups, X amount of push-ups. But I did that in the army every day. If you had the clout you could be five hundred pounds. But I passed it with flying colors. They sent me a letter. You're accepted, this is your starting day in the police academy. Bingo. I informed the army, they let me out early, it's on my record, and I went to school.

The academy was great. At the time it was on O'Brien Street, right off of Halsted, just north of Maxwell Street. It was an old rinky-dink place; they said it was a place where they kept prisoners in the Civil War. We were with thirty or forty guys; we had to go sixteen weeks. And in them sixteen weeks you were given aptitude tests. Every week we would take a test. Stuff that was a snap for me, but it wasn't for most of the guys. I'm a St. Ignatius student. That's an edge over most of them guys. So I breezed. I was class commander. That means I aced it.

The classes covered search and seizure. You have to give the man his rights, because Miranda rights had just come in focus. When you can shoot: You cannot shoot a guy that's running away from you, a fleeing felon. If you're in fear of your life, or in fear for a citizen's life, then you can use deadly force. It was interesting, and it was all good stuff. It was never dull. Everything that they were teaching, you needed to know. A lot of law.

The most useful thing we learned was defensive tactics. They got rough, they were good. They had some pros. I'll never forget, the guy's name was Sarbarneck. He was tough. "You want to mess with me? Come on. You don't like the way I teach you? Come on." Who's gonna fuck with this guy? He had no neck. But he was a good guy.

And it was good stuff. He showed you some moves that you could use. Then he showed you some vital spots: "You hit the guy right here, in the throat, he's gone. He'll cough, and he can't breathe. Come up like this, with the heel of your hand—you go too hard you might kill him."

Along with the defensive tactics was the physical training. You had to run. And again, the calisthenics. You had to do push-ups, you had to do pull-ups, sit-ups. That was throughout the whole thing.

After a couple of weeks in the academy, they send you out to buy the uniform. They give you a list; there are several places you can go to. I went to Kale's, on Roosevelt Road. I got ahold of Nucci Lombardo, Joe's brother. By this point Nucci was a booster, a guy who lifted clothes, a professional. He had oversized coats made, and he would stash stuff in these oversized pockets on the side, and he would walk out. I brought him to the uniform place with me. It was crowded.

He got my jacket. He got me half a dozen pairs of pants. He got me a dozen shirts, ties. He got me everything. He put it all in the coat. Every time he left, he made a trip to the car, he put it in the trunk. I come back, he's ready. I was shopping for a good hour, I was seeing guys: "How you doin'?" They get in line, with stacks of merchandise, they go to the counter and pay. When I left, I bought a whistle and a hat. That's it.

The clerk says, "That's it?"

"Yeah, I'll come back later."

Nucci got all my stuff. This is a policeman? There's where my career was headed.

⌇

They don't give you the gun training until your sixth week at the academy. The training was simple. They showed you the tactics, the technique. Nobody's gonna shoot like John Wayne, because you're not gonna be accurate. You've got to brace yourself or you've gotta find something to brace your hand on. You have to get your target in the sights. I was an excellent shot. I was an expert.

You got your gun, now you're a big shot. You're wearing the gun, and the last couple of weeks you put the full uniform on. And they put you in the squad car with a training officer, and he shows you what's what, you spend the day. Then you go into the Detective Division and they put you in the squad with someone. Now you're in the suit and tie.

You do all this stuff before you get out of the academy. On-the-job training, and you learn more on that than you did in that whole class. Then they come and speak to you. Each unit—the Patrol Division, then the Detective Division and this division and that division—everybody is trying to recruit you. But the best job was a detective. You didn't have the opportunity to make detective right away, but they came in and talked to you anyway.

Here's where I did have clout: when it came time to be assigned. You pick your district, where you want to go. I wanted to go to the Twentieth District, on Foster Avenue just east of Damen on the North Side. It was a good district, and I had a lot of friends there. Sammy Gambino was there already. My clout was Bill Hanhardt, and I got the assignment.

When I got there, it was soon after the big scandal in the district, the Summerdale scandal. Richard Morrison was a burglar, and he had the cops with him. The police were setting up targets and providing protection. It was such a huge scandal they had to bring in a new superintendent. And they changed the name of the Twentieth District from Summerdale to Foster Avenue.

O. W. Wilson became police superintendent—Orlando Wilson. He came from outside, from California. He was brought in to clean up the department, and he did a good job. Everybody still made money on the side. He didn't bother that. He was concentrating on the guys that were working with burglars. I wasn't on the force yet, but I know from other guys telling me, when they all met, he says, "You have absolution. Whatever you did, I don't want to hear about it. We start fresh. But from now on, you do something wrong, you're going down." That's the way he started his introductory speech to the men. He was good.

༄

Once Summerdale Avenue was just a street on the North Side of Chicago that lent its name to the local police district. Now, like Watergate, Summerdale is shorthand for a culture-changing scandal.

The 1950s were hard on Chicago's sense of security. A trio of sensational and unsolved murders of children between 1955 and 1957 wiped out the city's Eisenhower-era complacency and exposed its law enforcement bodies as dysfunctional. In October 1955 three Northwest Side boys went missing and were found raped and murdered two days later. A massive investigation scooped up hundreds of suspects but failed to identify the killer. The Schuessler-Peterson killings were not cleared until 1995, when longtime suspect Kenneth Hansen was finally convicted. In December 1956 it was the South Side's turn when the Grimes sisters, Barbara and Patricia, disappeared. Their bodies were not found until three weeks later, and the autopsy failed even to establish a cause of death. Geographic symmetry was preserved in August 1957 when the dismembered body of a West Side girl, Judith Mae Andersen, was found in two separate drums floating in Montrose Harbor a week after she disappeared. Nobody was ever charged. In all three cases, understaffing, lack of coordination, and interdepartmental bickering hindered the investigations.

Chicagoans had barely assimilated the idea that the police were unable to protect them from predators when a special task force of detectives operating on secretly obtained warrants fanned out across the North Side on the night of January 15, 1960, and arrested eight members of a gang that had been responsible for a spike in burglaries of businesses in the North Side neighborhoods of Edgewater and Rogers Park. Four truckloads of stolen goods were recovered in the raid.

Burglary was nothing new, but the identity of the eight arrestees made the city choke on its morning coffee: they were uniformed police officers working out of the Summerdale station at Foster and Damen.

The bust and the subsequent prosecution were overseen by Republican state's attorney Benjamin Adamowski. An inmate at Cook County Jail awaiting trial on burglary charges had gotten word to Adamowski that he had goods to peddle. The jailbird, a career burglar named Richard Morrison, was looking at twenty years and hoping to sell as many of his partners as the market would bear. The market turned out to be pretty good, once Adamowski realized what he had on ice down at Twenty-Sixth and California. Morrison's seventy-seven-page confession made riveting reading on the front pages of Chicago's four dailies for weeks.

According to Morrison, he had been trying to go straight after a wayward adolescence. A native North Sider, he had reconnected with an old school pal, now a cop, while delivering pizzas to the Summerdale station. Getting friendly with the local flatfeet had not, unfortunately, furthered his resolve to keep on the straight and narrow.

THIS IS A POLICEMAN?

When one of the officers proposed that he cut them in on some bur-glaries, Morrison found it hard to say no. What followed was a spree that caused insurance companies to stop writing theft protection poli-cies for businesses in the affected North Side districts.

At first the cops merely scouted likely targets and stood lookout for Morrison. But the thrill of the hunt appears to have worked its magic on the acquisitive coppers, and before too long the roles were reversed, with Morrison sometimes monitoring the radio in the squad car while the patrolmen tossed bricks through store windows and browsed through merchandise by flashlight.

In true Chicago style, the cops enhanced the racket by cutting in the local burglary detectives: they had the dicks haul Morrison in for repeated questioning and split the resulting shakedown money with them.

It all came crashing down in July 1959, when Morrison carelessly got himself arrested by the wrong kind of detectives, who weren't in on the scheme and couldn't be bought off. Having gotten a pretty clear idea from his cop buddies just where he stood with them, he made the rational decision to sing at the top of his lungs.

For the first time in his reign, Richard J. Daley saw he was deal-ing with something too big and nasty to sweep under the rug. Police Commissioner Tim O'Connor resigned, supposedly due to ill health, and Daley announced the establishment of a committee to pick a new commissioner.

Their choice, announced on February 22, 1960, was O. W. Wilson, the head of the School of Criminology at the University of California and the former chief of police in Wichita, Kansas. Wil-son was at the forefront of the movement to professionalize law enforcement, and Daley gave him real authority, even ditching the scandal-tainted title of "Commissioner" and reviving an older title, "Superintendent." Wilson consolidated police districts, computerized the records department, and built a state-of-the-art communications and dispatching facility. He picked Art Bilek to overhaul training at the police academy. In an unprecedented (and since unequaled) spasm of genuine institutional change, he brought the Chicago Police Department into the modern world before going off to a well-earned retirement in 1967.

There is general agreement that O. W. Wilson's reforms were effective and lasting, turning a police department that had been a largely impotent element in a political spoils system into a modern, professional organization. But Chicago's corruption problems did not start or end with the police department. A pragmatist and realist, Wilson himself admitted in 1964, "We have made little progress in our efforts to prosecute the higher-ups in organized crime."

13

STREET SMARTS

My first week, I'm in the squad, partnered with the guy who's breaking me in. Old-time policeman, Irish guy. I'm driving. I hear the call. "Burglary in progress." Well, my friend Louie Tenuta had told me he's gonna be around Ravenswood and Wilson on a score. And he doesn't want me to get in any trouble, but to listen to the radio. So my partner's all ready to be Dan August, and me, I want to make sure Louie's OK. So I put the siren on, the lights, and my partner's shutting them off. "No, no, no, no." And I'm screeching, and hitting garbage cans, making noise. And Louie gets away. And my partner says, "You gotta be cool." When we go into roll call, he says, "I can't believe this guy, he panicked." I knew more than he knew.

But my partner was looking to make money. So he says, "You're with me, I got the word that you're an OK guy, you're in good hands."

"Whatever you say."

So we go up and down Western Avenue. Here's his theory: after midnight, anybody on the street is dirty. Stop 'em, no matter what. I said, "OK."

"They shouldn't be out, they shouldn't be here, they're cheating on their wife." He's coming up with a scenario. "Stop that guy."

"OK." Stop them, he comes back, throws a five-dollar bill in the back. The guy paid him. "Stop that guy . . ." Another fin. We were loaded with fins, and three dollars, and four dollars, sometimes ten, which was big in them days.

We come in, and then he says, "Now, I don't want you to get in trouble. Never take money from a guy that drives a Volkswagen. Never take money from a guy who smokes a pipe. Never, for sure, take money from a woman. And if he's got a beard, run away from him."

When I left him, I didn't give a shit. The guy had a beard, was smoking a pipe, in a Volkswagen, I didn't give a shit, I took it. You stop a guy and say, "You moved over, you didn't put your signal on. Lemme see your license."

"Oh, please, let me go." *Badda-bing.* A fin.

They would offer it unsolicited. It was widespread. Because we didn't make a lot of money. They didn't want to go to court, they didn't want the ticket. So they say, "Listen, officer . . ." And some, they'd come out, they'd have the license, and the fin was right underneath. *Badda-bing.* A woman comes running out of her Cadillac one time. She throws twenty dollars. She says, "Officer, my husband told me what to do."

"OK, lady." If you didn't make a hundred dollars in a night, you were worthless. It was an amazing run. And it was fun. My day off came, I didn't want to take off. I was sick, I wanted to come in. "Hey, you gotta stay home."

〜

Now, Mikey Swiatek got caught for some burglary. So I go in there, I see my captain—another Irish guy. "We got a guy in there," he says in that accent. "He's locked up; he says he's your cousin, Pascente. How could he be your cousin and he's got a goddamn Polish name?"

I says, "Well, lemme see who the guy is."

He says, "And by the way, he's got a ring on his finger, it's eight sizes too big."

So this other Irish guy says, "What do you expect, Captain, when you get it out of a dresser drawer?"

Because of me, he let him go. They caught him in the area, but they didn't catch him with nothing. So instead of getting charged and going through the motions, they let him go, and that was it.

 ⌇

Three of us worked together in one car. My days off, the other two worked together. We rotated. Three Italians. One of them was Slugger's son Terry. Then a tac car became available. That's plain-clothes—then you really got freedom. So we're talking it over, the three of us. "We gotta go get that car. Terry, you're the closest with the captain, go in there and tell him you want the car."

Terry goes to the captain, he says, "Hey, Captain. This car's available."

He says, "Yeah, sure. What you got in mind?"

"Well, I'd like to have a shot at the car, with my partners." He gives our names.

"For Christ's sake, you guys will turn your back on murder for fifty dollars." He knew, but he never did nothing about it.

Yeah, the bosses knew—just don't get caught. And if you were on the ball, like I was, I'd go see the watch commander. "Here you are, boss." I'd give him a hundred dollars. A lot of them had the

Irish brogue: "And what would this be for, Pascente? Good, good. You're a good man. Take it easy."

That was then. You cannot do that today. It changed through the years; people were getting aggravated because they knew the policemen were making big money. It's all public opinion.

⌢

We didn't start making decent money until after the protests at the Democratic Convention in August of '68. The mayor, on a broadcast, he gave us a two-thousand-dollar-a-year raise because of that convention. Right on the TV he said, "I'm giving them a two-thousand-dollar-a-year raise—they deserve it."

The convention was when I just came on. Everybody was in uniform. Everybody. We had the shields, we had all the riot gear. Who's at the Conrad Hilton, who was at Lincoln Park—the police were spread out.

The police got a bad rap. The protesters were mean, mean-spirited kids. They were spitting, they were throwing bags of human excrement, shit. Bags of rocks, bags of glass, in the faces of the policemen. And we couldn't do nothing. We had to hold our line. And the abuse was just unbelievable. I mean, we're men, we gotta take this shit? This ain't right.

The best guys were the construction workers' union, the hardhats. They saw us taking the shit, they said, "Let us get them punks." They felt sorry for us. The commander says, "Get back over there." Probably most people, good people, were on our side.

A policeman got blinded in one eye from a can of Easy-Off oven cleaner. That was it. Everyone met at the armories. That was where our roll calls were. Five hundred guys at a time. We're in there, here comes the mayor. The real Mayor Daley. And he walked fast, that fat guy, and he had his bodyguards with him. He says, "I'm addressing the men." He says, "This guy here, he's the commander. Well, I'm his boss. I'm the commander in chief of everybody." He said, "This is my rules. A guy hits you, knock him on his ass. The guy spits at you, knock him on his ass. A guy loots, blow his fuckin' head off."

Just like that. And now you got these guys pumped up after two, three days of shit. "Yeah, let's go!" Couldn't wait to go.

Well, we chased them. *Boom.* Now they're screaming: "They're hitting us!" Oh, please. Now, we did go overboard. We did it because it was stored up—they did it to us, this is payback. They were running, the police were chasing them down LaSalle Street. Hundreds and hundreds, hordes. And there was a straggler. He had hair, he looked like Charles Manson. And he's just bopping away. I'm with my partner, he's big as a house and as tough as they come. We're in the breezeway of a store. As he comes by my partner grabbed him by the hair, hit him with his fuckin' stick. *Boom!* And he left him.

They put the heavy-duty guys on the convention floor at the International Amphitheatre. Because the mayor's there, his entourage is there. The most important people in the state are there. They put Bill Hanhardt right next to the overall boss of the Amphitheater detail, Commander McLaughlin of the First District. And Dan Rather's trying to stick the mike in somebody's face, and the mayor says, "Get rid of this guy." *Badda-boom.* He's on the floor. They got rid of him, all right. "They're attacking me!" Rather's telling Walter Cronkite.

Everybody we pinched, everybody, each kid, they had their bond money, a hundred-dollar bill. I got at least fifteen of those bills, the serial numbers all in sequence. I says, "Look at this. It's four or five numbers away."

"Lookit, I got another one. All close."

I brought it to the US attorney. I says, "Now, Mr. US Attorney, I'm not smart like you, but don't you think this is kind of a conspiracy here? Where are they getting all this money—in order? New bills. Somebody higher up is paying these people."

"Oh, we'll look into it."

They didn't want to say it was a conspiracy. And we got the short end of it. And today history brings it that we rioted, the police rioted. And it's not fair.

14

FUN AND GAMES

The fun we had in the Twentieth District. Before roll call, we'd get there early, and the liar's poker game was on. All the cops are playing liar's poker. And the lieutenant comes in: "All right, put the money away." That was the ritual. Today they'd suspend you. I loved that job.

One of the other cops in the district was a guy named Richard DiNicolo. DiNicolo was a funny guy. He'd have us in stitches every night. One guy would try to top the other guy. We had a guy named Bernie Feinstein. How's that for a name of a policeman? I loved this guy. He was a big fat guy. And he had this round face, with the glasses.

Roll call. We had Lieutenant Bessey, a sweetheart of a guy. Bessey wouldn't get you in trouble. At roll call he kept his head down, looking at the roll. "Pascente."

"Here."

Never looked up. "Pascente, DiNicolo, Feinstein . . ."

And everybody's laughing. Here's Bernie Feinstein, right in front of him, naked. He's standing naked, he's got his star taped to his chest, he's got the hat on, his glasses, and his socks, those little socks with his shoes, gun on, and his fat.

Finally Bessey looks up. He goes, "What the fuck . . . Get out of here!"

We were on the floor.

We had another Jewish sergeant. Another fat guy. His name was Sam Swerinsky. With a *y* at the end—he stressed it. "It ain't *i*, because I ain't no fuckin' Polack." We called him Kelly.

Now, Swerinsky, he wanted to hang out. He wanted to have coffee, bullshit with guys. Who's playing cards, who's resting, who's off of the street. Me and my guys, we did our job. But when we're on the midnight shift, four-thirty in the morning comes, we had our place to go. We went in Rosehill Cemetery. There would be eight cars in the cemetery. But we were listening to the radio. If a call came in, we'd run.

One night Swerinsky is a little more aggressive than usual, looking for us. He knew we were in Rosehill, but he didn't know his way around. It's pitch black, and if you don't know your way, you're lost.

Radio comes: "Twenty-eighty . . ." That was his number. He had a rasping voice. The call's for me. "Come over to Peterson"— the street right outside the cemetery—"and write a parking ticket."

Yeah, I'm gonna go write a fuckin' parking ticket at four-thirty in the morning. I said, "Yeah, OK." I never went.

Now, he's not gonna say I didn't go there on the air, so he called my partner. "Seven-thirty, get over here, meet me in the alley, there's a garbage can on fire, write the report."

"OK." He answered yes, but he didn't go. So finally Swerinsky's pissed. He has to come into Rosehill on his own. He comes into the cemetery, and he's lost. Now he makes a mistake. He comes on the air. "Twenty-eighty . . . Send a car in the cemetery. I'm lost."

Well, that's all I needed. "Gimme the fuckin' radio." I get on the phone, I wait a minute, I go, "Twenty-eighty"—I'm imitating Swerinsky—"I'm getting scared here."

"I didn't say that!"

Another guy goes, "*Woooo . . .*"

We're getting off later, it's eight in the morning. I'm in the line, he looks at me and says, "That was you on the radio, huh? You fuckin' mafioso."

Another time, a human leg washed up at the Thorndale Beach. A leg! You could see the foot, the toes, everything. Ugly thing. Swerinsky made me and my partner write a report. The real report is a hospitalization case report; for a body part, you describe the leg, found at this location, that's it. Simple. So I make the legitimate report, I got it stashed. Then I made a dummy report to turn in to Swerinsky: a lost-and-found case report. And I put: *Man swimming, lost his leg, unable to locate man, but we have his leg. We'll put it . . .* So Swerinsky is reading it, now he's got to put the OK on this.

"Come here, you fuckin' greaseball! What kind of report is this?"

I said, "Well, Sarge, the guy lost his leg."

If he didn't have a heart attack with us . . . But he took it in good stride.

We had another guy, Charley Smith. A sergeant, and he talked with a high voice, just a comical voice. *"Send a team over to Weiss Hospital."* High and squeaky—that was his voice. The nitwit, he's always on the air. *"This is twenty-eight . . ."* So now, he's around Weiss Hospital, and he's involved in a chase. Everybody's gotta get off the air. *"I'm chasing a station wagon!"* He's going on and on. *"I'm on Lakeside! There he is, on Marine Drive, now I got him! Just block off . . ."* He's giving the whole play-by-play. *"He jumped out of the car! He's in the parking lot by Weiss Hospital! I'm on foot! I'm in the alley!"*

So the squads are joining in. And now all of a sudden: *"Anybody got change for a dollar?"* He got into the parking lot—you gotta pay to get out. Guys are saying, "You fuckin' nitwit."

Barney Miller ain't shit compared to what I got.

⧓

It wasn't all fun and games. It wasn't a bad district, but there was always something. We got a lot of vicious stuff, a lot of stabbings. I had a lot of good pinches. Me and my partner caught a rape in progress. I get the call, and they said a lady was screaming for help in the laundry room, on North Winthrop. We get in there, here's the guy. He's got his pants down, she's propped up on the dryer. He turned around, but he never stopped.

I get over there, I hit him with the club. *Boom!* I got him. He didn't budge. My partner hits him with the flashlight, he broke the flashlight in a hundred pieces, and the guy just buckled a little bit. Then my partner, who's a huge guy, he hit him on the side of the head. Marciano couldn't hit him like that. He catches his head, and he hits the wall, flush, and it come out, and *boom*, my partner caught him. He's buckling, because he got two hits to the head. He was out. This guy was an American Indian, a big guy. He got twelve years for that. He should have got life. The poor woman. My partner took his coat off, picked her up, she was a little thing. We got a department commendation for that.

⧓

Two policemen were killed, and we were on the case. I'm at the station, I'm working, and it just happened. It was at Foster and

Ravenswood, there was a tavern. And the two cops were sharp, but they weren't sharp enough. They were tactical officers. They spotted this guy, and they wanted him. But they saw him and he saw them, and he had a shotgun, and he dropped it at the curb and ran into this tavern. And they went in after him. So they go in there, and here's where they let their guard down. He went into the toilet, they caught him, but as they're walking him out, they were feeling secure; they felt safe because the loaded shotgun was out on the street. And they didn't search him.

He had another gun. And as they're walking him out—they didn't even handcuff him—*boom*, he blasted both of them. He killed them both right there.

So, chaos at the station. And Bill Hanhardt shows up. And he sees me. He says, "You know that tavern?"

"Sure."

"Let's go back to the tavern." And he starts grabbing these guys back by the tavern one at a time. And he finds out that where the shooter holes up is in Milwaukee. So while they're looking at his house, they're looking at his hangouts here in Chicago, Bill went right to Milwaukee. Got the Milwaukee police, told them what he's there for, and they got the guy. That's Bill. He was sharp. He had a good mind, a police mind. He made a lot of pinches.

⏜

Hanhardt pinched Mikey and his crew one time. He had to pinch them, because the FBI was involved in the arrest with Hanhardt's crew at the CIU—the Criminal Intelligence Unit, that's like the CIA. They worked on big, major criminals. It was an FBI case, and they took our guys with them to execute this warrant. Bill wasn't a guy that's gonna go find these burglars and tip them off. I would have done that. Not Bill. Bill went with the FBI.

Mikey and his crew had a trailer load of TVs, electronic equipment, at a warehouse, and the cops are laying for them. And when they were accosted, they start running. Everyone's running for their life. And the shooting began. And Mikey gets shot.

Mikey's laying on the ground, and one of the cops was gonna finish him. And Bill stopped him. "Yo. That's it." And Mikey survived, he got fixed up. But Bill had to arrest all of these guys. Mikey went away for that. But he always says, "Bill saved my life."

A few years later, after I make detective, I'm at Area Six. I would see that cop every day going by and think about how he was gonna kill Mikey. And finally something tipped and that was it. I grabbed him. Right in Area Six. I can't tell you the words I used. I just ripped him apart. Right in the squad room.

I got in a little trouble. Not big trouble.

Cops used to shoot people all the time. My pal Jimbo Caporusso got killed in 1964, before I was a policeman. Two cops killed him. And he really was assassinated. He didn't deserve it. He was in a hot car with his partner and they got chased. So they bail out, they took off. Jimbo's in a yard, a trucking company, and he's hiding under a truck. He didn't have no gun. *Boom, boom, boom*, they killed him, and they threw a gun down to make it look good.

I knew the cops that killed him. They were detectives. One of them later got killed himself—he became a federal security guard and got shot in a prisoner escape. And his partner became a top guy in the police department. I had my discussions with them, but I couldn't go full force, because I'd be in a lot of trouble.

15

BAD COMPANY

This is a better explanation of Tony Spilotro than anything. This is around 1970. We're drinking. We're with Louie Tenuta and my friend Junior. We were in a place out west, near Harlem Avenue. The guy who owned it was Big George. The place is doing good business, but we got every girl in the place—the waitresses, the bartender. And the reason is, we're always giving them money. Every time they'd come by, Tony'd give them a sawbuck. Well, where you gonna go? We're not causing any trouble.

Big George comes to the table. He says, "That's your last drink. I want you out of here." Evidently he didn't know Tony. He felt that the regular customers weren't getting the attention from the girls because we were spending so much money, and he didn't like that. In fact he was a little envious because we were getting all the attention.

And I'm going, "What the fuck, is he nuts?" Tony's spending money like crazy. I'm telling you, a couple thousand dollars. That's a lot of money in a little joint.

Tony says, "All right. You want us out of here, huh?" Now he's hot. That vein comes out of his head and throbs.

Here's me: "Holy fuck." I ain't saying nothing. I don't act unless he acts. It's his show, he's the one that started it.

"He wants me out of here, this motherfuckin' guy. All right."

Junior was ready to go, fight everybody. "Fuck him."

Tony says, "Don't worry about it."

So we're leaving, we're packing up, and Big George is there. "Let me get you right, George." Tony's calling him his name. "You want us out of here."

"I don't want you in here."

"That means we're barred from here. Correct? All right. Now I'm gonna obey your command, your wishes. Whatever you say goes." Now he steps outside. He says, "Now, George, here's my rules. We can't enter these premises, from here on. Now here's my rule. You can't enter *out* of here. The minute you're out of here, you're barred out of everything. You're barred out of life. You step out of here, and you're mine. I will blow your motherfuckin' head off."

Here's me: "Holy fuck." And he meant business.

Now George, a big guy, backs away. We sit in the car. I said, "Tony, I never heard a line like that. That's a fuckin' good one. 'You're barred out of life.' "

It wasn't fifteen minutes. Willie Messina from the Elmwood Park crew pulls up with two other guys. "OK, fellas. Take off." Big George called them because they protected him. And Tony knew he was out of line. So that's why he didn't hit George in the head. But he scared the fuck out of him.

꩜

I told Bill Hanhardt, "There's a fence on Southport. These guys wheel and deal out of a tavern. These are a new crew, or they've been going on and nobody knows about them."

He says, "All right. I'm gonna put you with the CIU. I'll get you detailed from where you're at—you work with them." So I'm with the Criminal Intelligence Unit, we're on Southport. We have an apartment above a funeral home, and right there is the fence. We're watching everybody. We got cars staked out all over the place. We had a guy stationed in the tavern. He'd drink his beer, nurse it. Guys would pull up in cars, in trucks, have the fence come and look at their merchandise. Anytime that happened, we jotted the plate numbers down so we could get them at a later time.

Now we see a trailer coming down Southport. Tractor-trailer, right on this city street. Pulled up, guy came out. I say, "We gotta take this guy." So we followed him, and we stopped the guy down the road. We didn't want to let on that we caught it from the tavern, so we pinched him away from there.

But this guy was shitting his pants. He's got a load of fireworks, which is illegal. And when you got it on a truck, that's a federal crime. So, he's shaking. He says, "You guys wouldn't know Louie the Mooch, they call him the Mooch . . ."

I says, "Louie the Mooch, huh?" I don't say nothing to him; I leave him handcuffed, I go see my lieutenant at the CIU. I say, "Listen, this guy knows a guy I know. There's a score here for us."

Louie the Mooch, Louie Eboli, came from New York into Melrose Park. He was an everyday acquaintance of Joey Aiuppa, who was the Melrose Park boss. Aiuppa trusted him because he's from the town, and Aiuppa made him a boss. I go right to see Louie the Mooch. I says, "Louie, I gotta talk to you."

"What's up?"

"Your guy, we caught him with a load of fireworks."

"So what are you gonna do?"

"What am I gonna do? He mentioned your name. Now what are *you* gonna do, you gonna be hemming and hawing? I got the lieutenant, I got the sergeant, I got four other dicks. And then we gotta answer to the chief. So now, what do you want to do? You want to have him pinched? You want to have him testify to these G-men? You know you're coming in. You understand? You're already mentioned, because he says, 'You know Louie?'"

He says, "All right, you get it done, whatever it is."

Now, that's the key. *Whatever it is.* So I go back to Hanhardt, I says, "We got him, dead-bang. We got Louie, you know it's gonna be good, so figure out the number. Because he says, 'Whatever it is.'"

He says, "Well, we don't want to rob the guy. You put the number on it."

So I go back, I says, "Twenty-five thousand."

"Twenty-five thousand! What the fuck . . ."

He's got nine million dollars. What the fuck's he worried about, twenty-five thousand? I says, "Lou, that's the deal."

He says, "Nah, I ain't coming up with that."

"You ain't? All right, I'll be back."

I call Bill. He says, "You need to go see the boss. Go see the guy, you used to clean his house."

So I go by the Armory, in Forest Park. This was a hangout for these guys. Now, I don't know these guys. But I had Milwaukee Phil as my sponsor, there had been some phone calls, and I was expected. I walk in, I go right to Tony Accardo. Tony's sitting there, he had this rough voice: "Hiya, kid, how you doing?"

"Hi, sir, how you doing?" I was a gentleman.

Accardo says, "Go say hello to the boss before you talk to me." And that's when I knew the boss was Paul the Waiter. So I went over there.

I said, "Hello, Mr. Ricca. I used to clean your house."

Ricca says, "Good boy."

And then I went back, and Accardo says, "You tell that fuckin' guy it's twenty-five."

I went back to Louie, and the money was waiting, because he had been talked to.

But here's the deal. When Louie came up with the money, he says, "I get the load back."

I says, "Oh, no. The load is gone. It's recovered, and that makes us look good. We grabbed the load, we had a chase, we can't find him, but we got the load."

That was it. The guy that mentioned Louie's name? Caught a shellackin'.

⌇

The Armory Lounge, with its Z-shaped sign, is long gone, the building now occupied by an unremarkable neighborhood restaurant on an unremarkable stretch of Roosevelt Road in the quiet West Side suburb of Forest Park. There is no trace left of what might have been the most famous mob hangout in the United States after Sam Giancana made it his headquarters in the early 1960s. The FBI bugged it, Life *magazine published a picture of it, and it remained a favorite wiseguy hangout up through the 1970s. If they knew you, there was no safer place in the world to have a drink, with Outfit royalty on the premises and plenty of muscle to keep the peace.*

And keeping the peace was a prime function of Outfit bosses. Crooks don't have the range of institutions for nonviolent resolution of disputes available to legitimate people. If you are a soft drink distributor having trouble collecting on an account, you call a collection agency or take the deadbeat to small claims court. If you paid the contractor to fix your roof and he hasn't shown up to do the work, you call the Better Business Bureau.

The Outfit is the Better Business Bureau for criminals. You can't go to the police when the stolen bearer bonds you bought turn out to be counterfeit or the guy you cut the alarm for fails to come up with your end. But if you're up to date on your street tax, you might be able to go to the local crew boss. If things are working like they should, you'll get a sit-down and maybe some satisfaction, and nobody will get hurt.

When people get hurt, the cops come around, and that's bad for business. So a good boss makes sure things work like they should. As a class, criminals are not noted for their eagerness to follow rules, but they tend to respect the iron logic of force. In criminal organizations, might indisputably makes right, and the guys who are best at deploying force wind up on top.

Things generally work like they should for the bosses, of course; with everybody in the hierarchy kicking in a big chunk to the guy above him and all the thieves and hustlers paying street tax whether they consider themselves Outfit guys or not, money flows up to the top, defying gravity. It's good to be the boss. But you don't get there by being voted Most Popular.

〰️

By 1971, Milwaukee Phil was in jail. He still had his girl, the one who was hitting on me down in Hot Springs. Gorgeous woman. But she was no good. She went to see Phil in jail, and she told him that she and Sam Cesario, from Taylor Street, wanted to get married. Phil was livid. He went out and started running around the track, a hundred miles an hour, and his heart blew. He died on the running track of a heart attack.

And Sam Cesario? One day Sam was out in front of his house, sunning himself. Two guys walked up, blew his head off.

"Freddy, I like you." I can still hear her.

Street guys have a saying: I'm not intelligent, but I'm smart.

～

The Tender Trap was a hot joint downtown at Wabash and Delaware just off Rush Street. A guy named Herbie Blitzstein owned a piece of it, because the main owner was not a mustache, meaning an Outfit guy. Blitzstein wasn't either, but Blitzstein had a connection with Tony. So Blitzstein got a piece, and he watched out for the main owner.

I loved Herbie Blitzstein. Big, heavy guy. Herbie was real tight with Tony out in Vegas later. He got murdered in 1997. Some guys from Buffalo killed him, all to do with some credit card scam. Poor Herbie.

We used to go in the Tender Trap—the whole joint was named after the Sinatra song and the movie. The jukebox was Frank Sinatra, and all his pictures were on the walls. *Minchia*, what a joint this was. And Herbie Blitzstein loved me. He'd say, "Does your father know you're out drinking like this, at your age?" He was a good guy.

So I'm in the Tender Trap with Tony, Junior, and Sammy Gambino. And four guys from the Criminal Intelligence Unit show up—they want to pinch Tony. They wanted to take a new picture of him, prints, and they wanted to show that they got Spilotro. I said, "Sarge"—the guy's name was Bill Carroll—"I'm with him, you can't pinch him."

He says, "Well, whose side are you on?"

I says, "There ain't no side. I'm drinking with this man. He's a friend."

"Whatever he does, he's a criminal."

"OK, I'll bring him in tomorrow. But he ain't coming now. You ain't taking him from me."

Tony says, "Ah, I'll go. Don't worry about it."

I says, "No, you're not. It's the principle. I can't do it." I held my ground. "Sarge, you can't take this guy. If I'm not with him, do what you gotta do. But I'm not letting you go with this guy."

He says, "Well, we're taking him."

Now, I'm with Junior, who was as tough as they come. We were all together. I says, "No you're not. You got a fight on your hands. And let me tell you something. You ain't gonna win this fight." I told him, like that.

He insisted. I says, "Here's the deal. He's under arrest. I'm his arresting officer. The president of the United States can't take him away from me. Now, you want to? Try it. He's under arrest."

He says, "What's the charge?"

"I'll think of a charge. Aggravated mopery. Now what?"

So he left. He beefed on me to Hanhardt, which was good, because it meant they didn't take it any further. I got called in by Hanhardt. He says, "What are you telling this guy? You can't do that."

I said, "Bill. What would you do? You're gonna turn over your friend? Fuck them. He can't take him from me. That's a spit in the face. Let's switch places. What would you do if you're with some-body? You gonna let them take him? No, you wouldn't. Don't lie to me." I wasn't letting him go.

16

CARD GAMES

Marshall Caifano rode Sam Giancana's coattails to power when Giancana was elevated to boss status by Tony Accardo in the mid-1950s. Giancana sent Caifano to Vegas to be "Mr. Outside," the enforcer whose job was to make sure that none of the Outfit's inside men in the casinos took too much advantage of their position. Once in Vegas, Caifano legally changed his name to John Marshall and started throwing his weight around.

Among his accomplishments was the fingering of Willie Bioff, who had flipped and testified against Outfit bosses in an infamous Hollywood extortion case in the 1940s. Bioff had done a little time and was successfully flying under the radar after his release until Caifano spotted him in Vegas. Shortly afterward Bioff went out with a bang when he turned the ignition key of his pickup truck and ignited considerably more than the engine.

The less-than-discreet John Marshall was one of the first to have his name entered in Nevada's Black Book of undesirables banned *for life from the state's casinos; unlike most honorees, he promptly sued to have his name removed. In 1958 Caifano was called before a Senate investigative committee and invoked the Fifth Amendment seventy-three times, modestly declining to detail his accomplishments in Las Vegas.*

Caifano's high profile was frowned on in Chicago, where his patron Sam Giancana was also trying Tony Accardo's patience. By the mid-1960s, Giancana had drawn so much attention with his high-profile affairs, consorting with celebrities, and noisy defiance of the law that he had to be exiled to Mexico. After Accardo deposed Giancana, Caifano was demoted as well and was hauled back to Chicago in disgrace.

In 1971 Tony Spilotro replaced Marshall Caifano in Las Vegas as the gray eminence representing the Chicago overlords, launching him on the path toward bestseller and film apotheosis.

～

Marshall Caifano was the guy in Vegas, but he fucked up, bigtime, and they brought him back. I liked Marshall. He was a good guy. The broads were what pulled him down. That was Marshall. I mean, this guy was going all over. He was starting to be with movie stars. He hung with George Raft. But he worked for Mooney, Giancana. Marshall was Mooney's number-one guy, so nobody could fuck with him.

When Giancana lost favor, that's it. Then Marshall got dumped. Because citywide guys did not like the 42 Gang guys. There was resentment against the 42 guys. The old-timers brought them in way back when, because they needed them. Accardo and Paul Ricca made that decision. They were the bosses. They needed the 42 guys not to fuck with them, because they were heisting card games and crap games. They didn't give a fuck. So who's gonna go after them? What are we gonna have, Vietnam? Let's just bring them in.

If you go to a corporation and the new guys get promoted over guys who have been there, you go "Why? Who the fuck are these guys? Aren't they supposed to wait their turn?" No, they didn't wait their turn. They got made. As a unit.

So now, one by one, they went down. They killed Chuckie English, they killed Chuckie Nicoletti, they killed Giancana. They just demoted Marshall. As they got in, that quick, that's how they got out. All them guys. They were Taylor Street. The guys that stayed the longest were the Grand Avenue guys. Accardo, Grand Avenue. Lombardo was a Grand Avenue guy, Tony was a Grand Avenue guy. Schweihs was from Chinatown. But the Taylor Street guys did not last.

Now, Marshall had been a big boss. And they replaced him. This was the real insult: they put Lombardo over him. And Lombardo would order him around, and he ridiculed him a lot. You should never discipline a guy in those positions in front of anybody. Marshall was on the payroll and got his money because he was a big guy, but he had to answer to Joe. And that was really a comedown for this guy.

⌬

Tony went to Las Vegas in '71. I drove with him. He had a truck, and we drove the truck out there. I did the driving—he couldn't even see over the wheel. And once he was out there, *madonn'*. The fun we had.

Tony says, "Who do you like in the Super Bowl?" This was the year that Dallas played Baltimore. Now, Dallas was a three-and-a-half-point favorite. So he says, "What do you like?"

I says, "I love Dallas."

He says, "I like Baltimore. But I'm not gonna go against you. We gotta be on the same team. Come on, I'll take you by Herman." So he takes me to the book joint. Now at the time, the book joint was the Rose Bowl, on the Strip. There were no book joints in the hotels. Lefty Rosenthal started the first one at the Stardust, and after that everyone followed suit. So we go by Herman. Heavy guy, Jewish guy. This guy was a drone; he talked in a monotone.

"Hiya Tony, how you doin'?" And his head is down.

So Tony goes, "My friend wants to bet Dallas."

"OK, how much?" Now he writes, he's writing the ticket.

I says, "Five hundred."

"OK. Dallas, minus three and a half, five hundred."

"Herman. This is my friend."

"OK, Tony." Now he erases. "Dallas minus two and a half, for five hundred."

I got a full point. That's huge. And he's going in that monotone, "That's five-fifty."

"Herman. This is my dear friend, from Chicago."

"OK, Dallas, minus two and a half, five hundred. No vig."

"Now you're talking."

Tony, he was unbelievable. Fifty dollars I saved. We lost anyway.

I should be a gazillionaire. You know how many times I went to Vegas? Oh, my God. There was no nickel-ass room. We were in the tower at the Stardust, we had the suite. Tony had broads always waiting, we had fruit, and we had Crown Royal. He had everything for me. My pal.

We didn't use our real names. I was Mr. Wolf from Chicago. At the time, it wasn't like today, sophisticated. You signed your name. You're OK'd by Mr. Phil Dioguardi, you could play. "You have up to fifteen thousand dollar credit, Mr. Wolf." And he'd look at me, Mr. Wolf. "You look like a fuckin' wolf. I'd like to know what you're up to."

CARD GAMES

You got the credit, and you never paid them. After the Stardust, we'd go to the other Recrion joints, the Fremont and the Sundance. Recrion was the name of the corporation. There were about four joints under that. Al Sachs was the main guy at the company. I loved him.

I know the way the Outfit got the skim. That part I knew well. They did a lot of it by taking the change from the slots, and a lot of it was in the counting room. And they got it at table games. It was orchestrated, rehearsed, and it was done by guys like me. We were capable of doing it if we got enough rehearsal. It was done for whoever they had to give the money to in Chicago.

We'd have a table, and we'd have a whole set of players all ready to go in. We got our own cards, the same ones the dealers use—we got all the equipment because we got Lefty. The dealer's on our team. The floor man is on our team. The pit boss . . . Everybody's on our team. It's like a symphony. It's done in tune. And again, it's all Tony.

The table would have the six-deck shoe all ready to go. The players come in—third base is the end seat, first base is on the other end, second base is in the middle. The dealer shuffles up the cards, six decks, and he hands the shoe to the first base guy. Second base is the woman that's got the loaded deck—she's got a whole six-deck shoe in her purse. It ain't no little handbag, it's a fuckin' tote bag. And she's got it over her stool. When it's time to cut, third base stands up so the next table can't see any shenanigans, first base stands up so they can't see over there. Second base switches shoes, she leaves. Now, this deck was ready to go. They'd put it in the shoe and they'd start taking the money.

The deck is set for five players, all the cards in order. I open up, I got an ace, I'm a winner. Next guy, he's got twenty, that's a two-card win. The next guy, he's got eleven, and he's got one card coming, he doubles down . . . And ninety-nine percent of the time, you ain't saying nothing. The dealer's just going through the motions. And we take them down. Everybody gets a piece, you turn the money over to Tony, and that's it. I loved it.

The eye in the sky, if he spots it . . . "You better get over to table number six, there's a lot of winning going on." They'll come in, get a new dealer, tell the pit boss. We got the pit boss. So he stalls, he drags his feet. Now, by the time they break it up, it's done. It's amazing. And they took them down for a quarter of a million every time they did that.

Tony told me this. "Forget about baccarat, forget about blackjack, forget about craps, forget about all the table games. The slot machines in the casinos pay for all salaries, bills, mortgages, everything." So now, the rest is gravy.

When the MGM Grand opened, it was the biggest hotel in town. When you open a hotel, I don't care if it's the deadest time of the year, it's gonna be like New Year's Eve. But MGM opened almost on New Year's Eve 1973. So there's more chaos. So here's what Tony's guys did.

They beat them for a million dollars. Never, never reported. Because they didn't want that. They didn't publicize it. And they got them for a million. They got them through the baccarat room. Tony got some guys. One of them was the guard, dressed as a cowboy. He's got the guns. He escorted the baccarat captain to the cage. Nobody knew anybody. That's how much chaos it was.

So a fill was called. A fill is when you need chips for a table. The baccarat table has the biggest, a million dollars. That's the kind of money these guys play for. So the guy who's in, the captain, calls the cage from the baccarat pit: "We need a fill for the baccarat table."

"OK, we'll send it."

Now the captain goes there with the MGM guard. The people in the cage look, they don't know nothing. It's opening night. Here's the fill, the captain signs it, they never saw the guy again. Walks out of the hotel. A million dollars.

They were all Tony's guys. The guard, the captain who made the call: "Send me a fill." Now, these are all stand-up guys that nobody's gonna charge. It was clean as could be.

But what made it easier is that at the time it was done, you could take any chip and bring it to any hotel and change it. Now you can't. This is one of the reasons they changed the rules. Now the only hotel you could go to is the one the chips belong to. But then anybody could have done it. They probably cashed all the chips in an hour. Here's ten thousand, here's twenty thousand. They cashed them out.

How's that? When you're first, you're a winner.

⌇

The poker game in Houston is a classic. I met a kid from Saudi Arabia. Let's call him Abdullah. His father was a Saudi big shot. I mean a gazillionaire. Abdullah came to school here, and he saw the ways, the women, and he didn't want to go back. He was a real handsome kid. He was a prince, this guy.

I met him while he was living in Chicago. He was speeding, and he went through the light. We pulled him over, and he was with a beautiful girl. He got out of the car, knew exactly how to act. He wanted to give me money. So I took a liking to him. And I'm looking at the girl. I would have taken his money, but I liked the guy. So I says, "You got a pass. I'll give you the pass for two things. You're a good-looking guy, and you got a good-looking woman."

He gave me his card. He started telling me about Saudi Arabia. He had a freight company, near the airport. He had a couple of guys working for him. And he had a couple of accounts, nothing big. He didn't need more than that. He just had to stay busy. That was probably the rules of his father and mother.

That was my first encounter with him. And then he'd call me all the time, he'd come by my house. Now he's got a policeman friend. He loved that. Me, I'm thinking, this guy's worth hundreds of millions.

Then he moved to Houston. He opened up a huge business, airfreight and trucking. Doing well. I hadn't heard from him for a couple of years when he calls me out of nowhere. He says, "I need to talk to you. I'm gonna see you." So he flew in. He says, "These guys took me for my money." He lost his money in a big, big poker game, and he was cheated.

I says, "You know they cheated you?"

"Yes, I know they cheated me. I hear from this guy, hear from that guy, and after reviewing and going back, I know they cheated me. They got me for $125,000. I want to get them back and I'll save face."

I said, "What kind of rules is this?"

"I couldn't lie to my father. I told him, and he don't want no part of me until I get this squared away. I gotta get it. I gotta beat these guys. I figure you could do it."

I says, "OK." I call out to Las Vegas. "Tell Tony I'm coming to see him." I meet up in Vegas with Tony and an old friend who was living out there; we could call him Johnny.

"Tony, I need some guys to rig a card game. You got any of these guys?"

He says, "I got the best in the business. I got two guys, there ain't many guys that could do what these guys do. When you see them, you'll think I'm crazy. Because they don't look the part. But they're the guys."

And he was right. I looked at these guys, I wanted to tell him, "What, are you nuts?" To me they looked like two yokels from Oklahoma or something. I mean, these guys, they looked like mopes. One was a dorky-looking, buck-toothed guy. But that throws you off. "What idiots these guys are." Yeah, idiots.

Tony tells them, "We gotta get this guy his money back. If you do it right, there's ten thousand apiece for you guys."

They went for it. That's well worth a trip. So now the game is on. We go to Houston. Abdullah financed the whole thing. We got the high-line hotel—Abdullah's company was nearby. Johnny and I go to a strip club, high-line joint. We purposely run into one of the guys that cheated him. Big, heavy guy. Ruddy face. Not a sharp dresser, but high-line clothes. He was a pretty good spender. And we were spending money because we had Abdullah.

We told him that we were here on a visit. He says, "What business are you in?"

"I'm in the petroleum business."

"Got a card?"

I got a box of them. The card Abdullah had set up for me, it's some oil company. I'm an executive, John works for me. And he had the phone set up if anybody calls. Phone number in Houston, phone number in Washington, phone number in Chicago.

We had a good time until it was time to play cards.

We meet Tony's two guys, and we took a day for a little practice. They give us the rules. "Here's the way we're gonna do it. The guy who's the victim, he's gonna be second best in every hand. He'll have a full house, but you're gonna have a better full house. He'll have a straight, you'll have a flush."

They had cards. They called them "coolers." They had them in their boots—this guy had two decks in his boot! And I'm looking, I couldn't catch them. "If you want a diamond, just rub your finger, like that. If you want a heart, you go like this. If you look at your cards and say, "Christ!" you need a club. "Damn!" you need a diamond. "Hell!" you need the spade.

So then the one guy says, "If these guys decide, because they're losing, they want to switch games, we play blackjack. Now, in your hand, if you got sixteen, you hold your card like this, four fingers showing. Fifteen you put your little finger under the card. And so on. Sixteen, fourteen, thirteen, and twelve. Eleven and under, you're pat. I can give you any card and you ain't busting."

So now we got the rules.

The game was at somebody's house. There was twenty-, thirty-thousand-dollar pots. The guy we were after, he was sweating like a pig. He was the only loser. They kept him in the game by giving him good hands. Full house, he's gotta stay. And I'm watching these guys, and I couldn't see how they were doing it. I can't catch them. Now we're getting his money.

Me, I was good. "I raise . . ."

Johnny couldn't keep a straight face. So this one hand, the guy's losing so much money, and he turns to John, and he says, "I lost with aces full. This guy got four jacks. How the fuck can that be? Could you believe this?"

John says, "Yes, I could." And he gets up and he goes to the bathroom because he's laughing so hard, tears. I wanted to kill him.

Now they want to play blackjack. And we were getting ready for the game, we were all set. We were gonna take them for more. And suddenly the guy gets up and storms out of there. "I'm fuckin' through." So he ran out. But we got the money.

To make a long story short, we won a lot more than $125,000. Abdullah didn't get a dime. He just wanted them to get beat. He don't care if he gets nothing. It was his honor. Now he told his father, he's back in good graces. He gave us all the money. We took it to Tony, and he gave us the hundred and a quarter. He says, "Do what you want with it. Enjoy yourself."

A young and innocent Fred Pascente. I served Mass as an altar boy.
Collection of Fred Pascente

Rocco Pascente and sons (left to right) Billy, Fred, and Dicky, circa 1946.
Collection of Fred Pascente

Rocco Pascente. My father was not a tough guy. He was in a bowling league.
Collection of Fred Pascente

Rocco and Edna Pascente. My mother was a saint.
Collection of Fred Pascente

John "Johnny Bananas" DeBiase in 1944. In our neighborhood, people loved Johnny DeBiase.

By permission of John Binder

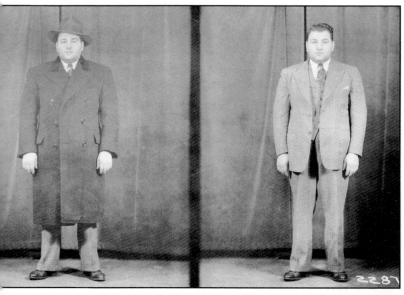

Fat Lenny Caifano in 1942. If they had listened to my father, Lenny wouldn't have got killed.

By permission of John Binder

Charles "Chuckie" Nicoletti. Chuckie was a dapper guy, handsome. And he gave a quarter to all the kids.

By permission of John Binder

A couple of young hoods from the Badlands: Jimmy D'Antonio and Joe Lombardo, arrested on April 4, 1951.

By permission of John Binder

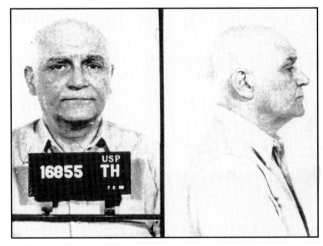

Paul "the Waiter" Ricca. You'd think he was a plumber or something, this old guy. He never looked like he was a mob guy.

By permission of John Binder

Ken Eto, "Joe the Jap." Really a good-hearted guy. And one of the best pool players you'll ever see.

By permission of John Binder

Felix "Milwaukee Phil" Alderisio, arrested by the FBI in 1963. So he became the guy with the premier hit squad: Milwaukee Phil.

By permission of John Binder

Sam Cesario. Milwaukee Phil's girl told him that she and Sam wanted to get married. One day Sam was out in front of his house. Two guys walked up, blew his head off.

By permission of John Binder

Jack "Jackie the Lackey" Cerone in 1965. Jack Cerone was the Elmwood Park boss. They called him Jackie the Lackey, because he had been Tony Accardo's driver.

By permission of John Binder

Marshall Caifano. Marshall was the guy in Vegas, but he fucked up, big-time, and they brought him back. He was a good guy. The broads were what pulled him down.

By permission of John Binder

Albert "Obbie" Frabotta. I don't want to be the guy who took Obbie's dog.

By permission of John Binder

Frank Schweihs. Schweihs says, "You gotta get this guy out of jail." He didn't ask. He told you.

By permission of John Binder

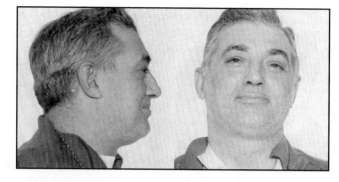

Mario DeStefano.
Mario actually broke
Tony in—that's
Tony's words to me.
By permission of John
Binder

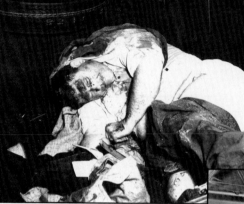

*Leo Foreman following a
workplace dispute with his boss,
Sam DeStefano.*
By permission of John Binder

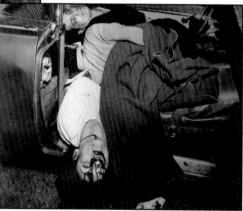

*Lydia Abshire and the Scalvo
brothers.* Anyway, the Scalvos
got killed. With a poor
innocent girl.
By permission of John Binder

Lee Magnafichi. "On something like this, you gotta go
with the best." So he got Lee
Magnafichi.
By permission of John Binder

Tony Spilotro with his son. Tony was thrilled when he got that kid, Vincent.

By permission of John Binder

Left to right: Michael Spilotro; his wife, Ann; Lefty Rosenthal; Nancy and Tony Spilotro.

By permission of John Binder

Fred and May on their wedding day. When I saw her, that's the true definition of "got hit by the thunderbolt."

Collection of Fred Pascente

Fred receiving an award from Chicago Police superintendent Fred Rice for breaking up a burglary ring in 1983. With Rice; Fred's mother, Edna; wife, May; and (left to right) son Rocco, niece Jamie Bulleri, and daughter, Nicole.
Collection of Fred Pascente

Fred with William Hanhardt. I never saw Bill do anything other than good police work. I don't know a better man.
Collection of Fred Pascente

Fred and May Pascente. I'm married all these years—this is still my girlfriend.
Collection of Fred Pascente

CARD GAMES

So I gave these guys ten apiece, and me and Johnny took the rest. That was a good score. And that's Tony. He got us them two guys. These guys knew what they were doing, buddy.

☙

There was another high-stakes poker game closer to home, in Itasca, Illinois. Huge money. A guy that knew a couple of the players brought it to me as a score. He laid it right out for us. The players were mostly Greek guys, restaurant owners. He knew the background—he was at the house once. Lot of money, lot of jewelry.

I went to Dinger, Gerry Carusiello, and told him what I got. He says, "Well, you got the guys?"

"Junior's coming with me."

He didn't know him good, but he says, "I got no problem with him. On something like this, you gotta go with the best." So he got Lee Magnafichi and Gino DeRoy. I knew them both. Magnafichi was a good guy. Gino later killed himself when he was doing life. He jumped off the roof in the prison. Like Dinger said, they were the best. In other words, he ain't backing away. He's getting it done. And if he has to hurt somebody, he will.

But I said, "I don't want nobody hurt. If anybody gets hurt, it's over. I don't want to hear about that. Because I'll run. And you know how tight I am with that little guy."

We knew everything. It wasn't like a sophisticated burglary, where you have to shut off an alarm. It was just a bulldozing thing. Kick in the door, they're right there. We knew from the guy that gave it to me that you could kick in the front door. It was not bolted. It was like a bathroom door; you could push it in. Maybe they bolt it when they go to sleep, but normally they're not thinking of that.

The plan was, we're parked in the town east of Itasca, which was Bensenville. We had two good cars, legitimate cars. We had the hot car stashed in Bensenville. It was a van, so we could change inside, put our stuff on over our clothes, our coveralls. We had the plates; it was clean. They got the plates first, then they stole the car to fit the plate. You look at the plate and run it, it's clean.

I had one more thing, and I didn't tell them what I did. I talked to my brother Dicky and said, "You gotta do me a favor." I told him, "I want you on Irving Park, going up and down. I want you to keep making the rounds. Just keep coming back." If there was a chase, if something went wrong, I wanted a fail-safe operation. I knew a spot to hide, off Irving Park. I'd gone by there a few times, looking for a place. There was a berm just off the road, and I would hide there. When I saw Dicky come by, I'd jump out and jump in his car. That was my escape. I said, "Dick, you gotta do this for me." But he didn't know what was going on.

We drove to Bensenville, parked. We changed in the van, went right to the score. We had walkie-talkies so we could communicate. And we had shotguns. Junior was driving the van. We pull up, pull down the masks, jump out. I went around the side of the house to the back. It was a yard, fenced in. The house was a tri-level. I could see everything through the windows. The game was on the first level. It was a room off the kitchen, a family room maybe, or a TV room. They had a nice table. There were seven players, and there was another guy waiting to get in.

We were all set. I'm in the back. That was the only way out. Junior's in the front; he's got the car, and he's got the front exit. That was it. *Badda-boom.* They kicked in the door. I heard it. I didn't need the walkie-talkie. And they all jump up, and the one guy left and took his money. He tried to come out. I see this guy running down the stairs. And he goes to the left, and he's hiding there. I could see him plain as day. And he's stashing stuff on a shelf. I saw him running down the stairs, right to the door. And I had him. So as soon as Lee came in, I said, "Get to the lower level."

Lee came down the stairs and I signaled to him, and he got him. The poor kid was scared, and as Lee brought him up, I went to his little spot and got the money.

We handcuffed everybody, and they were spread-eagled, handcuffed to each other. We took their rings, took their clothes off. The eight guys were all Greeks. Some of them couldn't speak English. And they were scared. You're facing a shotgun, a masked guy, you'd be scared, too. We put all the money in a big bag. A couple of guys went upstairs to the bedrooms and got all the jewelry they could find. And we got out of there. Simple as that. It was not a sophisticated thing.

I'm glad they were all right. In fact, I'm the one that insisted we call. We're home, I call from a public phone, Itasca police, non-emergency number. I said, "Go to this such-and-such a house and you'll find some people that are locked up and they need help to get out."

"Those morons? We know, we got them."

This was a big score. There was about $60,000. I knew there was a lot of money there, but the jewelry was the kicker. After the jewelry was sold, we got probably in the area of $170,000, $180,000. That's a lot of money.

17

CRIMINAL JUSTICE

Tony Spilotro was a suspect in numerous murders, but not until 1972 did prosecutors think they had enough to bring charges. In August of that year Spilotro was indicted, along with loan shark Sam DeStefano and Sam's brother Mario, for the 1963 murder of bail bondsman Leo Foreman.

After the murder, police had followed the usual procedures: evidence was gathered and bagged and stored. Nothing happened for nine years, while Tony Spilotro rose in his chosen profession and landed the Las Vegas gig. Then, out of the blue, on August 30, 1972, Cook County state's attorney Bernard Carey announced the indictment of Spilotro and the DeStefano brothers for Foreman's murder.

What had changed was that the FBI had persuaded Charles "Chuckie" Crimaldi, another old DeStefano associate, that talking to them was better than spending the rest of his life in jail. Crimaldi was given immunity and agreed to testify about the Foreman murder, in which he said he had participated. According to Crimaldi, *he, the DeStefanos, and Spilotro had lured Foreman into a bomb shelter built in the basement of Mario's house, where they had dispatched him after making him extremely sorry he had dared to cross Mad Sam.*

Spilotro was arrested in Las Vegas and waived extradition. He was brought back to Chicago and lodged at Cook County Jail, which was presided over by one Winston Moore, who had gained a national reputation as a reformer after taking charge of the mammoth institution on California Avenue on Chicago's Near Southwest Side. Larger than some state prisons, the jail was run largely by trusties called "barn bosses" who presided over a sizable internal economy that accommodated a variety of intoxicants and the usual assortment of shanks. Moore, a psychologist by training and the first African American to take charge of a major penal institution, put an end to the barn boss system, confiscated weapons and drugs, and cleaned up physical conditions, which had been notoriously squalid. He would last until 1977, when he resigned in the wake of brutality allegations that some said were trumped up in retaliation for Moore's refusal to play political games.

Tony was in Cook County Jail for the murder of a guy named Leo Foreman, along with Mario DeStefano, Mad Sam's brother. Mario actually broke Tony in—that's Tony's words to me.

Now, he's indicted. We're all sick about it. So I get a call from Joe Lombardo. I'm a policeman, and Joe knew I had my ways to get around people. He bought me and my partner dinner at Miller's Steakhouse on Western Avenue. He says, "You wanted to be a cop. Now's the time to make yourself useful." Lombardo says they gotta know about the evidence, what the state's attorney's got. And I gotta get it for them.

This is too serious. I says, "I ain't gonna promise nothing. But I'm on it."

I knew a guy who knew guys—he had friends in the state's attorney's office. So I go see him. Now, he's no shady guy. But for me, he did it. And he told me, "They have no eyewitness, they have no real evidence, they just know that he had dealings with him, but there's no evidence on the murder other than some paint chips they found." That was it.

Now I gotta get the word to Tony. Winston Moore was the warden of the county jail. He was a big, fat guy. Good, jolly guy. I had a lot of fun with him. He called me the funniest white man he ever met. Now, here's how I got with Winston Moore. I got a burglary. And the kid is Winston Moore's nephew. The kid is crying. He's not a crook, I could tell. He's got no sheet, he's in school. I says, "What's the problem, buddy?" And I helped the guy.

So who comes? The wife of Winston Moore. She says, "Officer, I am the warden's wife. This is my nephew."

I says, "Ma'am, you tell the warden that his nephew is in good hands. Because he's leaving here." I cut him loose.

Winston calls me. He says, "Anything you need, you call me." Gave me his private number. And I stayed in touch with him.

So now I call him, I says, "Warden. I got my brother in there." At the time, my brother Billy and a guy from my cousin Mikey's crew were there for a burglary.

"Come and see him. I ain't letting him go, but you come and see him anytime." So I go see Winston, and I tell him I want to see my brother. I brought Billy some food—I had boxes of food. I says, "I gotta interrogate these guys for a case I got." He knew it was just bullshit, but I had a reason. And he put down "detective interrogating these men."

I had two sessions. I saw Billy first. Then I says, "Can you bring Spilotro out?"

"Oh, man, they're watching that motherfucker," Winston says. "He's big time. But I'll get him down here." He calls the sergeant over.

Now here's what I did. I duked him a hundred dollars. "Take care of the boys." I gave it to Winston Moore, he gave it to the sergeant. Winston wouldn't take money. He was above that.

So Winston says, "Go get Spilo*toro*." Spilo*toro*, he called him.

Now, Tony comes down with another guy. Before I enter the room, Moore says, "Oh, yeah. I forgot. They got that room bugged. So watch yourself."

That's what I'm afraid of. Sure enough, they're talking in the room, we're outside, and we can hear them plain as day. Tony is telling the other guy, "Jesus. I have got the worst headache I ever had in my life. This is serious shit. I can't get rid of this—it's killing me."

So I told Winston, "Give me four aspirins." I put them in my hand. The first thing I do is I shake hands with Tony. "Hey, Tony, how you doin'?" And the aspirins went in his hand. And he knew they could hear him outside. That's how smart he was. He knew that I heard him talking about the headache and I knew he would catch it, because he's that sharp.

I wanted to tell him about the evidence, but I couldn't, because the room was bugged. I had to wait and get it to him through another guy. And Tony beat the case. Later he says, "What's that worth? What's that worth in dollars? Finding something like that?"

Think I'm gonna take money? I wouldn't take no fuckin' money from this guy.

Spilotro and the DeStefanos sat in Cook County while lawyers sparred over bail conditions. The trial was set for May 1973. At a pretrial hearing, Sam DeStefano insisted on acting as his own attorney, providing the kind of spectacle that promised to make the trial a major media production. News also emerged that Sam was suffering from cancer, and rumors began to circulate that he was vulnerable to pressure from the feds. Spilotro and Mario DeStefano successfully moved to be tried separately from Sam, and all three were finally released on bail pending trial.

On April 14, 1973, Sam DeStefano was shotgunned to death in his garage. The presumption that Mario DeStefano and Tony Spilotro were the killers was never backed up by an indictment. The Foreman case went to trial without Mad Sam, before Judge Robert Meier III. In the course of the trial Meier ruled inadmissible the testimony of expert witnesses that paint chips collected from Leo Foreman's body in 1962 matched samples taken from the floor of Mario DeStefano's basement in July 1972. Tony Spilotro testified that on the date of the murder he had been shopping for furniture with his brother and his brother's fiancée; check records and testimony from salesmen backed him up. On May 22, 1973, Mario DeStefano was found guilty of the murder of Leo Foreman, though the conviction was later overturned and DeStefano died of a heart attack while awaiting retrial.

Tony Spilotro was found not guilty and promptly returned to Las Vegas.

〰️

Tony and Schweihs, the German, grabbed a guy for me, because he was hurting me big time. This guy was an investigator for the state's attorney's office. He was a detective, but when you got the clout, you could go to work for the state's attorney. He was putting the bad words out about me. There was a whole crew there that didn't like me. I had just found out the information on the Leo Foreman murder. So this guy must have found out something.

And Tony and Schweihs grabbed the guy. They had so much patience. They watched him. He was divorced. Every Sunday he picked up his daughter and he took her horseback riding. Well, they caught him on the trail. Not where they pick up the horses, but when they're riding. They stopped him, took him off the horse; one guy took the little girl, and the other told him, "You see how easy it is to find you? If you ever fuck with that guy, there won't be no fuckin' warning."

He never bothered me again.

I says, "You can't do that, Tony."

He says, "Fuck them."

⚬

I knew Richard Cain had given the word that got my friend Guy Mendola killed back in 1964 when Cain was an investigator with the Cook County Sheriff's Office. But there was nothing I could do about it. Now in 1973 Cain goes into Rose's Sandwich Shop on Grand Avenue. Rose's was owned by Jimmy Cozzo's father, who was called Jelly Belly. Jimmy Cozzo was a guy from the neighborhood who was not a made guy, but he was tight with Lombardo.

Cain was in there and two masked men walked into the shop. "This is a robbery. Everybody against the wall." The guy's giving the orders. And that was sharp, because he made Cain relax. Jelly was dillydallying. One of the shooters says, "Come on, Jelly, get the fuck in the line." He mentioned his name.

They lined them up. And the guy that was lined up next to Cain was Joe Lombardo. Right next to him. And then the guy put the shotgun under Cain's chin and blew his fuckin' head off.

In the report there were two of them. But there's one more that nobody knows. This ain't in the report. Archie Gambino, Sammy's father, was just going into the restaurant. And there was a guy outside. He says, "Keep going."

His father says, "Yes, sir." He missed going in. So there was three of them.

There's lots of theories about why Cain got killed. Some say it was to keep his mouth shut about Giancana, because Cain was close to Mooney. Some say he had a beef with Marshall Caifano. Lombardo may have had his reasons. But I have my own guess.

The way it was done, the description of the guy, a small guy, and the way he did it. He blew his head right off. You don't do that. You do it with a .22, you put it right behind the ear, and it's all over. It's done. This, he disfigured this guy. So there's a little hatred there. It was personal.

There's a sidebar to this. Tony told me about this, years later. There was a policeman, an Italian cop. I don't know his name. He used to play the Grand Avenue overpass, and he would grab speeders. So the guys that got Cain are making their getaway, and this cop pulls them over. And a guy runs out of the car, and he throws fifty dollars at the cop. "Here, I'm going to the hospital."

"Go right ahead," the cop says.

How Tony knew about that, I don't know. I can only guess.

∾

In the 1970s rumors were circulating that dicks in a South Side district were getting confessions out of suspects by methods that were never taught at the police academy. The allegations of physical abuse of suspects involved detectives in Area Two, commanded by Jon Burge, a former army MP. They would remain rumors until February 1982, when a massive manhunt hauled in a career criminal who had shot two cops to death five days before. The suspect confessed after fifteen hours of interrogation, but his injuries were so severe he was taken to a hospital. His detailed description of the torture Burge's detectives had subjected him to started a three-decade saga of official denial and inaction, reversed convictions, and lawsuits that have cost the city of Chicago millions.

The alleged abuse went beyond the classic third degree, including the use of electric shock and burns. Much was made subsequently of the fact that Burge had served in Vietnam and had possibly acquired the dark arts there. Most of the victims were black, and a few of them were subsequently shown to be innocent. The case poisoned relations between the CPD and the African American community and sent out waves that reached the state capitol. In 2003 Illinois governor George Ryan pardoned four death row inmates who had confessed under Burge's ministrations.

Not much happened to Burge for a long time. He was hauled into federal court in 1989 in a civil rights suit; the case ended in a mistrial. He was suspended from the police department and then finally fired in 1993. A special prosecutor found in 2006 that the statute of limitations had elapsed on any misdeeds Burge might have committed. Federal prosecutors finally convicted him in 2010 of obstruction of justice and perjury for lying about the charges during his civil trial.

My brother Billy caught a terrible beating from Burge. Horrible beating. They caught Billy on the South Side—four guys got away. But they couldn't print it, 'cause they just caught him, and there's no case. But they beat him. They hung him out the window; they beat him with a phone book and baseball bats on top, because it left no marks. At the time, it was different. You could keep a guy two days, three days, move him to another area, let the other detectives view him and see if they got any cases on him. And that's what they were doing.

Billy looked like the Elephant Man. And he wouldn't talk to them.

So I go to Hanhardt, I says, "Yo. My brother's missing. My mother's goin' crazy, his wife, his kids . . ."

He says, "Fine, I'll find out." Bingo. He finds out Burge got him. So he called me. He says, "I got him located. You never set foot over there. I'll handle it." So he calls Burge, he says, "I'm coming for this guy. That's the end." Because Burge worked for him.

So now Burge takes that as Billy did a big thing. So he goes and sees him. Billy's head is up, he won't say a word. Burge goes, "We ain't gonna talk to you no more. The A Team is coming to see you now."

Hanhardt comes in: "Start your engines, you Irish motherfucker." And he spits at Burge. Then he calls me back, and he says, "Just forget about this. We got him, he's safe. Don't you go by this guy."

Because if I went there, I'd have pulled it out.

18

THUNDERBOLT

I met May nightclubbing it. Friday night was a big night. We'd go out, and we're cattin' it, we're going on Rush Street, Mannheim Road. Always hunting for girls. And having fun. And when I saw her, that's the true definition of "got hit by the thunderbolt." I mean, I never seen a woman look like this. She was a cocktail waitress. She worked at the Four Torches, which was at Armitage and Clark, the hottest place there was. Sinatra would be there when he was in town. He was friends with the owner, Jack McHugh.

She wouldn't give me two minutes. I never stopped going after her. Never. From the time I met her, I was struck. I used to drag my guys with me where she worked. Krueger and Junior, all my guys. And they used to get aggravated. "What the fuck. This girl, she doesn't even want to look at you. What are you doing here?"

It winds up, she caused us to have the biggest fight. I know she goes to Milano's after work. Milano's is an all-night restaurant, Division and State, and they used to serve alcohol after hours.

They'd give you your booze in a coffee mug. And you'd have dinner—you could eat there all night long.

I go in there, I'm with Junior, Sammy, Krueger, Jimmy Andriacchi, we're all friends. And all of a sudden we see Dicky, my brother, and Bruno Andriacchi, that's one of Jimmy's older brothers, and they're with two girls. I says, "Look at this. The two shortest guys, and they got the girls." But they didn't see us. And there's four guys next to them, and they're aggravating them.

All of a sudden, Junior says, "They're fighting." *Boom!*

Well, we get over there. Guess what? The fight leveled the joint. There wasn't a table standing. I'm fighting with a guy, and we both go down, the weight on my ankle—*boom*, and I knew it was broke. And he's whaling away at me, and I hollered to Sam. So Sam comes and hits the guy, cold-cocked him, broke his hand on his head. In the meantime the police come. We knew them all.

They take us to Henrotin Hospital. I'm over here, who's in this room, who's in that room. Now, me and Sammy are policemen. Dicky's a policeman. The nurse is a sergeant's wife. They're bringing the guy in, the other victim on the other side; he's all bleeding. Junior put the guy through the window. The guy got over a hundred stitches in his face. I got a broken ankle, Dicky got a busted knee, Sammy, broken hand, Junior, another bad injury. You can't believe this fight.

And after it's all over, they're going, "It's your fault, because of that fuckin' broad."

I pursued her for three years. I don't know how the hell she finally gave in. She had a guy she was seeing. He was a singer, from Chinatown. He was a little weasel. And her girlfriend Janice says, "That guy, he abuses her."

I says, "What do you mean, abuses her? I'll throw him in the fuckin' river. You tell her these words. She don't have to break up with her boyfriend, but she's gotta go out with me. I've been fair, I've been decent, I don't care if she likes me or not. But she's gonna go out with me. I'm gonna take her out to dinner, and I want her to meet me on my terms, and then she can do what she wants. And if she don't, I will throw him in the river. And I mean it. She won't have the boyfriend. You got it?"

"Oh, my God," she says. "You're a savage."

But she told her. And through Janice, May says "OK."

⌇

The first date was terrible. What I did, I don't know how she stayed with me. I was so tense. We were gonna meet at a place on Elm and State, nice place, and we were gonna go to a movie, *Blazing Saddles*. That was the first date. Now I go to the restaurant, she's at the bar waiting for me. And a guy's talking to her. She says, "Hi." The guy says hello.

I say, "Get the fuck out of here."

She looks at me, and here's the guy . . . he left. He knew I meant business.

She says, "You dirty animal. Who the . . ."

"What are you talking about?"

"You see those guys over there? They kept bothering me. And this guy came up, like a gentleman. He says, 'Lady, I see you're alone.' I told him, 'I'm waiting for my friend to meet me,' and he says, 'Well, I'll stay here by you. This way they won't bother you.'"

"My God." I went right to the guy. I grabbed him, I says, "I'm so sorry. I've been trying to date this girl for years. I was all . . ."

He says, "I understand."

I says, "Please. I apologize. Could I take you to dinner?"

"No, no . . ."

"I'm so sorry."

She saw that, and she liked it. "You're a savage."

"I'm not like that."

"Yes, you are, because you did it."

Anyway, we go to the movie, and she loved it, and that was it. She had a great time, she laughed. She saw I knew everybody in the world. I made sure I went to places where they knew me. I had umpteen people coming up to me. A guy even picked up the check. She says, "What the hell is this guy all about?"

I says, "I'm a policeman."

"Yeah, you're a policeman. Who are all these guys?"

She was living with her sister on the North Side, Albany Park. I met her son, Joey. Joey was from a previous relationship. He was about three, four. Wild kid, but I squared him away. And she saw how I was with the kids. I had all kinds of nephews, so I was good with the kids. My mother's what really did it, because she loved kids. It was like second nature. "Bring them over." And then she met my sister, and the brothers.

After the first date I married her in six months, and I adopted Joey. May and I got married on September 8, 1974. We had a big wedding. The wedding was at a place called Antoine's, on Elston and Pulaski, a nice place. Frankie Furio got us the place. He knew the people. We had Frank D'Rone, a great singer. We had the Dynatones, unbelievable entertainment. And this is the funniest part. The gifts. Now remember, this is 1974. Joe Lombardo, two hundred. You know what kind of money that is, in 1974? Joey Andriacchi, Jimmy's brother, two hundred. Spilotro, five hundred. Five hundred. Poopsie Ruggierio, three hundred. Everybody. Louie Tenuta, another five hundred. I mean, I can't tell you. Mikey was in jail, his wife came. She gave me a fifty-dollar check. I says, "Dolly, I ain't cashing your check. Thank you." Tony Borsellino and his wife. Danny the Greek. My friend the card player. On and on and on.

Now her side. Her aunt, salt and pepper shakers. And we made fun. "Look at these fuckin' people. Salt and pepper?"

May says, "I can't believe the money. These guys . . ."

"Well, they're good guys." She couldn't believe it. She says, "Where's all this money coming from?"

"Well, should we give it back?"

"No, no, no, no, no!"

And my mother, old fashioned, she says, "You be sure to keep track of who gives what, so this way, when you go to their wedding . . ."

I said, "OK, Ma."

~

Now May wants to go on the honeymoon. We had all the money in the world. I said, "Where do you want to go?"

She said, "Las Vegas," which is right up my alley, beautiful.

I told Tony, he says, "Freddy, don't worry about a thing." And those words are gold with him. "But why don't you come next week? Your man is gonna be here, Frank Sinatra." He's playing Caesars Palace.

"That's it." I says, "May, we're gonna delay it."

"You're gonna delay it for Frank Sinatra?"

"Yeah." I know she likes Blood, Sweat & Tears, and she likes Ray Charles. I says, "We're gonna see Frank." She agreed.

So now we're in Vegas. I go by Tony, he says, "All right, we'll get Cusumano over here."

That was his number-one guy out there. Joey Cusumano, wonderful guy. Joey says, "You're set. You just go see Wayne Gilbert, that's the head maître d' at Caesars. He knows you're coming. He knows you're my friend—all you gotta do is say who you are. And don't give him a dime."

By this point, Sammy was living in Vegas. He'd left the Chicago police and was a boss at the Stardust. So I brought May's sister Laurie to meet him. And they hit it off. So we go with them.

Do you know how hard it is to get in there? They have invited guests; then they got regular people. In the line, the invited guest line, Cary Grant. How big is he? Mike Connors, he was Mannix on television. Robert Wagner and Natalie Wood. They're in line. So I walk right up to Wayne Gilbert: "Mr. Gilbert?"

"Yes."

"Joey Cusumano . . ."

"Oh, right this way. Four?" What a classy guy this Wayne was. He took May by the arm, we walk. And we kept walking, past all of them. He took us right there, here's the stage. The table right next to us is Sinatra's mother—his whole family was there. We were right on the stage. They were looking at us: who the fuck are these people? We're mopes, you know. They were just smiling. But we saw Sinatra. Right on the stage—you could put your hands on the stage.

I gave Wayne Gilbert a hundred dollars, which was huge for a tip then. He says, "No, no, no."

I says, "I don't care if Joey Cusumano said not to. I can't do that."

What a show. You could see them blue eyes. My wife, she couldn't get over this guy.

"Check?"

"No check. It's on Caesars Palace."

⌇

So we're in Vegas, and I lost all my money. I was broke. Tony hung by the Las Vegas Country Club. And it was all older gentlemen, refined guys. He wasn't a golfer, of course. He'd play cards with these old-time guys. And they loved him—they loved to be around him. He would bring lunch. He would call the Stardust, they'd bring a big extravagant lunch for these guys.

I go see Tony there. He looked at me, he goes, "You're broke."

I says, "I just got here."

"No, you're broke. I could tell. Here, take the money." Now he takes it out of his pocket—the money was unbelievable. He says, "Take it."

I took three thousand, and that was more than what I lost. I says, "I'll get—"

He says, "Don't worry about it. Enjoy yourself. You gotta have money."

So I go. And all of a sudden I hear Tony says, "He's a bust out? You motherfuckin' Jew mother . . . Who the fuck do you think . . . That's my friend for life. If I got a dollar in my pocket, he ain't broke, you dirty mother . . ."

So I'm going back. Tony's yelling at one of his guys. It's this Jewish guy named Spiegel, wonderful guy. I says, "What's wrong?"

Here's Tony: "Get out of here."

I says, "*Okayyy* . . ." And I left.

So later I was meeting Tony for dinner, with May. I says, "What's up?"

Tony takes out a jeweler's pouch, which is velvet, and you open it this way, and you open it that way. I'm looking at all this jewelry. I see a beautiful gold chain, and on it is a twenty-dollar gold piece, diamonds on it. Tony says, "Here, May. This is for you. This is a wedding gift."

I says, "You already . . ."

He says, "This is another wedding gift. Here, put this on." He gives me a Baume & Mercier watch, all gold. Worth five thousand dollars. Beautiful.

"Where'd you get it?"

"Remember that guy Spiegel? He came back with all this jewelry, apologized to me. He gave me this jewelry."

"Well, what are you giving it to me for?"

Tony says, "Well, if you didn't come in there, I never would have got it."

The first apartment May and I lived in was in Elmwood Park. It was owned by a top guy in the Elmwood Park crew. This guy, my landlord, was the biggest builder in Elmwood Park, River Grove, and River Forest. A fortune, legitimate money. The building was on Harlem, right over the border from Chicago. It was a nice place. They were condos. He put me in there until he sold it.

Now, at the time, I was moving up in the police department with Hanhardt. I'm not supposed to live in Elmwood Park. I'm a policeman, I'm supposed to live in the city. But it was such a nice place. The price was right. So we took it.

My landlord's girlfriend lived right across the hall from us. She was from the Old Country, Italian lady. Beautiful woman, great cook. We used to eat there with her all the time. So we became friends with her.

One day a guy I knew from the neighborhood shows up at the building. In the car he's got his partner, who's a guy by the name of Moretti. And I despised this guy. Couldn't stand him. My friend says, "You're working on the North Side."

"Yeah. What could I do for you?"

"I want you to listen to the radio for us. We got a score." They want me to be the lookout for a score they're gonna do in my area.

I said, "I'm just gonna be going with Hanhardt. I don't want to blow anything. I pass." So that was it. It's over with.

Now my landlord and his girlfriend leave town. He takes her away, and all of a sudden, her apartment gets made. Somebody robs the apartment. Lot of cash, jewelry, furs. I says, "What the fuck?" We didn't hear nothing. So now, antennas go up, I'm thinking eyeballs are on me.

The landlord spread the word to all the fences and all the crooks. He says, "Listen, you find this stuff, OK? I got furs, I got jewelry missing, and this is the description. Here's a picture of the fur." And everybody's on the hunt for this.

A couple of weeks after, it's a Sunday morning, six o'clock or something, I get a call from my landlord. He says, "Meet me by the Golden Bear." The Golden Bear was at Harlem and North, in River Forest. Breakfast place. So I go there, my landlord says, "I got a jolt for you."

"What is it?" I thought he was gonna say my brother Billy did it.

He said, "Well, we got the stuff back. The go-between guy found it. And he says your wife is the one that set it up."

"My wife? My wife didn't set nothing up. Are you crazy?"

"Freddy. I'm telling you."

I says, "Who's the guy?"

He wouldn't tell me. Now, I ain't gonna let it go. "You got the burglar."

"The burglar was your wife's girlfriend's boyfriend. A Greek guy."

I says, "Really. I want to talk to this burglar."

He says, "It's over."

I says, "It ain't over. You accused my wife."

We grabbed the burglar—me and Junior Bisceglie. Junior was my best friend, but he was also my landlord's main guy. I says, "You're coming, Junior, because I want you to hear it and tell your guy. He's gonna believe you." We go see the burglar. Junior's also there to make sure I don't get crazy with the guy. I says, "You said my wife set it up."

"No, sir." Everything was "sir." He knew I was a cop, but he knew I was a badass cop. "No, I told that Moretti that your wife had nothing to do with it."

That's when I found out it was Moretti who found the stuff. I says, "Then how's my wife get brought into this?"

"Well, you know my girlfriend is tight with your wife. Your wife would tell her, 'Oh, he bought her a beautiful ring, he bought her a beautiful fur.' I would tell her, 'Get more information.' I told her what questions to ask."

This guy got it all from his girlfriend. He would ask her, "What shift is May's husband working?" To make sure I wasn't there. And then May tells her they're going on vacation. He's taking her to Las Vegas. May told her, but inadvertently.

"Ah . . ." Now we ain't around, they ain't around, I'm on the midnights, and they make it. They make the score.

I says, "You mean to tell me you knew whose place this was?"

"No, I didn't."

I don't believe him. What else is he going to say? That was your warrant for death, to make a place belonging to this guy. He says, "Please, I don't want no trouble."

Now, here's the part where I could have had him killed, but I didn't. "You don't have no trouble. The only guy who has trouble is the other guy." I says, "Are you listening, Junior?"

Junior says, "How about this fuckin' Moretti?" Moretti was pissed because I wouldn't be the lookout for his score. And that's why he fingered May.

Junior went and saw the landlord. He told him, "No, she couldn't know."

I told Louie Tenuta. He says, "That mother . . . I hate that fuckin' Moretti." So he went looking for him. Now, Louie's a little guy, Moretti's a big guy. Louie sees Moretti on Harlem Avenue. He says, "Come here, you motherf—" He takes out the gun. Moretti takes off like a deer. *Boom, boom!* He's shooting at him. Right on Harlem Avenue.

That's when I called Tony. I said, "Tony, Louie's in trouble."

"I hate that fuckin' Moretti. Don't worry about a thing. Go see Vic." This is Vic Spilotro, his brother. "He'll speak up for Louie, don't worry about it."

It turned out OK. You make this guy's house, a top guy in the Elmwood Park crew? That's death. He knew I didn't do it. But Moretti's telling him about May. Could have been big trouble.

Junior and Tony squared it away.

19

SHAKESPEARE

C hicago police districts are duly numbered as in any proper
police department, but they are interchangeably referred to by
name, usually borrowed from a nearby street, park, or other
geographic feature: Town Hall, Chicago Lawn, Grand Crossing. As
the city pushed north in the course of the 1800s, a series of streets on
the North Side was named by some forgotten cultural aspirant after
great literary figures, leaving succeeding generations to puzzle over
Goethe Street (generally pronounced "Goath" or "Goaty") and won-
der who Schiller, Homer, and Dickens might have been. The Four-
teenth District, now centered at 2150 North California Avenue in a
socially and ethnically mixed area with a large Hispanic population,
takes its name from the cross street just south of it, a little-traveled
residential avenue named for a man whom even most occupants of
the lock-up could probably identify: the Bard of Avon, who lends his
name to what must be the most grandly named police station in the
country.

SHAKESPEARE

We knew that Bill Hanhardt was going to be the big chief, the chief of detectives. That was predetermined by the powers that be. So I said to myself, "I'm gonna get my foot in the door with him now." At that time Bill was the boss of Shakespeare station, the uniform guys. His rank was commander—that's an exempt rank. Exempt rank is anything above the rank of captain. You make captain by your tests, meaning you're a patrolman, you're a detective, then you go to sergeant, lieutenant, captain. That's the rank that can never be taken away from you, because you earned those by testing. But you're only made commander by appointment. And when you're appointed, it's accompanied with a letter of resignation. When the next guy wants you out, you're out.

I wanted to go to work for Bill, but he was a connected guy—I wanted to make sure the Outfit guys gave me the OK. I could go there as a regular patrolman, but to get anywhere, I knew I had to go to them. Not that it was their decision. They can't tell Hanhardt what to do. He told them what to do. But I wanted to be in good graces with him. So with a word from them, especially Tony or Joe Lombardo, that puts me right in with him.

I wasn't that tight with Lombardo, even though he lived across the street from me. So I went to see Tony. Tony says, "Go see Irv Weiner. You tell Irv that I told him to make the way clear for you and Hanhardt." And that's what I did.

Lombardo felt offended. He sent his guy Chris Spina by my house. He says, "He wants to see you. Meet him by Jimmy's hot dog place."

Now, I'm a policeman. I don't have to take this shit. But I went. Lombardo was waiting for me. I says, "Yeah, what's up, Joe?"

He juts out his jaw like he always did when he was angry: "Why didn't you come by my door, ask me about Hanhardt?"

"Because I was in Vegas on vacation, with Tony, and the subject came up." This was a lie on my part. I'm starting to argue. I says, "So what about it? Would you give me the OK?"

And he said, "Absolutely." That was it.

When I went to see Bill, he was glad to see me. He says, "Sit down. You're the only guy in the history of the department that has a fuckin' Outfit guy call me to help somebody. Why didn't you come to ask me yourself?"

I said, "Hey, I know the priorities. I know what I gotta do."

"All right. I got a job for you. There's only one high school in the whole district, Kelvyn Park. You're assigned to the school. No uniform; I'm the guy you report to. You pick up nothing from the station—we'll have it brought to you. Report to the school. You don't come in here at all. School hours, you stay at the school. When you get off work, you go home. School's off, you're off. In the summer, I gotta put you on the foot post. You put your uniform on, and I'll put you on North Avenue and Crawford. But right now you got the school. That's where you work."

It's a great job. It's plainclothes, and that's number one. Number two, you don't have to answer to anybody but Hanhardt. Number three, the hours were unbelievable. School's out, I'm done. I never had to go into the station. The first day, I went right to the school. A squad car pulled up. The guy says, "I don't know who you are, but here's your radio."

The only time I went by the station was to pick up my check. The watch commander was another Irish captain. The guys had told me, "Watch that Irish mother—he hates Italians."

One day I'm there picking up my check. The captain never sees me, so he asks the secretary, "Who's this fuckin' guy?"

"Pascente. He's the school guy."

The captain calls me. "Pascente, come here."

"Yes, sir." Always a gentleman.

He says, "You come to roll call, OK? And your radio, you sign it out. I want to see you every morning. I want to see your face in here before you start your shift. You understand what I'm talking about?"

"Yes, sir."

So I call Hanhardt. "Man, this guy is on my ass."

Bill says, "All right, don't worry about it. I'll talk to him."

The captain came into Bill's office, without Bill calling him. He says, "You know, Commander, not for nothing, but this greaseball comes in here, picks up his check—I don't know if he's living or dying. Who the fuck is this greaseball?"

Hanhardt gets up, he says, "Listen to me. I'm gonna tell you one time. My mother is Italian, my wife is Italian, my children are Italian. So if you're referring to them with that slur . . ."

Here's the captain: "I guess the conversation's over."

Bill says, "You're fuckin' right." He had a way with words.

～

At the school in Shakespeare district I got close with the gang that ran the school. They were a Latin gang called the Imperial Gangsters. They used to fight with a white gang called the Gaylords. They would flash signs at each other. And I'd play along. Instead of being a tough guy, I'd joke with them. They liked me. I got close to them to where, when a fight started, I could tell them "Yo" and they'd stop. Not because of fear; they liked me.

There was a fight in the lunchroom, which was the worst place to start, because of the mess. And I'm calming them down. And then the sergeant comes—someone called from the school. That was it. The way he got up there and belittled these kids . . . "Hey, fuck you." They start throwing things. And the tables went up. If he leaves me alone, it's done. I had them guys.

The boss of that gang was a guy named Carlos. He was sharp as a tack. Smart kid. He's a big-shot activist down in Texas now. I said, "Tell me what kind of rules you got."

"Well, this is our territory. And the Latin Kings, they want to take over this spot. And we don't have anybody to match these guys."

"What do you mean, match these guys?"

"If we have a meeting with them, it's under a truce flag. And we state our case. And sometimes their guy fights our guy, and the decision is made after that. If we win the fight, we get what we want."

I said, "That's all you need, is a tough guy? I got a guy who'll beat the fuck out of all them guys. I'll do you a big favor."

I knew these three guys named Tommy back in the neighborhood. The three Toms, they called them. They were a team. They were bad kids, younger than me. These guys were tough, monsters. And I brought the toughest one to the school. He could fight—he was like a pro. The fight was in the schoolyard, after school, at Wrightwood and Kostner. Tommy came with me and he represented, like he was one of them. And he beat up the boss of the Latin Kings. It wasn't even a contest. One minute. Annihilated him. And they let him go.

The Gangsters jumped on it. "You want in?"

Tommy said, "Fuck you. I did it for my friend."

The Latin Kings honored it—they let the Gangsters have their little couple of blocks. They were no match for the Kings, but for that day, after that fight, they were.

〰

I had a guy who was with the narcotics unit. I went to school with him. He was a good policeman, but he told me about these major drug dealers that they had. He says there's this one particular guy that lives in the suburbs. They had pinched him many, many months prior. He's not a gang guy. And he's got money in the house. My guy says, "This guy'll be back into the same mode. He's that type of a guy. Comfortable."

I took three guys with me. I took Junior Bisceglie, I took Dinger, and I took a guy we called Bobby Q. I couldn't be the one knocking on the door and going in, but I gave Dinger my stuff, the badge: "Police. We want to talk to you." And we knew where the stuff was, from my guy in narcotics.

So we get him. Of course, no resistance. White guy, just a generic guy. I told them what to do, then I came in. I was the supervisor. In disguise. My hair was gray, I had sunglasses on, and I had a fedora. There's no way you could see me without the disguise and say, "This is the guy." And you're not gonna see my ID—you saw the star.

They got him down, and I told them to handcuff him, right away, and he's the only guy home. He had a dog, which he put away. Dinger says he'll kill the dog, and these guys would. So they get the guy down, and we started searching. We searched his pockets. They found thirty-five hundred dollars in his pocket. So they took it out, *boom*. "You got any objections about this?"

"Not at all." He was afraid.

He was in the vending business. So check the slot machines. Check the cabinet, which is like a safe—it's where he keeps guns. *Boom*, he opened it up. He didn't want it broken. And here was marijuana, maybe a hundred pounds, in twelve-pound packets, sealed, good stuff. Took it out.

Then we found the money in the slot machines. Just like it was described, exactly. How does a guy continue with the same thing if he gets pinched? There was a slot where you open up for the money. He had stacks of hundreds. And the next one, stacks of hundreds. And the next, stacks of hundreds. It was a little over three hundred thousand, cash. A hundred pounds of marijuana. There was a collector's shotgun. It was like an Annie Oakley special, whatever it was. And this fuckin' moron, Bobby Q, wanted the shotgun. And Dinger says, "You ain't taking no fuckin' gun out of here. You understand?"

And Bobby's, "Oh, OK."

Dinger meant it. That's all you have to do is get grabbed with the gun, and then they know. And he couldn't trust him to shut up, because that's a hundred-year sentence. Home invasion.

Around 1974 or 1975 there was a Puerto Rican reverend in Shakespeare. And he got robbed of thirty thousand dollars, on the street. Thirty thousand cash. He was on the street, two cops stopped him for traffic, they took his money. They knew his background. He dealt with the drug dealers. He'd transport their money—they used him a lot.

So he's complaining. Now IAD's got the case, Internal Affairs Division; they know it was guys in Shakespeare District. So Bill calls me. I'm at the school, I'm not in uniform. Bill says, "Where were you today?"

"At work. I'm here at the school."

"You weren't on the street?"

"No."

"You come on in. I want you to stand a lineup."

I go in, we go to the lineup, he tells me what happened. I put my uniform on, in the locker room. He was worried because a guy we knew was in the lineup and he might get fingered for this thing. He says, "You got anybody that looks like this guy?

I says, "Yeah, a guy named Dennis DeBoer. I know him from Twenty."

"Get him over here." So DeBoer came, in uniform, and he stood the lineup. The guy Bill is worried about was there too, third spot in the first row.

So now the IAD comes in, and they look at the line before the reverend comes in.

Bill goes, "Are you finished?"

"Yeah."

"Get out of the fuckin' room." Just like that. He had no use for them guys whatsoever. So they leave the room. He says, "You, get over there. DeBoer, get over here. We'll switch. You get over there." He put me in front, right next to DeBoer. He moved everybody around. "Take your stars off." We take our stars off. "Take your shields off." We take our shields off. Now we're there, no stars, no shields. Because he didn't want them to use a number, and he didn't want our guy to be in spot three in the first row. He wanted DeBoer to be there.

Now they come in. The reverend comes in, identifies DeBoer. He didn't even look. First he says, "That's the guy." Then he looked at the other guys.

Hanhardt says, "Is the identification process over with?"

"Yeah, it's over with."

"Get out of the fuckin' room. You identified Dennis DeBoer, a Twentieth District policeman who wasn't even on duty."

That's Bill Hanhardt.

⌒

Obbie Frabotta had been with Milwaukee Phil and all those guys. Now this is a killer. Obbie lived on Rush Street. And he'd walk his dog, every day. He had this beautiful poodle. I think he had gone into the liquor store, tied his dog, and someone nailed the dog, kidnapped the dog. So now the dog is missing and Obbie is hot. "My fuckin' dog." I don't want to be the guy who took the dog.

Hanhardt gets the assignment. He tells Obbie, "You gotta make a report."

I'm the guy that's got to take it. So I go see Obbie. He says, "I want my fuckin' dog."

So I says, "All right, I'll find him." And I got the word out. I have my own sources. Other guys didn't have connections like I did.

Guess what? I find out who's got the dog. His name was Joe Brown. Really a good guy, but stupid. He's put out a ransom for the dog. He figured Obbie's an old Jewish guy walking his dog, and he's gonna pay. I says, "You ain't gonna get no ransom. You ain't gonna get nothin'. The only thing you're gonna get is, I'm gonna save your life, OK?"

I go back by Hanhardt, I say, "Bill, I got the dog."

"On your person?"

"I'm gonna get it. But the guy that did it, you ain't gonna know who it is."

He says, "Aw, beautiful. Go by Obbie."

I go by Obbie. I says, "Ob, you want your dog?"

"Yes!"

I says, "That's the end of it. No report, nothing. You'll get your dog, no repercussions."

He says, "Please get my dog. As long as he's safe . . ."

I bring the dog. He's kissing it. He puts the dog down. "All right, who took the fuckin' dog?"

I says, "Obbie, I told you before. I ain't telling you. I did my job, I got the dog. Now let it be that way, OK?"

"I wanna know who got—"

"I'm not telling you."

It took Tony to come there. He says, "Listen, you old mother-fucker. He did you a favor. This is my friend. Don't aggravate him. Enjoy your dog, and that's the end of it."

That was it. Tony had a lot of authority, big-time. They were afraid of him. And Joe Brown, he wound up getting killed later, but not for that.

20

WORKING BOTH SIDES

My daughter, Nicole, was born January 29, 1976. May had lost one the year before, which wasn't full-term, so now we were happy. When I went home from the hospital I went by Myron and Phil's, a joint on Devon Avenue, with Matt Raimondi. Matt was the big bookmaker that Tony and his crew had; he lived down the street from us. He and I had nothing but fun at Myron and Phil's—we were with all the Jews. "You're part of us. Your wife's a Jew, that makes you a Jew."

"Nah, you are what your father is."

"No, no you are what your mother is." And they were arguing, and we were laughing. Those two guys, Myron and Phil, were wonderful guys. Irv Kahn was in there, Ralph Greenberg, all Jews. "What's the name gonna be?"

"It ain't gonna be fuckin' Milton, that's for sure."

⌇

I never felt bad about making a score. But I was always afraid of getting caught. I didn't want to go to jail. And I was in serious trouble once because a guy beefed on me. And I never had anything to do with the guy.

Matt Raimondi was a huge bookmaker, huge. He got big because of his knowledge of the bookmaking business and because he was Tony Spilotro's cousin through marriage. Matt threw Tony's name around. Tony didn't like that. And he said, "Keep an eye on him."

I liked Matt. He was a big-hearted guy. So one night I'm with Matt, and we're having dinner, we're having fun, we got drunk, we're on Rush Street, and we're at a place called Augustino's. And a guy I know comes to me, in front of Matt, and asks if he can talk. I trust Matt, so I says, "Absolutely."

The guy says he's got an in with the State of Illinois. They have an office where they keep property that no one claimed. It's from persons that died, and they're waiting for the heir or somebody, and they don't know who to give it to. And I'm talking about money, cash, jewelry. In this case, he had stocks, bearer bonds, where he could do whatever he wants with them. And it's a lot of money.

I says, "Hey. I don't know nothing about stocks. Forget about it."

Matt steps in. "Wait a minute. I got the guy who can do this."

I says, "Matt, if you want to take the chance, go ahead. I don't want to do it."

The guy gives them to him. Now, he don't know Matt, but on my OK, he did it.

Well, Matt gave them to this guy who had a high-line restaurant on Lake Shore Drive. And the guy knew a lot of stockbrokers, and that's why he knows he could do it. So he did find a guy to take the bonds.

But now they put it through the system, and fireworks went off. The FBI grabs the stockbroker—he gives them the restaurant owner, the owner goes, "I don't know. I got it from the policeman, Fred."

Me? He didn't get them from me.

There's a party at my house, a birthday for Joey or Nicole, and they're at the door, the FBI. Three agents. I see them, I says, "Hey, how you doin'?" I know who they are. "What can I do for you?"

"Well, we'd like to talk to you. But I want you to remove everybody from this room. Because you don't want anybody to hear it." So I proceed to do it. My wife is in there, my mother. Oh, my poor mother. She was praying.

I was sick. "Look at this."

So my brother Billy says, "I'm staying right here."

The guy says, "What, is this your lawyer?"

Billy goes, "No, I'm better than any lawyer, you motherfucker." Told him, just like that.

"Hey, you don't need to swear."

Billy says, "You want to arrest me? Arrest me. I'll fuckin' swear any motherfuckin' place I want." That's Billy.

So the guy goes, to me, "You know this guy so-and-so?" The restaurant owner.

Billy says, "He don't know the guy."

I says, "Billy. I'll answer the question. And if you don't shut up, I'm gonna send you downstairs." I say to the FBI guy, "I can't answer this question. Please understand, I can't answer. My lawyer, you know."

He says, "Well, here's a subpoena for the grand jury." He had it all ready.

I call Matt. I say, "Matt, your motherfuckin' friend . . . You better go talk to this guy."

The restaurant guy wasn't around. Matt goes to see Michael Spilotro, Tony's brother. He calls me. I go see him. I says, "Hey, Mike. You better talk to this motherfucker. Understand? It ain't me, it's Matt. Why didn't the guy beef on him? He's the one that brought them to him."

Michael says, "You can't hurt this guy. He brings us tons of money." He didn't just run a restaurant, this guy—he was a book-maker, too. Michael didn't want to lose a source of income.

I said, "Mike, I ain't getting the right answers here. What kind of rules is this? I don't give a fuck about no book. I'm not gonna let this end. If it ain't over tonight, I'm . . ."

"Don't hurt that guy."

"This guy beefed on me. Now what are you gonna do about it?"

If you couldn't reach Tony, there was a guy we'd get in touch with. He was with the heavy machinery union, local 150. I used to go to hockey games with him. He was real tight with Tony. I says to this guy, "Get ahold of him."

"It must be important."

"You're fuckin' right."

So Tony comes to town, I told him. He says, "Freddy, don't worry about a fuckin' thing."

That's all I had to hear. I go to sleep. Next thing I know, the restaurant owner goes to the grand jury. Now he tells the grand jury. "I was in the hospital when they talked to me. I don't remember what happened. It was a guy named Fred, but not that one, that's a policeman." And it was all over.

Tony and Irv Weiner visited him and that was the end of it. When Tony says it's over, it's over.

‿つ

Bill Hanhardt was the guy that placed everybody. He would detail us to the Criminal Intelligence Unit. I did many things for the CIU without being a member. Once Hanhardt put me there with a guy I'm going to call Bobby who was a sharp detective—very, very sharp. Bobby was a guy that I would have to say helped me along, broke me in as a detective. He was a protégé of Eddie Vrdolyak, the alderman, came from his ward, way, way south. But Bill Hanhardt loved him, because he was a pretty good guy. He was a gutsy guy, too. He had some killings under his belt. Bobby killed eight people on the job. In the act of a felony, fleeing, whatever.

So now Bobby shoots another one, and this time he gets bagged by the superintendent, James Rochford. Off the street, suspended indefinitely until the hearing. And Bobby is pissed. He says, "I'll kill that motherfucker." He's telling Bill Hanhardt and me.

And Bill says, "Listen, leave it up to me. You'll be on the job within the week."

Jack Killackey was a deputy superintendent under Rochford. Great guy, good for the men. Jack Killackey was a heavy-duty guy, politically. He worked directly for Rochford—he was his man. Now, Jack Killackey had a snitch on Rush Street who would keep an eye on policemen. If they were getting a little too drunk, if they were abusive, if they were hanging with bad guys, whatever. And the stool pigeon was a guy named Duckie Bills. He ran the Singapore on Rush Street.

So Hanhardt sent us into Singapore on a Friday, and Duckie Bills is there, and the plan was all orchestrated by Hanhardt. He told Bobby, "Here's what you do. You start it off, make sure you go in blind drunk." He wasn't drunk, but he was acting the part. We're sitting with Duckie Bills. He's laughing, we're having fun, here's Bobby: "Duckie, I like you, buddy. That dirty, motherfuckin' Rochford, I'm gonna blow his brains out."

"What?" Duckie turns to me: "You hear this?"

I says, "Hey, Duck. I don't want to know nothing."

Bobby says, "I'll kill that . . . He ruined my life, he wants to take my living, my kids'. He's dead. I don't give a fuck." And he's making it worse.

Duckie Bills is getting red. "Freddy, this is your friend. Can't you talk sense into him?"

"Hey, Duck. I'm not involved."

We did our part. And we walk out.

Now, Bill Hanhardt knows that Duckie's gonna go to Killackey, and Killackey's gonna tell Rochford.

Well, this was a Friday. Monday morning, ten to eight—I'll never forget this, Bill gave me the story—Killackey calls Hanhardt in. He says, "Is Bobby So-and-so capable of murder?"

Hanhardt says, "Is he capable of murder? He killed eight guys."

"You're sure about that? You wait right here." Now Killackey goes by the superintendent, comes back in a couple of minutes, he says, "Come with me."

Now he walks in there. Here's Rochford, sweating bullets. It was zero degrees outside, but he's sweating. He says, "Bill, I'm the superintendent."

Hanhardt told me, "He never called me Bill in my life. Now I'm Bill."

Rochford goes, "What's going on? Give me the bottom line here. If you talk to Bobby, do you think he'll come back to the job and will forget about his back pay?"

Hanhardt says, "Let me talk to him. The guy's crazy."

He calls us. "Meet me at Gene & Georgetti's." We go there. He tells Bobby, "You're back on the job, you jag-off." He's giving it to him. Finally he says, "The hearing's over."

Here's Bobby: "What about my fuckin' back pay?"

"Just let it be." Hanhardt pulled it off. He knew how to do it.

I told Bill Hanhardt, "Put me in the organized crime unit. Please."

He says, "No, I can't put you there. You'll have everybody in jail. Are you fuckin' crazy? You can't go there."

I says, "I know more than anybody. Put me in there."

"That's out."

"How about the gambling?"

"No." So he kept me away from it.

Now I'm with Bobby from CIU in a restaurant on Rush Street. The name of the restaurant was Billy's. It was next door to Faces, a famous, famous place. Two guys walk in—guess who they're from? Organized crime. Nice guys, shook hands. "Hey, Bobby, how you doin'? Breaking him in, huh?"

"He knows more than me." Then Bobby says to me, "Could I ask them to sit with us?"

I says, "Sure. You want to sit?"

Now they sit. Who comes to the table? My old boss Joe the Jap. "Hey, Freddy. How you doing, Freddy?"

That's it. So he goes to his table, we have a nice dinner, big dinner. The waitress comes, says, "Just so you know, Joe the Jap picked up the check." So I waved. I didn't even go over there. "Joe, thank you."

"That's OK, that's OK."

So one of these guys from organized crime, we're talking, he says, "Man, what a nice gesture, that guy. Who is that guy?" These guys are organized crime. They're supposed to know every organized crime member, everyone there is.

"Ah, he's a pool player."

Bobby went: "What the fuck? Who the fuck they put in organized crime? Those guys didn't know Joe the Jap?"

WORKING BOTH SIDES

In 1976 Frank Sinatra did a concert for the police in Chicago. It's at the Four Torches, and he's got the big entourage. My wife's there, my sister. Michael Spilotro is there; instead of sitting at the table with Sinatra, he's sitting back with us. But then he says, "All right, come on." So he takes my wife, he takes my sister. The other girls didn't want to go. They were afraid. So we walk over to the table—it wasn't far from us—and we're talking to Sinatra. And then May sees a few friends that she knows next to them, so she's talking to them. And Frank grabs her arm and says, "Hey, *chiacchierona*, I'm not through with you." So she takes out the picture of our daughter, who's only six months, and he signs it. It says, "To Nicole, welcome to the world, love and kisses, Frank Sinatra." We still got that picture.

So now I go to the bathroom. Frank's in there, he's combing his hair, he washed up, and I'm talking to him.

I says, "Nineteen fifty-eight, the Stadium, you were there for the title fight."

"What a fight," he goes. "Couldn't even see, Basilio. Robinson and him, big fight. Too bad he had to close the eye. Otherwise he was in the fight."

I says, "You don't know me, but I stole your handkerchief."

He remembered. He goes, "You son of a gun." He calls his guy, Jilly. "Jilly, this guy stole my fuckin' handkerchief." It's eighteen years later.

I says, "I wanted the hat." He started laughing.

So he leaves. I says, "Yo! My wallet."

"Go on . . ." He hits me in the back of the head. He got a kick out of that.

21

GAMBLERS

In the late '70s Tony's brother Vic came up with the off-track betting, the messenger services. That was legal bookmaking. It went on for a couple of years. And we made nothing but money. The deal was, we're not booking. We're just taking your bet to the track for a service charge. We would charge you 10 percent. That was the way it was outlined. In other words, we'd take your twenty-dollar bet, and we'd add two dollars to it—that was our fee, to bring that bet to the track. Give 'em a receipt. The idea was, we were just providing a service. It was legal, until the state did the research and caught on, under Governor Thompson.

～

The short-lived existence of racetrack messenger services in Illinois in the late 1970s was only the last, anticlimactic chapter in Chicago's long and glorious history as a place where a man can always get a bet down without going too far out of his way. It was Chicago's Mont Tennes who brought gambling into the modern world with his visionary adoption of the telegraph and then the telephone to get race results instantly from the track to the poolrooms and handbooks dispersed about the city. The race wire defeated the track owners' attempt to keep the betting, and consequently all the profits, on their premises; it allowed a bookie with a wire connection to set up shop in a basement or the back room of a tavern. Tennes made Chicago the handbook capital of the United States by allying with the upstart company AT&T to make his innocently named General News Bureau the top purveyor of race information while paying off compliant Chicago policemen and politicians.

Tennes was bought out by Moe Annenberg (father of Walter, later made US ambassador to Britain by Richard Nixon), who allied with Al Capone to drive out rivals and dominate the race wire business with his Nationwide News Service. When Annenberg was prosecuted by the feds for tax evasion, he simply walked away from Nationwide, which mysteriously continued without missing a beat as the Continental Press, under Annenberg's old pal from the West Side, Mickey McBride.

McBride then promptly sold the concern to James Ragen, another fellow who went way back with Annenberg. Ragen was ambitious but unwisely stubborn. Outfit bookies used Ragen's service for free due to a long-standing agreement made with Annenberg, but the Outfit didn't own it. When Outfit bosses made Ragen the classic offer, he did the unthinkable and refused. The Outfit formed a rival company, Trans-America, but the hoods were just biding their time. In 1946 Ragen was shotgunned in his car from a truck pulled up next to him at a stoplight. He lingered in the hospital but died, possibly poisoned, weeks later. The Outfit then closed down Trans-America, put Mickey McBride's son Eddie up as a figurehead at Continental, and sat back satisfied at a job well done.

At this point, the Chicago Crime Commission's Art Bilek says, "Chicago was sort of the central mecca for the gambling empire in America. All the slot machines in America were being made in Cook County or the city of Chicago. All of the machines in Cook County were Outfit-controlled. It was an amazing world that existed here. Every district in the city had bookie joints—some of them were just, for example, the cigar stand at the El station. People went to work each day on the El going downtown and then came back at night, if they were lucky, to collect their winnings.

"And this was not considered to be a bad, evil thing, because there were a large number of policemen that were part of this underground empire of gambling. The feeling was that if people wanted to bet in handbooks, which they did in great numbers in Chicago, that wasn't something that should be taken away from them. That's a very sacred kind of a thing, to deal with people's vices when it's on that wide a scale, as was the bookie business in Chicago."

Continental stayed in business until the feds got into the act and banned the transmission of betting information with the Wire Act in 1961, which, combined with O. W. Wilson's police reforms, ended the era of overt handbooks in Chicago. The bookies didn't go away; they just went further underground.

They stayed there until a man named Frank Oliver wondered in 1975 why it should be illegal for a person to convey a bettor's money to the racetrack for him, as a service, and started the first wire messenger service in Illinois. Imitators soon sprang up, many accused of having organized crime ties and booking the bets themselves rather than simply conveying them to the track. Worse, some offices experienced mysterious fires or thefts, or simply vanished, when a bettor made a big score.

The state legislature promptly outlawed the business model, but the services appealed, and until the issue was resolved, with the state Supreme Court upholding the prohibition of the messenger services in

GAMBLERS

July 1978, Chicago bettors saw a brief resurrection of the golden days of the neighborhood handbook.

〰

We booked everything that was coming in. We didn't take nothing to the track. Lombardo, Tony, the German, they were all in it. And the money was unbelievable. Our company was the Western Messenger Service. There was Finish Line, there was Western, there were three or four of them. Tony had four or five joints. There was one on Lincoln Avenue. Jimmy Cozzo was watching it, so he got paid for that. There was one on the South Side, and Louie Tenuta and Vic Spilotro were watching the one on Fullerton.

Tony had me on the payroll for the Fullerton joint. All I had to do was be there and watch the money, because I had the gun in case somebody got heisted. This was the main drop-off spot. There were four Western joints from all over; they'd come in with all the money. The South Side place would come, Lincoln and Paulina would come. And we'd go in the back and they'd count it. They'd bundle it up. And then whoever took it to the bank or took it wherever, I'd go with them. That was my job. They paid me $150 a day, which was huge. Cash money.

Vic took care of the guys that came in to bet. He'd have a big spread for them—they'd have corned beef and this and that, sandwiches, everything, all through the night. He had booze if they wanted a drink. The joint was mobbed. And these Gypsies would be in there, and they'd be betting all night.

We beat them out of so much money. We were getting the results and giving it to them on a delay, because we had somebody at the track and we'd get ahold of his information, real fast. We knew who won already. We had a guy in the back, and we had speakers all over, and he called the race. So we'd get the information, it would be a couple of minutes after, and . . . "Post time, here they come . . ." He didn't know who was second or who was third. But he knew all the horses. "And coming around . . ." He made it such a generic call, you couldn't even follow it, you couldn't tell. "And here's Seabiscuit around the turn . . . and it's Whirlaway!" And they'd be jumping for joy. Now, if the guy comes in with the winner, there's a couple of minutes left: "Too late, the race is off. You're out." If he comes with the loser, we took the money.

The bettors never got wise.

Tony had told me, "Don't get behind that counter, because as long as you're on this side, you're just coming in to make a bet. That's legal. There's nothing wrong with that." So every time I'm in there, I was like a customer. But one day, I'm sitting behind the counter, relaxing, bullshitting with the girls. The one time I'm back there, Joe Lombardo comes in. "What the fuck are you doing here?"

I said, "What do you mean, what am I doing here? I'm working. You don't know? I'm here."

He says, "You ain't working no more, 'cause you're out. You're fired."

"I'm fired? Why?"

"Because you're gonna fuck up your boss, Hanhardt. You don't belong in here. You're a policeman."

Well, I'm not gonna argue with him. These are incidents that cause a lot of friction. So Vic says, "Come over here, I want to ask you about this bet." In my ear he says, "Go by Tony. Fuck this guy." Just like that.

So I call Tony. I says, "Tony, I got a red alert here. Vic told me to call you."

Tony says, "Well, that dirty . . ." Because I'm Tony's friend, Lombardo couldn't just do that to me. Tony says, "You stay away, don't worry about it. You go by Hoagie's"—Hoagie's Pub, that was his brother Michael's place—"he'll give you the money, don't worry about it." I went by Michael, he gave me my money. I didn't even have to be there. It came off of their winnings. And it was better, because I didn't have to go to work. That's Tony. He looked out for me. How do you not love a guy like that? I loved that guy.

⌇

One day my neighbor Matt Raimondi says, "Freddy, I want you to meet this guy." The guy's name was David Ballog. He was a Gypsy. Matt knew all these Gypsies. He booked them in the messenger joint. And they borrowed money from him, for betting. Now he's giving them money, and sometimes they couldn't pay. So they bring him merchandise, they give him TVs, they give him this, they give him that. So he's got them pretty well locked. Ballog ran out of money and couldn't pay him, and he says, "How about if I get you a TV, a color TV?" And he did.

So I met Ballog. The first meeting I had with him, he had $175,000 cash in the briefcase. He had currency exchanges that he used to do business with. He used to give them a percentage for cashing the checks. They were kinky guys, but the checks were legitimate. This was an insurance check he cashed.

He showed the cash to me. He knew he could trust me, because I'm with Matt, and I'm a policeman. He said, "I want to drop it off by somebody. Take a ride with me." He didn't need me; he did that to impress me. And he did. I almost was gonna take it away from him.

Ballog had a guy that booked horses in an office at Foster and Pulaski. The guy must have known the people—they were Koreans—that owned the building. And he had the whole bottom part. There was no reason for a customer to go downstairs. You couldn't see in it, you had to be buzzed in, you had to be a member. So the Gypsies used to go there. He had sheets on the wall for different racetracks: Gulfstream, Hialeah, Santa Anita. This was like an old-time deal. And he booked these guys.

The Gypsies came up with a scheme. They said they need me, otherwise they won't do it. Ballog says, "We got how we're gonna beat this guy. He's taking the bets after the race goes off. Because nobody can find out in time who won the race." You would be in this place, there are no phones, there is no communication. There were no cell phones at the time. At the bookmaker's desk, he had a phone. There was a lock on it, and he never left it. He was the only guy with a phone.

The way the Gypsies would do it, though, was with beepers. Ballog says, "I'm gonna have my brother in Gulfstream, in Florida, and he's gonna call me on the beeper. And we're gonna know that like, within a minute, who won the race. And the guy will take the bet."

I says, "OK, you got it figured out."

So the brother goes to Florida. But prior to that, Ballog was making bets all week. Just to set him up. He lost between two and three thousand dollars. He was sharp, the Gypsy. "Here, gimme three hundred on this horse." The horse lost. Now he writes the time down—eight o'clock or whatever, and it's five minutes after the race went off. But the guy still took the bet. The bookmaker sees Dave right there, he knows he didn't get any information from anybody. There's no phones.

Now D-Day was coming. And the D-Day payoff was forty-some thousand. Because he paid track odds. Bookmakers, because they're cheap scoundrels, they only allow you bookmakers' odds. They'll give you, let's say, up to twenty to one, even if it's a hundred to one. That's all you'll get from the bookmaker. Track odds is what they pay at the track.

Davey went in, and the brother sent the race results over the beeper. It's on vibrate; you can't hear it. It comes over, *6-6-6-6-6*

. . . And then he sees *8-8-8-8-8* . . . Well, six and eight is the double. He makes the bet, *badda-bing*, it wins. All the combinations he bet comes to forty-some thousand.

The bookmaker says, "I ain't paying you. This is past post."

Davey said, "You can't do that to me. I mean, I'm playing the same way, all week. I lost a thousand, I lost five hundred, I lost three hundred, I lost every day. They were the same times. Don't do that to me. I have to go to the guy who's betting with me. He's expecting this money."

He says, "I don't give a fuck who you're with."

I walk in. I said, "Your day is done."

"Who are you?"

I says, "I'll tell you who I am, motherfucker. I'm the police, and I know the boys." This guy didn't pay the street tax, to the Outfit. He was scared of them more than anything. "So you *want* to get pinched. You don't want me to tell them you're an outlaw bookmaker. I want the money now, I want the money in cash. I don't want no 'I'll give you five now and six later.' "

He paid him right there. Opened the fuckin' book.

⌇

A guy from the neighborhood was in the horse business. All his life he bet horses, and he eventually bought some. One day he comes up to me, he says, "I got a horse for you. We've been pulling the horse back for the last three outings. Holding him back. This time he's gonna hit, and he's gonna pay big. It's gonna be fifty, sixty to one." This was a trotter, a harness racer.

I says, "I'm in."

"Don't give it to nobody. Because that'll make the odds go down."

"OK." I call Tony. "Tone, this is it." I tell him about it.

He says, "I'm coming to town for this one. I don't want you to bet a nickel. You're in with me."

The day that this went down, Tony comes in, he had his brother Vic, he had all these guys. So now we're at the track. And the horse was eighty to one. By the time these guys bet it, it was down to seven to two. Tony must have bet a fortune. He must have given it to other guys, too.

My friend's watching the board. And every time the fuckin' thing moves, he looks at me. Now I got nervous, because I gave it to Tony. My friend goes, "How many fuckin' guys did you tell?"

We had the jockey, a good driver. He comes up, I remember he had these teeth missing. He says, "Here's the way it's gonna go. I'm gonna come by right here where you're sitting. We'll see if the horse is ready. I'll know once I get him to go around a couple of times on the track when we loosen them up. Now, if I come by like this, sitting straight up in the cart, don't bet it. If I come by leaning to the right, like I'm checking my equipment, that's the sign: go bet it. Now, if I go this side *and* the other side, bet your house. Go steal more money to bet it."

We were in there where you eat, the Derby Room. We're waiting, and here comes our guy on the buggy. And he was going crazy. He was going back and forth. He's going over to this side, and over to that side, he comes to this side, and then he goes this way—and he falls off of the fuckin' cart. And here goes the horse. The horse is going, the buggy's flopping up and down, they had to scratch the horse.

Tony wanted to kill him. The vein was coming out of his forehead. "Get that motherfucker! I'll . . ." He's so mad.

My friend says, "Ah, what the fuck." In fact, he was happy, because now it was scratched and he could get it the next time.

I was afraid for the poor jockey. I don't even know the guy, but I'm afraid for him. I run down to the paddock. I says, "Buddy, get the fuck out of town. When you leave, go another way. If you come up there, you're gonna fuckin' get your . . ."

He says, "What's wrong, what are they so mad about?"

"It's not why, it's *who's* mad. Just get out of here."

I saved him. Because Tony was gonna throw him off the fuckin' balcony.

22

OCCUPATIONAL HAZARDS

I n late January and early February 1978, in the depths of a brutal Chicago winter, burglars started turning up dead. The first was Bernard "Buddy" Ryan, who was found with three holes in his head in a snow-covered Lincoln Continental that had been called in as abandoned in Stone Park, a west suburb with long-standing Outfit associations. Next was Steve Garcia, found with his throat cut in the trunk of a car parked at a motel near O'Hare. Two days after that a police officer brushing snow off a Cadillac left next to a bar in the southwest suburb of Stickney found Vincent Moretti and Donald Renno in frozen intimacy on the backseat. They had been strangled before having their throats cut. When John Mendell turned up in the trunk of a ticket-bedecked Oldsmobile Toronado next to a fire hydrant on the South Side on February 20, also strangled and slashed, a pattern was noted. If you were a burglar working in the Chicago area, it was time to head for warmer climes. Somebody had pissed off the wrong people, and the Outfit was thinning the herd.

It took years for the full story to emerge. The final pieces were not put in place until the federal Family Secrets trial in 2007 featured testimony from several of the killers. But the word was on the streets and the outline of the story known within days of the first killing: somebody had hit Tony Accardo's house.

This made jaws drop on both sides of the law. Who was stupid enough to do that? A prison term was one thing, but prison was survivable. There could be no greater deterrent than Outfit dictates. The "M&M boys," Jimmy Miraglia and Billy McCarthy, had supposedly been killed in 1962 for their bad manners in committing murder inside Elmwood Park city limits, and their victims had nothing like Accardo's status. Making Tony Accardo's house was folly beyond understanding.

Insiders pieced the story together, tracing the die-off to an earlier burglary, which had taken place on December 17. That Saturday night, a team of skilled professional burglars had gotten into Harry Levinson's jewelry store on Clark Street just north of the Loop and cleaned him out, getting away with a million dollars' worth of jewels and thirty thousand dollars in cash.

It was a terrific score, a career highlight, and there was only one problem with it: Harry Levinson was an old pal of Tony Accardo's. All it took was a phone call and the word went out: the score was no good and the money and jewels were to be returned.

∽

They made Levinson's. And it was sophisticated, they did a great job. Levinson's was near Clark and Chicago. Whoever had the information had it good. John Mendell was the boss of this gang. He put this thing together. Johnny Mendell was an electronics expert. Plus he could do some drilling of the safes. But they brought in other safe guys, in case. There were, I think, seven guys on the score. You got Johnny Mendell. Vince Moretti, who was an ex-policeman and a relative of the Moretti who tried to pin that burglary on May. You got Steve Garcia, who was good. You got Buddy Ryan, who was a known burglar, and he worked with the Elmwood Park crew. Those are the main guys.

They cut the alarm, they shut the phones. The phones in the whole area were shut down. They had to go that far to do it. And it was a weekend. They did their homework. The Chicago station is not far from there—the Eighteenth District, between LaSalle and Clark on Chicago Avenue, maybe a block or two away.

So they get it, sophisticated as could be, big score. When they made it, the whole Area Six was on it—I think it was Jimmy Biebel who was assigned to it. But we helped out. Now, me, I'm doing my own investigation. Because there ain't many guys that can do this. This is no junkie burglary. This is sophisticated. And I got on it through friends, and I'm not gonna reveal it to the cops. I'm on it because if I could approach them, then there's something in it for me.

Levinson went for help. They had a network like nobody. Levinson goes to Accardo, Accardo puts out the word that they have to return the stuff. Find out who did it. Nobody's in trouble, but they wanted the stuff back.

So now I got the word from a guy I knew on the Elmwood Park crew. He said, "Stay away from that stuff." He didn't even say why. He says, "They got the guys." So I know something's up. After a while I found out, and everybody else found out. Except the cops.

The only guy I saw was Steve Garcia. This was after he had returned Levinson's stuff. And he says, "Fred, I don't even want to talk about it." So I didn't get anything from the guys directly. But I know from the sources that after they returned it, they waited a little while, not a long time, and they went to Accardo's house, and they made the house. I don't know how they thought they'd get away with it. Nobody in their right minds would take a chance on hitting Tony Accardo's house. Because there's people would come out of the woodwork, retired guys, to get these guys for doing that.

∽

John Mendell wasn't out of his mind. But his judgment was probably clouded by anger. The story as it emerged eventually was that Mendell had hidden the loot from the burglary and started looking for a fence, only to find that nobody would take the stuff; the word was out. Understandably reluctant to simply give back a personal best score, Mendell dug in his heels. So somebody took it from him. Outfit discipline kicked in and somebody gave up his secret stash. The loot disappeared and word made its way to Mendell that the matter was closed. If he had left it at that, he might have lived.

∽

Here's what I think happened. I'm sure, knowing these guys, if they're sat down, everybody knows you're the offender, and this guy, the boss, he wants the stuff, they better get it back in hours. So they brought it back. But here's something that I'll tell you. They asked the boss for money. Mendell said, "This is our score. This is how we make a living. We want to be compensated. What about the money?"

"There ain't no money." Told them point blank, there ain't no money. And that ain't right. He should have given them money.

Or he should have got the money from Levinson, by all rights, because he was gonna get compensated from the insurance company. So I guess it was bitterness. But they knew the score.

So they says, "We'll wait, we'll make his house." But it was only three weeks or so. Wait three years!

John Mendell couldn't wait three years. Knowing that Accardo was wintering at his Palm Springs home, Mendell opted for guts over brains. In the wee hours of January 6, Mendell and Garcia broke into Accardo's house in River Forest and recovered the Levinson's haul from a vault in the basement.

That made twice in a month that Mendell could claim to have pulled off the score of a lifetime. The only problem was that Mendell's lifetime was rapidly shrinking. Accardo's houseman, an old Sicilian named Michael Volpe, called Accardo to report the burglary. Accardo told Volpe to keep his mouth shut and flew back to Chicago immediately. The break-in was never reported. Accardo had more efficient ways of dealing with misconduct available to him.

Accardo's executive officer at the time was the old Cicero veteran of Capone's gang Joey Aiuppa. It is assumed that he took care of the cleanup. The last of the crew that had originally hit Levinson's turned up on April 14: John McDonald was found shot to death in an alley near Racine and Grand. And that should have been that. But power is a blunt instrument, and Accardo was no surgeon. Career burglar Bobby Siegel, who had nothing to do with either burglary and took a lie detector test to prove it, testified at the Family Secrets trial that his fears that he was on the hit list were confirmed by one of the killers, Gerald Scarpelli, who told him that Accardo intended to make a point by hitting one burglar of every ethnicity. "You just happened to be the Jew," Scarpelli said.

The FBI had opened an investigation into the murders, designated with the agency's usual poetic flair BURGMURS, and in September 1978 they convened a grand jury and hauled Accardo in to ask him about the burglary. He took the Fifth. Next up was Michael Volpe. The septuagenarian houseman, who had faithfully served Accardo for decades, saw no alternative but to tell the truth about what had happened at the house. On October 5 Volpe was seen for the last time, driving off to work at Accardo's house. Neither he nor the car was ever seen again.

In November the FBI obtained a warrant to search Accardo's house. They found and confiscated cash, which was later returned to Accardo after he won an appeal of the seizure. The cash was found to have originated at a Las Vegas bank and was probably money from the Outfit's casino skim. They also found an incinerator in the basement, and among the ashes they found fragments of eyeglasses like those worn by Michael Volpe.

Among the evidence the FBI compiled in the BURGMURS investigation were the phone records of Gerry Carusiello, also known as Dinger, who was Joey Aiuppa's driver and gofer. The records showed repeated phone contacts between Carusiello and each of the victims shortly before their deaths.

The last chapter of the story came when Carusiello himself was shot to death in September 1979, in Addison, Illinois. He was dressed in dark clothing, had no identification on him, and was probably casing a building for a burglary. A witness heard him plead with his killer just before being shot. In 1988 Gerald Scarpelli, looking at serious jail time on federal charges, flipped and confessed to a long list of crimes to the FBI. One of them was the murder of Gerry Carusiello. Shortly after that Scarpelli recanted his testimony and, while held in the feds' Metropolitan Correctional Center on Van Buren Street in the South Loop, hanged himself in a shower stall. Persistent rumors that it was an assisted suicide have never been proven.

Dinger did them all. He never told me. But you know. Joey Aiuppa, his bodyguard and driver and confidant was Dinger. Dinger knew them all. Dinger worked with them. Especially Mendell. So for him to call them . . . "Yeah, I'll see you." *Badda-bing.* That was all. That was a simple thing.

That's the only guy who can get you, your friend. If Joe Lombardo told me to meet him in Joliet . . . Yeah, fuck you. If Tony told me, I'd be there. And he'd get me. Only your friends get you, with those guys. No strangers. Who in their right mind would go see these guys?

And then Dinger got it. They killed him. Why? Because him and his crew got all these guys. Now, they buried the secret of who did it all. Now he's out of the way. He did it all, got it all back, and he whacked all them guys, him and his team. And they wound up killing him to clean it up.

How do you fuckin' kill a guy like that? What a sick business. That's why I want people to know that these guys are not hero types. They're lice. You can't kill your friend.

Here's how I always thought about it. If they come up to me and say, "All right, you got the assignment. You gotta get Tony."

"OK. I got it, buddy. He's as good as gone." And then, "Tony, get the fuck out of town. That's all I'm telling you." And back to the bosses. "I can't find him. He's gone."

Can't they do that? Let him go. What kind of human beings are these? They're just evil, evil. There's no words to describe them.

23

RIGHT-HAND MAN

In 1979 Jane Byrne was elected mayor. She had come out of the Machine but proclaimed herself a reformer and started to clean house. Her first acting police superintendent promoted William Hanhardt to deputy superintendent. Hanhardt had been made head of the CPD Burglary Section in 1971, beginning a climb up the department ranks, to commander of the Shakespeare station and then deputy chief in charge of Property Crimes.

As Hanhardt's profile had risen, so had the murmurs that his ties to underworld figures were not entirely antagonistic, and his appointment as deputy superintendent set off a tug-of-war in the CPD between reform and business-as-usual factions. Within a few months, Byrne's second acting superintendent, Joe DiLeonardi, had demoted Hanhardt from deputy superintendent to chief of Traffic.

They made Bill chief of Traffic, and he put me in the Hit and Run Unit. Reason? Daytime, he wanted me by him, to hang with him. He said he's only gonna be there a year, and then, after everything clears, he's gonna become chief of detectives. He says, "But you stay with me in Hit and Run. You'll investigate major accidents, you'll do whatever you want. It's gonna be an easy job. But you'll be with me."

And that's what we did. He just wanted me with him. In fact, I was on the desk. He was in there, the big office, I was right outside his door. I did my reports, I did my job. He used me a lot, as a matter of fact. "Go by Kenny Curin, let him know this. Go by Brzeczek, tell him this." Things like that.

I was his driver, too. I'd drive a hundred miles an hour. He'd say, "Slow down."

"Yes, sir."

"I'm telling you, slow down." I'd keep on.

He'd pull out the gun, he'd say, "You don't fuckin' slow down, I'm gonna blow your fuckin' foot off."

We'd have more fun at night. He figured for a year, we could do that. I didn't object. It was a great job. I'm getting my check. Every day, lunch. Gene & Georgetti's. And I meet his guys. We go to Counsellors Row, we see Roti and Marcy. And we got on the tapes the FBI was recording there. I was notified. Never questioned, but I was notified by mail that I was picked up on the tape.

An overzealous busboy nearly blew an FBI investigation sky high when he stumbled across a miniature video camera under a cushion while cleaning out a booth at the Counsellors Row restaurant at 102 N. LaSalle in 1988. Apparently not content with the phone tap already in place, the feds had planted the camera to cover the joint's famous Booth One, where the triumvirate of Fred Roti, Pat Marcy, and John D'Arco had held court for years.

The food was not the main attraction at Counsellors Row; the draw was the location, across the street from city hall. The booth at the front of the restaurant was permanently reserved for the bosses of Chicago's downtown First Ward; it was garlanded with signed photos of politicians and featured its own private phone. The First Ward, comprising the Loop and surrounding fertile ground, was the heartland of connections and clout and had been in the Outfit's pocket since the 1920s.

Roti, the son of a Capone-era syndicate boss, was the alderman of the First Ward from 1968 to 1990. D'Arco had been the alderman until 1962, when the Outfit decided he was not up to the job and shunted him into the figurehead post of Democratic ward committeeman, trying out a series of replacements until settling on Roti in 1968. The real power was always Marcy, whose birth certificate read Pasquale Marchone and who had done time for robbery in the 1930s. Marcy held the somewhat vaguely defined post of secretary of the First Ward Democratic Committee and was the Outfit's political boss, ruling on matters at the hazy intersection of crime and politics.

One or more of the trio could usually be spotted in Booth One, dealing with the steady stream of cronies, subordinates, and supplicants who slid in and out in the course of the day, dispensing favors, calling in markers, and murmuring orders into the phone. The FBI got a judge to approve a tap on the Booth One phone and the video camera, but the real damage to First Ward clout was done by Robert Cooley, an attorney who had won a big chunk of Outfit defense business before gambling debts and a change of heart led him to offer to put on a wire for the feds. The resulting operation, GAMBAT (for "gambling attorney"), survived the discovery of the spy camera after Marcy had the restaurant swept and declared it clean. The phone tap remained and ultimately, along with Cooley's testimony, led to a cascade of indictments that put Roti and Marcy on trial along with numerous associates and forever busted up the Booth One crowd. Three years after the camera caught the busboy's eye, Counsellors Row was gone, another Chicago institution falling prey to changing times.

⌇

One day I'm sitting, Bill comes out hysterical. He cannot leave the office because the superintendent's coming, so he sends me. He says, "Get over by my brother-in-law." This brother-in-law, his name is Vito Gobbo. He was married to Bill's sister. He says, "Get over there. They just shot at him."

So he threw me his keys, I shoot over there. From our office I get to Sheffield and Armitage, that's where Vito's realty office was, in five minutes. I go in there, Vito is bleeding. I says, "Vito, what happened?"

"My brother did this to me."

"Your brother?"

He starts crying. He says, "He thinks I stole the money from our mother who died. I was in charge of the money, and I didn't divide it properly." And there it is, holes in the wall, like *boom, boom, boom.* He came in the office, he hit him with the gun, then he shot over his head. You could see all the pictures with the holes.

Bill don't want to make a report—it's all a family thing. So I says, "What does he look like?"

"He's a big guy."

With that, here's the guy at the door. Now, it's winter, he's got the topcoat on, and in his fedora, he's bigger. Fills the whole doorway.

Vito goes, "There he is!" and he runs. He leaves me.

I says, "Holy fuck." In the process of running here, I forgot my gun. So I'm there, and the guy's looking at me, I'm looking at him.

And he goes, "I know who you are."

Here's me: *I'm gone*. I was scared. But I says, "Oh, yeah?"

He says, "Take me."

"Take you? Where's the gun?"

"I left it at home." Now he's crying.

All of a sudden, from the back, Vito grabs me around the neck. "Don't hit my brother!" And he's crying, and choking me. His brother's sitting down crying.

Now Bill comes in. Well, you never seen a guy get so hot. "I should have killed you twenty years ago." *Badda-bing*, he hits the brother. The couch goes over. He's beating this guy something terrible. Blood all over the place. Vito says, "Stop him!"

"Fuck you, you stop him."

OK, now the fight is over. Bill says, "I ever catch you by here, I'll kill you." The brother's gone.

I says, "You don't have to be so rough on him."

Bill says, "And fuck you, too."

ᔐ

I wanted to go to the Overweight Unit, because the Overweight Unit was money. You go out in uniform, mostly day shifts, looking for trucks that are above their weight limit. Now here's where the money comes. You catch someone with overweight violations, and there are two different charges you can write them up for. You write a city charge, it's a very minimal fine. If you write the state charge, it's huge. A hundred-dollar fine for a city charge. State, two thousand. For the same violation. See the leeway you had as a policeman? I wanted to go there, but Bill says, "No, you'll get everybody in jail."

Now, Bill's out of town. Two weeks. All I wanted was a couple of weeks. So I go to the secretary, I says, "Put me on the Overweight Unit."

"Well, I don't have an order from the chief."

"Hey, I talk to the fuckin' chief five times a day." So he says OK, and he moved me on there.

Well, let me tell you something. Everybody I stopped, state charge. I was stopping trucks of all kinds, all fuckin' day.

"I'm overweight? How do you know?"

"You want me to give you another one?"

A couple of days later I get called in by the terminal manager for all these big companies: Consolidated Freightways, Yellow Freight. "What the fuck? Can't you write the city charge?" I tap on the table. Then they says, "Here." So I rescinded the state charge at the court date.

The money I had in just a couple of weeks . . . When Bill saw me: "You're off." And he hollered at me. So what? I made money.

I went all over with him. Every so often, maybe once a month, all the exempt ranks have to take a turn being acting superintendent for the night, on the midnight shift. So if there's a serious call on the midnight shift, you get it. Whatever it was, we had to go. So he puts on his uniform, with the braids and everything, and I put on my uniform and I drive him around. I hated that job, because I had to work midnights, I'm in uniform, and I'm driving him around, the whole night. And I got the radio.

One time we go into this place on Rush Street, Rush and Delaware. They had a card room. Big card games. Who's playing gin, who's playing call rummy, who's playing *klabiash*. No money on the table, just keeping score. I got the radio, I'm in my regular uniform, and he's going around saying hello to everybody. I knew everybody in there. I knew more guys than he did. But I'm saying hello behind his back. I don't want him to know I know all these guys.

Another brother-in-law of his is in there. His wife's brother—

Googie, they called him. Googie Morici. "How you doin'?" So Bill comes to a table, four guys are playing cards. He says hello to the three guys; he don't know who the fourth guy is. I know him. His name was Louie. He was a good burglar, a good-hearted guy, who worked with my stepbrother, Frankie Furio. Louie was a gregarious kind of a guy. He liked me.

So Hanhardt goes, "What's your name?"

Here's Louie: "Who wants to know?"

Well, that was the biggest mistake he could make.

"Who wants to know?" Bill punches him. He's like Magua in *The Last of the Mohicans*. The guy goes off of the chair, his legs are in the air. Gone. And everybody was standing at attention.

Here's me: "What the fuck?"

And everyone's looking at me. "Can't you stop this guy?"

Bill says, "Get the fuckin' wagon."

"Yeah." I go out of the room, I make like I'm calling them, but I didn't. I want him to calm down.

"Did you get the wagon?"

"Yeah. Don't worry about it."

And these guys are all just sitting there. No one wanted to mess with him. So he calmed down, Louie's bleeding, Bill says to his brother-in-law, "Who's this jag-off, Googie?"

"I really don't know."

I says, "Bill. Come here. I know that guy."

"What! Why didn't you tell me?"

"I didn't want to get hit."

"Cancel that wagon."

"OK." I never even called for it.

So now Louie comes to, he gets up. Bill says, "My name is Hanhardt. And don't forget it. I ask you a fuckin' question, you answer the question."

"Yes, sir." Now it's "Yes, sir."

My son Joey is playing Little League. They made me assistant coach. I don't know how to coach a baseball team. The coach, he's like a Green Beret: "You will do this. You committed to this, and if you go on vacation we want to know," and this and that. The kids are shaking. "And Coach Pascente has something to say."

I had nothing to say. But he's the boss. So I walk by, with my arms folded. I said, "I got one rule." And they're looking at me. I says, "There's no fartin' in the dugout." They started laughing, and the coach goes, "What the hell kind of . . ."

I said, "Hey, what are you, crazy? These are little kids."

Spilotro came to town and wanted to see me. He and Matt Raimondi come to the park. Man, am I glad to see him. So he's watching. My son, he's the star. I mean, he's good. He's pitching. He's firing the ball, strikeout, strikeout. But now we have to take him out. He could only pitch three innings. All of a sudden he's out of the game.

Tony goes, "Hey, why are you taking him out? He's the best player on the team."

I says, "Tony. In Little League the rules are, you can only pitch three innings, and then another guy's gotta pitch."

He says, "Freddy, are you nuts? He's the best guy. Here's what we do." My wife's listening to him. He says, "Take the other kid's jersey, put it on him and let him pitch the other three."

"Are you crazy?"

My wife says, "I knew this guy was gonna get you in trouble."

That's Tony.

24

THE BANK DICK

August 23, 1979, dawned warm and humid as August days in Chicago often do. A reader of the Chicago Tribune *bringing the paper in off the porch would have checked the weather report on the front page and seen that thunderstorms were forecast for the afternoon. The headline shouted that Mayor Jane Byrne was calling on the school board to resign en masse, showing the confrontational style that was coming to characterize her months-old administration. Other front-page news concerned the sickly national economy, with layoffs spiking to levels last seen in the 1973–74 recession. And a Chicago icon had disappeared: author James T. Farrell, creator of Studs Lonigan, had died at age seventy-five.*

A reader interested in world affairs would have noted fighting in Iran, with Ayatollah Khomeini's new Islamic regime cracking down on the Kurds; Anastasio Somoza, the recently exiled dictator of Nicaragua, complaining that the United States had abandoned him; and the start of talks in a now-vanished country called Rhodesia involving a man named Ian Smith. The reader would have had to turn all the way to page 12 of section 3 to note the following small item crowded by ads into the upper left corner of the page:

POLICE, FBI PROBE THEFT OF $85,000 AT MADISON BANK

Chicago police and Federal Bureau of Investigation agents are investigating a loss of $85,000 discovered Wednesday at the Madison Bank and Trust Co., 400 W. Madison St.

A. Andrew Boemi, president and chairman of the board, reported the money missing shortly after 8 a.m. when bank employees opened the auxiliary cash safe, where the money had been stored.

Yolanda Deen, a vice president at the bank, said the money was in several metal containers and had been locked in the second-floor safe at 6 p.m. Tuesday. She said police found no evidence of breaking into the safe or the main banking area.

Police said the bank's alarm sounded in the central alarm office at 6 a.m., but no evidence of a theft was found.

Proceeding to the sports section, the reader would have seen that the Cubs had lost to the Dodgers the previous day despite the efforts of their slugging left fielder Dave Kingman and their untouchable relief pitcher Bruce Sutter.

Two months later it was football season and the cool weather had arrived when the following item appeared in the Tribune *on October 23:*

LOOP BANK OFFERS $5,000 THEFT REWARD

A Loop bank has offered a $5,000 reward for information leading to the conviction of the persons responsible for an unsolved $87,000 theft.

Anyone with information about the missing money, taken from a second-floor vault of the Madison Bank & Trust Co., 400 W. Madison St., last Aug. 22, is urged to call Chicago police or the Federal Bureau of Investigation.

Apparently the FBI's investigation had succeeded only in adding two thousand dollars to their assessment of the thieves' haul. And that was that; no further mention of the heist was seen in the pages of the Tribune. *The Madison Bank booked the loss, collected the insurance, and continued in operation until 1995, when it was closed.*

The crime was never solved.

⌒

The bank job was an easy job but a big, big score. It was the Madison Bank at the time, at Madison and Canal Street. I know exactly the year because I kept a log, because of the statute of limitations. That was '79. I was in Hit and Run. Out of the blue, this guy, Hardy, a policeman, says, "Listen, I just got a position at the Madison Bank. You want to be security? They pay good, and you work in uniform. It's a clean job, there's no trouble."

So I says, "Let me try it." My ulterior motive was to nail the bank. But he don't know that.

So with my charm, and I'm not bragging, I maneuvered. With the jokes, with this guy, and everybody. They ask me what shift I want to work, and I say I want to stay with the girl who does the deposits and things.

This girl, she loved me. Now I see her, she says, "Come on with me." I go with her, we go to the deposit, the deposits from the night. That was our first assignment. When the bank is closed, restaurants would put their deposits in this outside deposit box. I don't know how she can't memorize it—she does it every day. She takes the paper, and I see, here's the drawer. I says, "That's the fuckin' combination. She just takes it out of here, and she puts it back. Holy God. Look at this."

So now I got the combination for the downstairs, the night deposit. I had the keys for certain rooms, where they kept money orders, cashier's checks. Every teller has so many at their station. "Fred, will you get some . . ."

"Yeah, sure." I go get the checks, I bring them to whoever requested them.

I got the key made. I had Junior come to the bank. He brought clay, kids' modeling clay. And we made the imprint, and boom, they come out beautiful. They worked. I tested and I know there's no alarm on the perimeter. For some reason, they don't have a burglar alarm on the bank, the outside, in the doors. The vaults, yes. You can't get in there without the alarm going off.

I says, "Man, this is gonna be a kick in the ass." So I put Junior outside, at like one, two in the morning. I went in with the key, opened right up, I opened the night deposit safe, I took the money. They're all in bank bags, with their deposit slips and the cash. Five minutes, *boom*, I took it. It was only a couple of thousand dollars, but the blame went to the depositor. Because all the papers were in there.

Nobody came. There wasn't even mention of it. Never. So I says, "All right. We can get in the bank. This works."

Here's the next step, the big score. The main vault is on a timer. That was a huge monstrosity. I never even gave it any thought about that. But there was another safe that was used for when tellers' stations stayed open after the main vault was closed. I got that combination, because of the girl again. She's got it written down. But I watched it, and she used the numbers, but then there was a little catch. She pushed the dial in and turned it to the last number. And I watched it many times, and I got it down.

So the day we were gonna do it, we figured out we had to do it early on a working morning. I took two guys with me—we called them the Polish gang. One of them grew up in our neighborhood.

Here was the plan. We'd all be in suits and ties—again with the disguise. I went, too. I couldn't leave it up to them. And I'm disguised. You could not tell who it was. We could walk in the bank, and who's gonna recognize you? There's no alarm going off. And we walk up to the second floor, where the safe is. We got in, there was no trouble.

Now, when you open that door, that's when the alarm's gonna go off. We didn't need anybody on the calls, because we got the calls on us, the radio. We have three of these carry-on bags, luggage. Very, very sturdy, strong pieces. We had to work fast, because you probably got about five minutes before the alarm goes through and they arrive.

So, *boom*. It opens up, just like I figured. And there are the tellers' drawers. When they bring up the money, the whole till, their drawer, goes in the safe. I take a drawer out, I put it in my one guy's bag, I put a second one in there. He's walking, he's out. The other guy and I took one. There's five tellers' spots. So we get them out, and we're walking. We're going to the van. If the police are coming, they're not gonna stop you. You're not conspicuous. We blended in. There was a lot of people. Because the train was there, and a lot of traffic from the train. We're walking right with them. And we get there, we're in the car. We got on the expressway, 90. And we hear the call. "Bank alarm at the Madison Bank." Here's the guy, he's calling the other cop: "Yeah, one-oh-three. That fuckin' thing went off many times."

So now the aftermath. They asked everybody to take a lie box. All the employees. But I wasn't working that day. So they didn't get to me until long after. They went through all the people that worked, now they come to me. This was months after I had left there. I never thought I'd be called in, but I got called in because of my name, my associations.

I says, "Absolutely."

So I go. I passed the test. A drug guy gave me the tip. He says, "You take some Librium," which was a relaxant. "And I want you to put a thumbtack in your shoe. And press on it, you understand? And that's all you'll be thinking about, is the fuckin' pain in the foot." And I was bleeding in the foot, but I passed the test.

Next I hear from an FBI guy by the name of Ryan. He was their guy in charge of the banks. The reason they come by me was because of the background. My brother Billy, the guys I knew. So I talked to him. And he couldn't get anywhere with me.

That was all over the news. They wanted to nail me on that, and they didn't have nothing. I waited five years for the statute of limitations to run out. So I know in 1984, I'm home free.

25

DETECTIVE PASCENTE

I became a detective in 1979. The test is very hard, harder than the sergeant's test. There was sixty-some hundred that took the detective's test. And they're only going to put on the list two hundred. Everybody had their own clout guys, and some made detective based on big arrests. Me, I had help, because Bill gave me the answers. I would read them, go through it three or four times, and I'm ready for the test. I passed high. I made it in the first week.

You went to detective school after you made it, and they gave you the fundamentals. That's less than a week. You're in suit and tie. And it's the best job on the department. You got freedom, you have a car. That's big, a car. And you're with the chief. You got so much freedom. I took my car anywhere I wanted.

After I got out of Hit and Run, Bill Hanhardt put me in Area Six, which is Belmont and Western. My first commander was a guy named Ed Wodnicki. He was tough. Big, tall ex-marine, tough as they come. He was a rough-and-tumble guy. He would take no bullshit, and he was a straight shooter.

Bill Hanhardt said, "Freddy, I know you're from the Badlands. And I don't want you working on your friends. You don't have to go after guys you know. Anybody has a problem, bring them in. I'll talk to them. Guys in trouble, there's nothing we can't beat. But if it's a drug deal, I don't want to hear about it. Don't even bring them in." He never would do a deal involving drugs.

And that's the rules we kept. We helped a lot of guys. I started off like that with him, and I was with him ever since. The line was this, simple and sweet: if Hanhardt knew the guy as a friend, like in my case of my brother Billy, he'd help him. Billy was a rootin'-tootin' burglar. If Hanhardt grabbed Billy he'd get him the fuck out of there. He would protect his own, who he knew. He knew a guy we called Larry the Bum. One day he brought me into the office. Larry the Bum's sitting there; I see him, I don't acknowledge him. And Hanhardt says, "This is a friend of mine." So we had to watch out for Larry.

It wasn't an everyday affair. It was people you know. He wasn't gonna take it from Lou McFarkle, go out on a limb for some guy off the street. You do stuff like that, you're gonna get in trouble, you're gonna go to jail. You better be correct in who you bring in.

Another thing is, if he trusts the deal, the money will let you go. He never had to see the guy first—I would be the front guy. It still had to be screened, OK'd. You just couldn't do it with anybody. He had certain guys. Guys would come to me: "Hey, Freddy, you think he . . ."

"What is it?" I'd weigh it myself. If there was a score for me, I'd jump on it. I wasn't going to do it just because a guy asked me. "Let me go talk to him."

It was the unwritten law. We knew what we were doing. As policemen—this was many years ago—it was widespread that policemen would take money. It was a low-paying job, a thankless job. And we did our job, but it was no money, so policemen used to take money. It was wrong, I know that, but it was common practice.

⌇

In, like, '80, I'm Area Six, I'm on burglary. A gang is working at night, hitting all-night convenience stores, like 7-Elevens. Anything that was open, they would heist them. This was a terror gang. Two people were killed by these guys.

This is for the robbery section, property crimes. But they recruited everybody. Both sides—burglary, robbery—we all went together and were assigned to this. So an informant let one of the robbery detectives know, he knows where they're holed up. That's big information.

Now we go, eleven strong. Because these were dangerous guys. So we get into the house—they're not there. But we know this is their safe house. This is where they come with their money, their guns, everything. It's an apartment in the Logan Square area. So we're searching and searching, the lieutenant's there, the sergeant, and we're all in there, looking for something.

We find some illegals that are staying there. These people are scared. The lieutenant's saying, "You'll lose your kid, you'll lose your aid, you'll go back. Where are they?" They wouldn't say nothing. So we're on our last leg of the search, I come up with an idea. I didn't tell the sergeant, didn't tell the lieutenant, didn't tell nobody. I took my gun, emptied it, and I made out like I found the gun. And I started screaming, "I got it! We got 'em!" And I show the gun. I said, "We got it!"

Sergeant said, "Beautiful."

Lieutenant says to the illegals, "You're going down, we're taking your kids. You want to lose your kids? Fine. We got the gun."

Well, what do you think they did? They told us where the gang members were. I says, "How do you like this?" So I waited, I got everything down, inventory this and that, the gun. I grabbed the lieutenant, I says, "You got the information, right?"

"We got it all. You found that gun, that was it, because now they're part of the crime."

I said, "Lieutenant, that's not the gun. That's my gun."

"What the fuck?" Then when he calmed down, he says, "Well, that was good. We got what we wanted."

They got them at the address where they told us. We got them, dead-bang. They were charged, and they all got life. The whole crew. The illegals were deported, with their kids.

〜

My kind of guys, they are standoffish with everyone—Jews, blacks, they don't like them. Not me, I'm the opposite. When I was little, my dad took me to Wrigley Field to see Jackie Robinson. He was the big deal in those days. And I saw these black guys, I mean, dressed to the hilt. They had straw hats and suits. They were there to cheer on the hero, like we would do with Marciano. And these white guys were yelling, "Nigger, nigger, nigger . . ." Animals. Why would you bum rap them guys? My father whispered, "Who's the bad guys?" That stood out with me. Never forgot it. "Who's the animals?"

DETECTIVE PASCENTE

In about 1980, we had to go to the Ida B. Wells housing project to pick up a kid. The kid was wanted for a shooting. Not a murder—no one died. The kid was twelve years old. So we go there, the kid's not there. And what caught my eye was the old woman. Her name was Mrs. Chester. She's got like seven kids, running all over the place. Little kids. In diapers, and they're a mess. And she's the only one, with all these little kids. And I had to ask her. I says, "Lady, what are you doing with all these kids?"

She says, "Well, one of my daughters is dead, I got her kids. Another one's in jail, I don't know where the other one is." You don't know how my heart went out to this woman. I felt bad. She was such a nice lady.

It's Christmas, I say, "What the hell?" I told my partner, "Get the policewomen here, from Juvenile. Now. Take care of these kids. Get them square. Lady, you're coming with me."

I took her in the car, I drove her by my friend Freddy Minelli. He had a grocery store in Niles, huge. I says, "Freddy, whatever it costs, fill up the van for this lady. She got nothing."

He didn't even question it. He says, "Yeah, don't worry about it." So he filled it up, and I wanted to give him the money. He says, "This is on me. Christmas."

I says, "Fred, I didn't come here for that." But he insisted. He saw that I was doing a good thing, so you do it.

I gave her fifty dollars. I says, "Lady, go get yourself some whisky, go get whatever you want. This is for you. This is for you personal."

She couldn't believe it. I says, "Just take it. It's Christmas." And that was it. And we go. I forgot about the kid. I left it up to the policewoman. I was out of the picture because he was a juvenile.

That was not the only time. Minelli sent her other stuff. And then one year I took the niece and her, and her son, I got them situated, at one of the hotels downtown where my friend was security.

And they had Mother's Day. I brought them in there, they sat them down, and I was on my way. I said, "This is Mother's Day for you."

～

The best case was the gay guy. I was on that case for two years. This was a shrewd guy. The name was Saban Dreas. He was half Yugoslavian, half Italian. He was a small, good-looking guy. And he knew where the gay community hung out, and he would prey on them. He'd get them to invite him to their apartments, and once up there, they'd have a drink, and he'd drug them. He had the stuff with him. Whatever it was, phenobarbital, a mixture of stuff. Once they were out, he took their cash, jewelry. No big stuff, but he had some artwork, rolled it up and took it. The total was over a million dollars in all his scores.

We got him for attempted murder, because one of the guys almost died, an old man. There were seventy reports that were made, but when I went to the *Gay Life* magazine—they wrote me up, I was a hero over there—they said, "You know how many don't make reports? They feel they're not given a fair shot."

It was good. I got him off of the street, and he got over twenty years.

Here's how I got him. I asked one of the guys, "Tell me, how did he get the stuff in you, in your system? How'd he do it?"

He says, "Well, it had to be when he was flirting with me."

"What do you mean, flirting?"

"He started to kiss me, and he must have had it in his mouth and put it in."

You gotta know, where I come from, we look down on that. But you gotta have a little compassion—you're a policeman, trying to solve a crime. Anyway, this guy gave the description. He was so accurate. I had the sketch artist draw it up. He was excellent, this artist. He went and saw the guy, and they come up with this. The guy says, "That's him."

Now, this was the best lead we had, a description. So I get the telex, with the description, and I put it out to all the major cities. Chicago, of course, all the suburbs. I send it to New York, all the East Coast cities, West Coast. I send it to Montreal, Toronto, all that. And don't I get a hit, of all cities, in San Francisco. He was arrested and charged in San Francisco with the same thing that I was looking for. So Bill said, "Go ahead."

The San Francisco PD, they were wonderful. I fly out there, they picked me up. "This guy did the same thing that you're looking for. Drugged the guys . . ."

I says, "Give me some time?"

"All the time you want."

"How about three minutes?" And he told me the stuff. He said yeah, he did all the Chicago things.

So they says, "We got him first." They're gonna try him in San Francisco, and then I'll come back and pick him up.

Guess what? When I went back to get him, I took my wife. We went to San Francisco, all on the city. We pick up Saban, he says, "I'd like to get something to eat."

I says, "You got it, buddy. What do you got a taste for? You like Italian food?"

"I love Italian food."

I took him to a place called Scoma's, on the wharf. How's that for a policeman? I says, "Saban, don't make a move, or I'll kill you."

He told my wife, "Listen, I'm going away. I got over twenty-five thousand, cash. Why don't you have it, because you guys took me to dinner."

Here's May: "Can't you let him go? He's so nice."

He wanted to give me his money. "I got money stashed. I want you to have it." He's got a safety deposit box. He had gold, gold coins, cash, he had everything.

Bill says, "Don't even go near this." But now we're talking half a million dollars. So there's no way I'm gonna listen to Bill. How the fuck do I get it? So I went to the Gypsies, because they were schemers. I said, "This guy's got a safety deposit box. I got the keys. Do you know a way to do it?"

"We'll figure it out."

We never did get it. I tried my best. But we got him. And he got over twenty years.

26

FOUND MONEY

I stayed in touch with Davey Ballog. And he started telling me about his scams with the insurance, the accidents. He had brothers, he had a moving crew. These guys were Gypsies, but they were not fortune-telling guys. They would do slip-and-falls, make claims against insurance companies. He had a guy, his name was Tony Ziga. This guy had a broken back. He never got it fixed. He endured the pain for years. He used that break to make many accident claims. The settlements were unbelievable.

I went everywhere with Ballog. He took me and my whole family to Disney World, for nothing. He had connections. He used to get the airline tickets for nothing. He scammed the airlines. We'd go under different names. We were the Horvath family once. We'd get hotels on the grounds of Disney World, for nothing. He'd hand me four or five thousand dollars' worth of Disney money. You can spend it like cash all over the place down there. He had a connection in the Disney office. I went there many times.

He took me on cruises, too. I was on a cruise with him, and he wound up getting into an accident—he made over forty thousand dollars. It's in the evening, and we're on the deck, outside. It's a beautiful night. It's dark, and we're looking at the moon and the stars, and it's just gorgeous. He's sitting there and a bolt comes, *boom!* Hits the deck. Later, they found out it came from one of the lifeboats: it's hooked up together, and this bolt must have come loose, and *badda-boom*. He picks the bolt up. And his wife gets the razor, and they cut his head. Not deep, but he cut it so it looked like it was slashed. And the blood is coming out.

The wife and him knew what to do. They scream. *"Ahhh . . ."* And they're screaming, and I'm: "What the fuck?" And they get him, they put him on a stretcher, they take him off by Coast Guard cutter and they bring him to the local hospital. He collected a settlement, over forty thousand dollars, in two months. He was geared for that stuff. I mean, this guy was smart. Me, I'm going, "What the fuck are you doing?" He gave me money out of that.

෴

One time I'm on duty, I'm with a partner for the night, a rental. His name was Jerry Wojnar. This is not my regular partner, who had the night off. I see a guy, he's driving erratic on Lawrence and Clark, where the Rainbo Arena was. In fact he came out of the Rainbo. And he's going north on Clark, and he's going back and forth. It was a slow night, so I put a stop on the guy.

So I get out of the car, go over there. He comes running out of the car, right at me. "There's a lot of money in that car!"

Here's me: "No shit?"

He did have a lot of money in there. He had it in a cigar box—there was thirty-one thousand dollars. I said, "Yeah, this is a lot. What are you doing with this kind of money?"

"I got a real estate deal coming on Saturday, and I'm gonna . . ."

"What kind of an answer is that? A real estate deal, you're gonna go buy a house with cash money? This is bullshit. I'm gonna run you."

Jerry wants to pinch the guy.

I says, "Pinch him for what? He's got money. What kind of a charge? Because he's got money? You don't know."

So we go to his house. It's on Sacramento just south of Chicago Avenue, and on the property, you gotta see what he's got there. He's got livestock. This is in the city. There's a pond, you go up on the hill, and over here he's got this secluded place, and he's got two cows, he's got goats, he's got a mule. I go, "What the fuck is all this?"

So now Wojnar is nervous. He knows I'm up to no good. He says, "Listen. I want to arrest this guy, I don't want no nothing."

I says, "You don't want to take the guy's money?"

He says, "No."

"Come on, hey."

He don't want to do it. And when you got a guy like that, it's no. So we bring him in to Area Six. Inventoried the money, and we turned it back to him. They charged him with reckless driving, danger to the community. Because he was weaving.

I call my guy in narcotics. I says, "You know this guy?"

He says, "Oh, Fred. This guy's on our list. He's a guy to watch."

I says, "OK. That's all I gotta know." I call Junior. "June, meet me by Boston's." Which is at Chicago and Grand. It's a roast beef stand.

I left Wojnar. Now, remember, they pinched the guy, they charged him, he's waiting to make a bond. But they wanted to hold him and run him a little bit. Like I did. So we know he's dead for the night. And there's nobody in his house. What, the cow's gonna be in there?

I get Junior, Junior gets Frankie Furio. They go into the garage, and I'm outside listening on the two-way. They pop the trunk: a hundred thousand even, to the dollar, in the trunk of the car. So

Junior says, "Man, the garage was good to us." I know we're in good shape when he says "Good to us." Now there's a safe. Junior knows how to open the safe. *Badda-bing*, we get into the safe: cocaine and cash. Out of the safe we get another sixty. But the cocaine, we kicked it around. "Dump it in the fuckin' toilet." So that's what we did with the cocaine.

We made a big score, just by luck. And I'm sure they were looking at me after that was done. But I never heard a word on it. Never heard a word.

I never, ever didn't have a hot car. The guys would get me a car. They'd take them right from the car lot. Brand new. Warren Buick, Fanning Cadillac, whatever. They took them right off the lot. They'd get the car, they had the keys made up. At the time you could do it. You'd get the plate, and you'd get it registered through clout at the Secretary of State. And we'd alter the VIN number. Now it's not hot. The plates are registered to this other address. So if I got a ticket it goes there. It always checked to a woman. And it worked. I'd trade them off. I'd give it to the guys: "Here, get rid of it. Give me another one."

"What do you want?"

"Give me a Lincoln." All for nothing. Only thing I paid for was the plates. My wife could not drive it. No copper could drive it. No one could drive it but me. I was too comfortable in what I was doing.

The only time I got caught was when they towed the car. A new Lincoln. I go to Rush Street, I got my sister and her husband, and I parked on Rush Street. Bad spot. The car is towed. Here's me: "Screw it." Then I go, "My wallet's in there, my star is in there, all my identification." I still could have overcome that: "They stole my wallet." But I had four rolls of film from parties, with me, my wife, the kids. I had to get it.

They towed it; it was about midnight. I got May home, the guys picked me up, and we shot over there. This was the auto pound a little bit off of Chicago Avenue on Sacramento. I went with the guys, but they couldn't go in there. I gotta go. So I went in like MacGyver. Went over the fence. There was a dog. But I get along with dogs. I brought him some meat. And I found the car. I got my stuff.

I got grabbed. The guy says, "What are you doing?"

I showed him the star. "I'm looking for some tires."

"You don't come here for tires. You know where you get them."

I says, "Well, thanks. I wanted to spot them, and then I would have bought them." That was it. They didn't know from nothing.

〜

Tony is in town, and he and Louie Tenuta come by my mother's restaurant with a van. They pull up, they're emptying out the van, they're bringing in cheeses and salamis. So I'm sitting there with my suit, it's Sunday, I'm working, I'm a detective, I'm alone. And my mother's getting ready for lunch. And I see Tony's coming in with cheeses and hams, Krakus hams. Holy shit, what's going on?

My mother says, "He's so nice, Fred. I love Tony. He went and bought these at a closeout."

I says, "Yeah, I know his fuckin' closeout." So they're putting it in the big walk-in box, I says, "What's going on?"

He says, "This Polish deli on Milwaukee Avenue, they're supposed to have money in there, and we couldn't find the money. So I'm not gonna leave empty-handed, so we're bringing this stuff by your mother."

"How much money?"

"Well, there's supposed to be over twelve thousand."

So here's me: "You stay here. Sit down. Ma, they're gonna have breakfast."

"Whatever they want." She's happy she got all this stuff.

I says, "I'll be right back." So I'm working, I go to the address, he tells me how he got in, so I walk in. I get on the radio. "Twenty-eighteen," whatever the number was at the time, "I'm at a location, there's a break-in. But don't send anybody, I got everything covered. OK? I'll call you with the information. They're all gone."

Now I start looking. I call back. I said, "Give me the phone number, the emergency number." For every store, there's always a number, in case of fire, flood, or this. There's a contact number.

I call. And the guy answers. I says, "Mr. Popolski?"

"Yes?"

"This is Detective Pascente, Chicago police. I'm at your deli on Milwaukee Avenue. Somebody broke in."

"Oh, son of a bitches . . ." He's got this strong Polish accent. He says, "Did they get the money?"

"Where's it at?"

"It's in the pickle barrel. You go into the refrigerator, it's in the pickle barrel, it's on a hanger." I found it in there—it was in the bank bag, wrapped in plastic, on a hanger.

I go, "It's gone."

"Son of a bitch!"

So now I get the uniform car. I says, "Make the report, send a copy to Area Six, my name. Get the fingerprints and that's it."

I go back to my mom's store. I throw the plastic away, and I bring out the bank bag. And I throw it at Tony.

"How the fuck did you get this?"

I says, "He told me."

We cut it up three ways.

27

THE CHIEF

The battle between reformers and the champions of the status quo within the Chicago Police Department had seen Bill Hanhardt promoted and then demoted by successive acting superintendents within months of Mayor Jane Byrne's election. The conflict was finally decided by Byrne's permanent choice for superintendent, Richard Brzeczek, when he named Hanhardt chief of detectives in April 1980.

A CPD insider who watched the whole thing play out says, "The story was that Jane Byrne was afraid of the Outfit. So Brzeczek convinced her that the only guy that could protect her was Bill Hanhardt, and that's why he was resurrected. Bill was a tough guy, so he'd be able to control them. And it seems that they may have controlled him instead."

᠊ᢒ᠊

Jane Byrne was wonderful. She loved us, me and Bill. I had more fun with her. You could joke with her, she'd laugh out loud. I loved her. She was a drinker, big-time.

When the firemen were on strike in 1980, one day Bill says, "We gotta be in city hall, we gotta guard the mayor. Get ready."

"All right." So we're in plainclothes. We're at the mayor's office. And right outside of her door was a guy named Ronnie Nadile. Ronnie Nadile was four hundred pounds, a big monster. He had tailor-made uniforms. But he had a nice job. He was assigned to the mayor's office. The mayor's inside, me and Bill are right outside the door. Nadile's propped up with a chair and he's reading the paper. And the firemen are over there. And there's a line of police, so no one could get near the mayor.

The mayor comes running out. There's reporters there, she comes running out screaming like you never heard. And she's shit-faced. She points. "I want him arrested!"

Poor Ronnie Nadile thought she was talking about him. He fell. Now he couldn't get up, because he's four hundred pounds. He's like a turtle. Me and Bill are laughing. Bill called four or five guys: "Help this motherfucker up."

So Bill grabs Byrne by the arm, like, "Come here!" He didn't want her to get noticed by the reporters. So we walk in her office. "What is it?"

"I want him arrested."

Who is it? Her husband. Jay McMullen, he's stone drunk, slumped on the desk. He was like this: "Rockin', fuck-a fuck-a . . ." Just blind. Right in the mayor's office. He's on her big desk: "Rock, fuck-a motherfucker . . ." He's falling off.

So Bill says, "Get him home."

I say, "Come on, Jay."

So we get him in the car, I got the address—they live on

Chestnut, high-rise. So we got him, and he's singing, a drunk Irishman. *"Rah, da rorda rorda hoora . . ."*

I says, "Jay, we're gonna get you home."

"You fellas married?"

I says, "Yeah."

He says, "Kill the motherfuckers. None of them are . . ."

We're laughing. I mean, he was such a comic as a drunk. He's falling over. So we get him up, he pulls out money. I'm telling you, hundreds. He says, "Take this fuckin' money. I got plenty of money."

I says, "Jay, no." We didn't take any money. We put him in his house and we left him.

So we get back, she's a little better. "What did you do with that fuckin' drunk?"

I says, "Mayor, we got him safe. He wanted to give us money."

"You should have took it."

〜

We were working with other towns on a guy we called the North Shore Burglar. They got hit by the same guy, with the same MO and everything, that had hit places on Lake Shore Drive. So my informant calls me, he says, "I know the guy, and he's leaving town. He's leaving for L.A. His name is Ettendorf."

It was an unusual name. And they check the airlines and an Ettendorf is on the flight to L.A. from Midway. So we jump in the squad and shoot, four guys. I'm driving, because I was the best. Height of rush hour, we get from Belmont and Western to Midway in less than twenty minutes. How's that? I'm on the shoulder; if there's someone on the shoulder I go back on the road. These guys, they didn't budge.

We get there, we take the guy off the flight—wrong guy. He's a little guy. Scared, poor guy. We went through his luggage. He says, "My name is Ettendorf, and I work in quality control at Ford Motor Company in Detroit. I never did anything wrong."

In the meantime, Hanhardt's at the office. We call, he says, "You got the wrong flight. He's going to L.A., but he's going from O'Hare."

So we tell Ettendorf, "Listen. We're gonna get you on another flight."

"Oh, thank you."

So we get him in the car, and we're going to O'Hare. Now we're five. He's in the middle in the back. And we're flying. And after five minutes he goes, "I could leave tomorrow."

We got to O'Hare. Now we got it planned. We got another car that's meeting us there. We got the tac team. This is a big, big score. The boss says, "You can't miss him. Tall, blond, handsome guy. Dark tan."

He's in the line. We see him there. From down there we can see him. He's got a briefcase, nothing else. "There's our guy. He's in the line at the check-in counter. We gotta be cool. This is loaded." We got this guy positioned here, this guy positioned here. We're gonna go up to him real slow, take him out, no one gets hurt.

Well, it didn't work out that way. We had this sergeant with us, he gets in like he's in Vietnam. He's on the ground, screams out, I mean loud, he goes, "Drop that luggage!"

Everyone dropped their luggage but the crook. People dropped their luggage, and we looked at him, and here goes the guy. He starts running, he's jumping over stuff. Tony DeLeonardis was fast, he tackled him, he got him down.

I go up to the sergeant, I says, "You jag-off. 'Drop that luggage'?"

But we got him. And we got the stuff.

I called Bill. "Bill, I got a big surprise for you."

"Yeah?"

"That North Shore guy? We got him. And the goods."

He says, "All right. Just bring it in there. You do the inventory, I'll tell the commander." He tells the commander, "They got the boy."

"Yes, I know, chief, good job, my guys got him."

He says, "Yeah, when they get there, your office is gonna be used for the inventory. I want it locked, I want no disturbances, Pascente does the inventory."

"Yes, sir, chief."

I know why he wanted me to do the inventory. I inventoried one pair of earrings. That was it. I put the earrings into Evidence and Recovered Property. The rest I took.

Bill says, "What did you inventory?"

"One pair of earrings."

"That's it?"

"That's it."

"You . . ."

I handed him his end. "Will it be all right with this?" And it was. Money turns people around. Money does magic.

〜

There was this cop named Lewis, a fuck-around guy. And he was a funny-looking guy, a big fat guy. And him and this other cop, an Irishman, always went at it. So we're at a Chinese restaurant. And Lewis has got this .45 on. This was Friday. Every Friday we went to the Chinese joint on Fullerton and Pulaski. Small joint. On Bill—it's his dinner. So we're having our dinner, we're in the bar section, we're drinking. And the Irishman goes, "Look at this fuckin' gun you carry. You can't even use it."

"I'll use it on you, you sawed-off mother . . ." Bantering.

Bill's getting pissed. "Enough of this nonsense," he's telling these two guys.

There's a pheasant on the wall. The Irish guy says, "You couldn't hit that."

So Lewis takes the gun, and a gun going off inside a closed place, you know what that's gonna do. Well, he lets it go. *BOOM!* The smoke, and the noise. All these Chinamen, they're all running around like crazy. Bill takes Lewis, slaps him in the fuckin' head. "You jag-off . . ."

I run outside and I come back. Just joking, I says, "Bill, they got an ambulance coming. A woman was waiting for a bus, I think Lewis hit her." He sobered up like *this*.

⤴

Bill Roemer was a fighter from Notre Dame, and he made his mark as an FBI agent. He was a tough fellow with his hands. He'd take you on, he was that tough. I'm sure there are other FBI guys that are capable, but he was one that would use it. He was tough but he was a glory seeker. He was no bargain.

The book he wrote about Tony was bullshit. "Tony 'the Ant' Spilotro"—bullshit. Roemer says he gave him the nickname "Ant," but there was no such thing. He never had that name. It was like this: if I had him on the phone, I'd say, "Hey, Ant," in other words short for Anthony. My mother would say, "His name is Anthony, it's not Tony." So I'd call him Ant. We laughed about it.

I knew Roemer. I was on a case, a kidnapping case. We did all the work. Bill Hanhardt was in charge of it. A Colombian family lived on Leland and Leavitt. Drug dealers. Middle of the night, six black guys, three in the front, three in the back, come to the house, and they broke right in, kicked the door. Husband was there, they threw the husband down, and they want the money.

He wouldn't give it up. They said, "OK, we're taking the kid." And they took the baby. This kid was three years old.

We got the case. As chief of detectives, Bill Hanhardt sets up a command post at Area Six. Everybody on duty, there's no burglary, no robbery, we're all one, we're all on this.

So it's a big case. The FBI comes in, because kidnapping is federal. Who's on the case? Roemer. He starts giving orders. Hanhardt says, "We'll conduct the investigation. Don't you tell my detectives nothing." Ultimately it's the FBI's case, but we got control of the investigation.

We go to the house. The father, the tough guy, will not cooperate. Bill Hanhardt says, "Listen. We know what you do. We just want your kid back. And the longer it goes, the less chance we have of getting him." And the guy puts up his hump, he's refusing to talk. This is the victim!

The wife hears him. "You son of a . . ." She's screaming at him. Her boy, her little son.

Bill gave him an open hand. From this wall he knocked him into that wall. *Badda-boom*. He grabs him. He says, "You scum motherfuck, worry about your fuckin' drug business . . ." Kicked him. *Boom!*

Here's her: "Yeah, kick him again." So she told us, with her accent, "These guys, all I could tell you, they have a business. And they work on the truck. They sell food."

Catering trucks. At the time there's only a couple in the city. Thunderbird is a big company. So we go see them on the South Side. Bill goes, "Get the list of all the employees." We get the list, and he sees a guy named Hamilton. Black guy. He says, "Bring that guy in." He knew, like that. "That's the guy." He had him pinched before. Bad dude. He tells us, "I want you to bring him in. And when you get five minutes from the office, I want you to tell him that Sergeant Hanhardt is in charge of the investigation." Hamilton don't know him as Chief Hanhardt; he knew him as Sergeant Hanhardt. "You tell him Sergeant Hanhardt is in charge of the investigation. And he was taken off a wedding to come here. Make him really sweat."

OK, so we got him handcuffed. He ain't saying nothing. We got him in the back. He says, "I don't know what you're bringing me in for."

I says, "A serious crime." I didn't say what. We're driving all the way from the South Side, now we get off of the expressway, I says, "Call Sergeant Hanhardt. Tell him we're bringing him in. We're gonna be right there."

"Who that fella you just said? Sergeant Hanhardt?"

"Yeah, Sergeant Hanhardt."

He says, "Let me tell you something. I never did nothing. I never do no fuckin' women, I never hurt no kids."

Hurt no kids? Now that hits me.

So I tell Bill, "This is the motherfucker."

Hamilton must have got a shellackin' from him before. He walks in, he sees Hanhardt, and Bill was an impressive-looking guy. Especially then. Bill takes off his suit jacket, he says, "Here, hold on to that."

Here's Hamilton: "There's no need for that."

We got Hamilton, we're bringing him up, Roemer says, "Work him over."

So I go in and tell Bill. "That mother . . ."

"He says work him over, huh? Who in the fuck is he to tell my detectives to work somebody over?" So Bill gets out there, he says, "I'm gonna tell everybody on this floor, you want to work somebody over, come and work me over." Bill got the message to

Roemer. "If you want to work someone over, do it yourself, don't tell nobody else to do it. Because the first guy who's gonna beef and put somebody in jail for working a guy over is you."

Without getting hit, Hamilton gave up everybody. We got him. We got the kid. Everybody else on the job got thirty years, Hamilton got twelve.

～

Hanhardt's a serious policeman, believe me. So every month he's got a meeting. A pep talk. And he scares the shit out of you. Picture this: he's got the whole Area Six at Belmont and Western, upstairs—he's got a hundred detectives at the meeting. "Listen. I don't want no more pot-and-pan thieves, I don't want no more junkie burglars, I want quality arrests. I want fences, I want . . ." So I'm in the back, I go in the office, and I got the list of their beeper numbers. We didn't have cell phones. We had beepers. I start calling them, while he's talking.

And *beep-beep, beep-beep, beepity-beep* . . . Dozens of them are going off, and he's going nuts. He saw me in the back, he knew right away. It was so funny, because he got red. And the cops are going, "Only you could get away with it." Oh, *madonn'*. What I did to him.

28

FAMILY GUY

When May and I got married, she was a waitress, and I said, "You're never gonna work again." She stayed home, took care of the kids, sent them to school—she did her homemaker's job very well.

Rocky was born on October 24, 1980. And May lost another one between Nicole and Rocky. We'd have had five. Joey, Rocky, and Nicole were all raised in Catholic schools. That was May's choice. Even though she's Jewish, she wasn't real religious. I gave her the choice. "You could do what you want. But if you do it Jewish, you gotta follow through with it. I think you're more likely to follow through in the Catholic thing."

The school they went to was Queen of All Saints. It was on Devon, just east of Cicero. They loved the school, they played ball for the school, they participated in everything. They were pretty good kids. I never had trouble with them. I only had one rule: Bring your friends home. I want to meet them. Because if the kid's a junkie, you're a junkie. If the kid's a sports guy, you're a sports guy. That's my belief.

My shift was days as a detective. We'd work round the clock if we were on something, but I was around all the time for the kids. I helped them with the homework when they were stuck. I had season hockey tickets, and I'd take them to the games. I was a dad.

My paycheck went right in the bank. The cash I was hiding. I'd hide it in the house. I mean I had a pile of money. It built up. I had half a million in cash in the house. I didn't even tell May. I had my clothes in these wardrobe cases, like a leather covering for the suit. Half a dozen suits, I had thirty, forty thousand dollars here; thirty, forty thousand here; thirty, forty thousand in there. "Just don't let nobody in my closet. Understand?" My brother wants to borrow, he can't.

My wife knew, but she didn't know. She knew the general picture. But she wouldn't know an incident. She'd know I was out. Then I come back with money, she's: "What did you do?" The kids didn't know, but she knew.

She would say, "What are you doing with these guys? You're such a smart guy. I hear you talking to guys, lawyers. They come by you. You got the answers. What are they asking you for? You're not educated. But you're a smart guy." She really pumped me up.

She encouraged me to stay away from these guys. She would say, "You know, you got a future, you got your pension coming." She'd always throw that pension in there. And look how it turned out.

There was no problem with money, ever. Money would come in all the time. It came fast, it went fast. I was in Vegas all the time. Days off, you go to Vegas—you only need one day. Every show, every dinner. But you can lose your money.

And besides the scores, I was full-time with the Gypsies. Vacation, you can't believe vacations. Now the kids are getting a little older, we're in Disney World a couple of times a year.

For zero. With the Gypsy plan. The Gypsies had the flights, the hotels. One time we went seventeen people. That's my kids, my sister and her kids, a friend of mine and his kids. The Gypsy set it up. He had somebody inside there. I didn't want to know. I just enjoyed it.

When I bought my first house on Devon Avenue, Ballog furnished the whole house, for zero. Here's how he did it. He goes to Wickes, which was a big furniture joint. He went in there with his wife. We never showed our face, my wife and I, except we went in there and we picked out what we wanted.

Ballog goes with his wife: "I want this living room set, I want this dining room set, I want this kitchen, I want this bedroom." The total was well over six thousand dollars. And he says, "Can I give you seven hundred dollars downstroke, cash?" Pulled out the money, cash. "And when it's delivered, I'll finish the payment. I don't want no credit. I want to pay."

"Yeah, you could pay."

He says, "Could I give you a personal check?"

"Absolutely."

Well, Ballog knew the time the bank closed. He told the furniture people to deliver everything on Friday after he gets home from work. So now you cannot call the bank—it's closed. They bring it late, and we had trucks ready. As they brought it in, we moved it out the back. The whole house was furnished for nothing, seven hundred dollars. Ballog did it for me.

༺༻

We used to tease my mom that my brother Dicky was the favorite. Dicky never, ever got in trouble. And she would brag. I was at my mother's house once, and my sister was there. I always went there, I'd give her money, whatever I could do. So I'm there, and she starts with me about Dicky. "Dicky comes here, he takes the air conditioner out, he puts the air conditioner in. He takes me to the bank, he takes me shopping, he does everything."

I said, "That's it, Ma. I'm through. You love him more than us."

She says, "I love all my kids." My sister's laughing—she knows I'm joking.

I says, "I'm gonna teach you, once and for all, that he's not so lily-white, Ma."

So I give her the phone, and I dial on the extension, and I call Dicky up. Now I disguise my voice, he don't know it's me. "Mr. Pascente?"

"Yes?"

"I have a police report here. Says that you witnessed an accident at O'Hare airport." He worked at O'Hare as a policeman.

"I never witnessed an accident." Very indignant.

"I'm sorry to bother you, Mr. Pascente. It must be for the other Pascente, Fred. I have a check for the witness for eighty-five hundred dollars."

"What was the date of that accident?"

My sister's laughing, my mother goes, "That wasn't fair."

I says, "Well, he's not so lily-white. You always call me and Billy bad guys. Now look at what he's trying to do."

⌒

My brother Billy's friend Johnny Santucci, Schiavone was his real name. Billy knew him all his life. He was an actor. He was in *Crime Story* later, and many other things. It was him that got Billy hooked on drugs. He also beefed on him. Santucci had a couple of FBI agents that he was tight with, and he put Billy down.

Billy's first beef, he got a slap on the hand. That was when he got pinched with Frank Furio. And then the second one was another hijacking. He had about eight guys. And the judge was a bad judge. Man, what a mean cocksucker he was. He put Billy away, gave him eight years. But he did his time. He did a little over three. The third beef was, he had to drive a shipment of some liquid, something to do with drugs. And he got grabbed in Florida. And Santucci's the guy that set him up. Billy got like three or four years. And he did his time, and that was the end. He still continued to do stuff, but nothing of that severe nature.

Santucci was a rat, a stool pigeon. In fact he was an informant for Bill Hanhardt. And Bill told me, "Don't you fuck with Santucci." When he told me that, I knew. Santucci was Hanhardt's guy. He tipped him on a lot of stuff. And I couldn't do nothing.

In 1980, Dicky and my nephew Rocco, Billy's son, they come to me. Billy was on the shit, on drugs. Now, they knew I would blow my stack about that. There's nothing I'm more against than dope. So they didn't tell me before. But now it's gotten too far. It's the end of the world, now they come to me. And I was pissed. I says, "Now you're coming to tell me? Why didn't you tell me before?" They were afraid. Now they're crying to me.

I says, "Where's Billy at?"

"Well, he moved out of the house. He took a few things, he's staying downtown, at this hotel, just east of Michigan."

So I'm working. I got two guys with me, Tony DeLeonardis, who was my partner at the time, and Bill Devoney, who was the boss. He was the lieutenant. I says, "I gotta go get my brother."

"Let's go." We go downtown. We go into the hotel, I know the security guys. They're all detectives. And they see I'm hot.

Billy's not there. Across the street was an all-night restaurant, Cambridge House, where Billy used to eat. I go in the restaurant, and I see him way in the back. And there's this black guy there with him, and Santucci. I told Devoney and DeLeonardis, "Don't you lift your hand on my brother. I'll take care of my brother. I don't even want you to lift your hands on the other two unless they jump in. Then you take care of them."

Billy's eating like a crazed man. He's eating a hundred miles an hour. He's got salad dressing all over him. And he keeps shoveling. Now he sees me, and he's looking at me with these eyes.

I went right for him. I grabbed him by the throat. I picked him up, I threw him against the wall, *boom!* I says, "You dirty . . ." He's shaking. And the black guy and Santucci are standing. Devoney says, "Don't you move." And they didn't move.

I slapped Santucci. I says, "You scumbag mother . . ." He's down.

I dragged Billy by his hair. I don't even know if we paid the check. We got him, I marched him across the street. "Where's the room?" I took them all with me. The security guys were there, I says, "Get the fuck out of my way." They turned their heads. We got into the elevator, took him upstairs, we go in the room. They had like a change of clothes, that's all. I get Billy in the room, and I just slapped him. Johnny Santucci, I broke the phone on his head. "You dirty motherfucker."

I'm looking, and I find the junk. This was crack cocaine, in a hard block. They had a couple of kilos. This is life in prison. I start breaking it and throwing it in the toilet. Santucci screams, and I slapped him again. This was thousands and thousands of dollars. The black guy's watching, I says, "What do you got to say?"

"Nothing, man." The guy was there to make money. I didn't touch him. But I threw him out. I says, "I ever catch you north of Roosevelt Road, I'll kill you." That was it. And I threw Johnny Santucci out, I says, "Go to the fuckin' hospital. I ain't taking you." He was beat to a pulp.

And Billy knew it was curtains. He knew.

Devoney says, "I got a place for the rehab." We took Billy there. They got him strapped in; he turned out pretty good. The rehab got him started, but his kids and his wife, they made him. I mean, he had a good mind and he squared away, but he was sick because of all that abuse, to the day he died. He had a bad heart, he was diabetic, he had emphysema because of the smoking, he had everything wrong with him.

You see why I'm so dead against drugs? He was terrible with that stuff. He was an intelligent kid. Billy was a top guy at St. Ignatius. He was a bright, bright guy, but he was stupid with the people he hung with. Tony used to tell him, "You'll never be nothing but a pot-and-pan burglar." Fooling around with him, but he was serious, too. "You want to be a crook? Come with me." Tony offered him that. Maybe if Billy would have paid attention to him . . .

29

RATS

I was assigned for a month, because of vacations, to do misdemeanors. It's about the third week of the month, and I'm calling guys in: "You had a fight with your neighbor. Come on in."

"What do you mean?"

"You had a fight. He signed a complaint on you, so you gotta answer it. I'm gonna set up a court date, your signature's enough for the bond." That's the way I did it.

I had a guy named Salvatore Romano on a small case. I knew him. He was a burglar. And there was a recent arrest. So I call him up. I said, "Listen, Salvatore, Detective Pascente. Gotta talk to you. You threatened a guy, it's an assault. It's no big thing, it ain't the Great Train Robbery, come on in."

He says, "I'll come in, but I ain't got no transportation. Could you pick me up? I'm not far, I'm in Melrose Park."

"All right." You're supposed to go out and get the guy. But most of the time they come in, because it's not the end of the world. So I go there, toot the horn out front, he comes down. No handcuffs, no nothing. He's coming in voluntarily. He rode in the back, I'm driving, I'm bullshitting with him. We get to Belmont and Western, I get him upstairs, put him in the room. I says, "I'll be right back."

Now, I learned this from Hanhardt, and I abide by it. Bill says, "You search that fuckin' car. You never know. A guy could drop a gun, drop a knife, drop anything. So just make sure." So I go down, because I always did it when I had a strange guy in the car. I go in the car, I'm searching, and all of a sudden I put my hand down behind the seat, and here's a Crown Royal bag, I take it out of there.

Jewels, emeralds. I said, "This motherfucker." I called Hanhardt. "Bill, I don't know what this means. I put a guy in the interview room, I go downstairs, and in the backseat is stashed this bag of jewelry."

He says, "Who did you pinch?"

"Romano."

"That dirty motherfucker. He's no fuckin' good." He sees, right off the bat.

"I pinched him for a misdemeanor. I called him in, he asked me to come and get him."

"He's got a fleet of cars, that guy. What the fuck's he need you to come and pick him up for? He's a no-good rat. He's an informant."

So now I'm thinking. The IAD, Internal Affairs, was always looking at me. They knew I was tight with Spilotro and Lombardo and those guys. And the IAD knows what I'm working this month, if they inquire.

I ask Bill, "Why didn't you tell me about this guy?"

"I can't tell you about everybody. Here's what I want you to do. Go inventory those pieces."

The pages in the inventory book are numbered from one to a hundred. And one of the copies stays with the arrest record, another copy goes down to Evidence and Recovered Property with the goods, and one stays in the book.

Bill says, "What page you on?"

"I'm on sixteen."

"Go to the very back of the book. But don't take number one hundred. Go to ninety. Because that won't be missed."

I knew what he was doing. He was sharp. If I used the right number, seventeen, other policemen would have used eighteen, nineteen, twenty, twenty-one. The Evidence and Recovered Property is gonna call the commander. "Where is number seventeen?" We don't want that inquiry. Plus, if we ever did get a chance to keep the jewelry, page ninety can go away and nobody will miss it.

Bill says, "Inventory everything on that page. Now, you're gonna put it in the commander's office, with the inventory slip, and I'm gonna order the commander to keep the property in his locker. Don't send nothing down to the Recovery Section yet. Tomorrow morning before you come in, I'll tell you what to do. Got it?"

"OK." So I did what he said. I listed it. Emerald earrings, matching emerald bracelet. Matching emerald brooch—all emeralds. I gave it to the commander, with the slip. I wrote up Romano, I let him go. I gave him a signature bond, he's gone, he's on his way. He says, "You don't have to take me home. I got a ride. I called a guy, he's gonna pick me up."

"OK, good luck." He's gone.

The next day I call Bill. He says, "I want you to go through the burglary reports of the last two months. Look up like a dozen burglary cases where they lost jewelry. Victims in your area. I want you to call every one of them in, and I want them to view the jewelry. We know it's not theirs, so no one's gonna claim it. We'll give it six weeks. Nobody claims it, it's yours. But let's see how it goes."

"Whatever you say." And I called them in. I got a dozen, fourteen, fifteen. They came in, I spread the jewelry out, they looked at it, I got their signature. "Oh, thank you, officer, it's not mine." And I made the report. I had a whole big folder on this particular case.

Two weeks pass. I'm in the office, the cavalry comes in. Fourteen agents stormed Area Six. There was IAD, FBI. Threw me against the wall, handcuffed me. "You're under arrest." That was the IAD lieutenant, Irish guy.

"Against the wall? What the fuck is this?" Everybody's looking at me.

"You stole jewelry."

Stole jewelry? Now everything comes to me. They set me up. They wanted to arrest me for stealing Romano's jewelry.

So I told the commander, "Call the chief."

The chief says, "What's going on?"

"We have your man, and he's under arrest. Grand theft, jewelry, interstate shipment." They knew where everything came from.

"I'll be right there." Bill gets there. He says, "What's he charged with?"

"Theft of jewelry. We got him dead." They even had pictures of the pieces.

"Oh." He goes into the commander's office, he says, "Commander, open your locker. You mean, this piece? You mean this piece? Is this what you're looking for?"

The IAD guy's face looked like a tomato, it was so red. Now he's stuttering. "Why wasn't it inventoried?"

"It wasn't inventoried?" Page ninety. "What's this?"

Now he's stuttering more. "Why wasn't it sent to Evidence and Recovered Property?"

"That was my orders. Because a lot of jewelry gets lost. Somewhere it gets lost. Maybe IAD, maybe Recovered Property. I wanted him to show it to the victims."

"Where's the reports?"

Sixteen fuckin' reports.

RATS

They start calling the Bureau: "Oh, yeah. He showed me all the jewelry."

Here's Bill: "Get the fuck out."

Man, they thought they had me dead-bang. That would have been a big feather in their cap, if they got me.

〜

Salvatore Romano had his fifteen minutes of fame at the 2007 federal Family Secrets trial in Chicago before disappearing back into the Witness Protection Program. Testifying from a wheelchair, he recounted his long criminal career and his six years as a federal informant, from 1981 to 1987. Recalling bygone days in Chicago, he described how a connected burglar, if he was careless or unlucky enough to be arrested, could get money to a judge via the right lawyer to buy an acquittal.

Moving on, Romano talked about his sojourn in Las Vegas. Romano was a locks and alarms man, and in 1979 he was invited by Peter "Duke" Basile to come out to Las Vegas to work with a crew that had coalesced under Tony Spilotro's protection and was putting the arm on stray bookies and pulling burglaries, always making sure Spilotro got his end. The gang included Frank Cullotta, a longtime acquaintance of Spilotro's from his Grand Avenue days, and various other associates, some already in Las Vegas but all with Chicago ties. One recruit brought in by Cullotta was Larry Neumann, who was not a professional thief but rather a killer who had, remarkably, been paroled after serving only eleven years for a triple murder over a matter of a two-dollar dispute in a bar. Since his release Neumann had teamed up with a burglar named Wayne Matecki, and he brought him along. Other core members of the crew's somewhat fluid roster were career thieves Leo Guardino and Ernie Davino and a former Las Vegas police officer named Joe Blasko who had been fired for passing information to Tony Spilotro.

Romano's skills were apparently not crucial; the group found it most convenient to simply knock holes through the flimsy stucco and chicken-wire walls of Vegas buildings to bypass the alarms, earning themselves the press nickname of the Hole in the Wall Gang. They ruled the roost in Vegas for two years, until on July 4, 1981, they hit a large antiques and jewelry store called Bertha's, only to be jumped by a joint FBI and Las Vegas Metro police team that had been lying in wait. Cullotta, Davino, Neumann, Matecki, Guardino, and Blasko were caught red-handed.

Sal Romano had also participated in the Bertha's job; when he didn't turn up in a cell along with the rest of the crew, it became clear to all who the feds' man on the inside had been. Romano disappeared and continued to draw good money from his gig with the government (including forty thousand dollars in one lucrative lump-sum payment in 1987, according to his testimony in 2007) while, apparently, telling the feds what they wanted to hear.

A couple years before the Bertha's bust, we had a friend named Bob Brown. He had a jewelry spot on Belmont and Nordica, right in that area, a little east of Harlem. Tony put Bob Brown in there. Bob Brown was a good man. Tony would move his jewelry from Vegas, wherever he got it, and Brown would sell it. Plus, he sold other stuff in there, too.

One day I'm on duty, I get a call from Michael Spilotro. He says, "Freddy, where you at?"

"Well, I'm on the east side, but I'm not doing nothing important."

"Shoot over to the store. Go see what's with Bob Brown." This was before the police got it—somebody must have tipped him.

So I shoot over there. Now the police are just arriving. They know me on sight; I'm a detective. I'm the first dick on the scene.

And boom, here's Bob Brown, beaten to a pulp. His face, his hands are beat up. Maybe he was fighting back. He's on the floor, his face is to the side, eyes open but blood all over the place. And he had a dagger through his back, stuck in the floor, and that was what did it, finished him. And they robbed him.

No sooner was I over there by Michael, Louie Tenuta comes in. He goes, "Freddy, I gotta talk to you. I know who did it. The guy that did this is Cullotta."

I says, "No." We knew Cullotta. He was from the neighborhood. He worked with Mikey Swiatek. The guy that made him was Mikey, not Tony. Tony didn't even like him.

Louie says, "Yeah. Cullotta did it."

Louie Tenuta had a club right next door to the jewelry store. And he would see Brown all the time. A few days before this guy got murdered, Louie says he spotted Frank Cullotta parked in a car along the street. "Why would he be parked here? I saw him one day, never said nothing, then I see him a second day. So I made it my business to go talk to him in the car, just like light talk. So what was he doing here two days?"

Then he says he saw Wayne Matecki and Larry Neumann. Bad-asses. Neumann was a horrible guy. Now, Louie knows these guys, where the police wouldn't know them. And he didn't forget it. When you see a guy like Cullotta laying on there, he's scoping it out.

I think they did go to rob him, and maybe Neumann was the guy who actually killed him. Because he was a big, mean guy. But I think Cullotta was there.

I told Michael, "It's in your hands." Michael took it in stride, and he probably got ahold of his brother. Soon after that, Cullotta went on to be an informant. He was in protective custody. What are you gonna do with him?

The Hole in the Wall Gang, Tony didn't put it together. These guys put it together. Leo Guardino, they called him Bubash. He lived on Erie and Damen, a few blocks away from me. He used to come by me all the time. He says, "I'm going to Vegas with Duke Basile and a few other guys. We're gonna set up shop there." Leo worked with a guy who was an ex-policeman in Vegas, Joe Blasko, who I knew well. Good guy. Tony liked him, liked Bubash, liked Duke Basile.

And Cullotta. Now Cullotta got in, not through Tony, he got in through these other guys. They knew him.

These guys were terrors. My God, what they did. They had it down pat. They pulled up to a joint, now they got a trailer. Pulled up against it, backed in, parked. They're against the wall, they're working on cutting a hole in the wall. Which was sharp, as long as there's no alarm. They weren't qualified to cut the bugs. Then you had to bring the A team in. But they did a lot of scores, because out there the police weren't geared for this. They didn't school the vendors in security. Here in Chicago, they got bugs that you can't touch.

On the scores they went to, they knew what they were after. They went for the money. They got the safe and they took the money. But the merchandise they never took. And once the score was done, then the place was open, it was clean. The police didn't come.

Tony would never go on anything. His days of that were over. But one time, I'm in Vegas on vacation, he says, "Why should we leave all this stuff? I want you to go finish it off." Because he wanted me to make money. There was a high-line dress store, and they were gonna make it. "There's dresses and suits. Silk, the most high-line. You gotta do this score. Don't worry about it. I got every-thing covered. I'm gonna be your guy outside. I'll be with Herbie." He didn't want nothing to happen to me. He and his friend Herbie Blitzstein knew all the cops; they knew everything.

RATS

I brought Junior with me. It's in a mall, a pretty good-sized mall, and it was sheltered—from the street nobody's gonna notice you. It's a weekend. The alarm is cut. Nobody knew anything about it. Nobody could see.

Tony says, "Now, when you hear the horn, just come out. Once you're out, you're in the clear."

I says, "OK."

So he goes, "I want you to hear the horn."

He wants me to hear the horn? If it's a different horn, I'm just gonna stay here? But he wanted me to hear his horn. "Here's the horn." *Beep.*

Herbie rolls his eyes. I says, "Is he nuts, this little cocksucker? If I hear *any* horn, I'm coming out."

We made a ton of money. I mean, thousands and thousands of dollars. We brought the clothes to a warehouse. This guy was in the slot machine business. He had a big warehouse. So we brought the stuff there, we left it, Tony had somebody's nephews or whatever, they sold it. And we got our money. Tony says, "Look what you can do here."

⁓

In July 1981, two weeks after the Bertha's bust, Tony Spilotro was arrested along with his brother John, Herbie Blitzstein, and Joe Blasko on a nine-count federal indictment for "a pattern of racketeering activity." The feds had been working overtime on Spilotro since 1978, when they raided the Gold Rush, Spilotro's Vegas jewelry store, only to have the evidence suppressed by a federal judge on the grounds that the warrants were "unconstitutionally general." Bertha's gave the FBI what it needed to make an indictment stick.

With top legal talent on his side in the person of Oscar Goodman, long a top defense lawyer and later the mayor of Las Vegas, Spilotro would put off his day of reckoning on the racketeering indictment until 1986. When he finally came to trial, two key witnesses against him were Sal Romano and Frank Cullotta.

Sitting in jail facing serious time for the Bertha's job, knowing the Vegas police were close to nailing him on a killing he had carried out for Spilotro and aware that Spilotro had washed his hands of him, Cullotta had flipped and run for cover with the FBI. He was given "transactional immunity," essentially a free pass for all crimes committed in exchange for his testimony against former associates. A better deal is hard to imagine for a man of Cullotta's accomplishments.

Since testifying in Spilotro's trial and others, Cullotta has maintained a fairly high profile for a protected witness, collaborating on Nicholas Pileggi's book Casino *and his own biography, appearing in TV documentaries and the film version of* Casino, *and making numerous public promotional appearances, apparently unafraid of legal or extralegal consequences.*

∽

Cullotta's story was that he was afraid Spilotro was going to kill him. But they had Cullotta on three murders. This was around the time when they started grabbing guys for that trial in Vegas, when they tried to bribe a senator.

The Bob Brown thing alone, he's a scumbag. To let Neumann do that, to a guy like that. And one time Joe Lombardo grabbed Cullotta, on Louie the Mooch's request, ordered him to come to our neighborhood. Leavitt and Grand. I'll never forget it. I was there. It happened across the street from where we hung at Bert's Tavern. So here's Frank Cullotta, Joey Lombardo, and Louie the Mooch, and Louie the Mooch is beating Cullotta with a fuckin' brick, a house brick. And Lombardo says, "Don't you lift a hand." I was shocked. I said, "Look at this, this guy's not even swinging back." Then later we find out he was there to take the beating because he had been in a place on River Road that was owned by Louie the Mooch's son. And Cullotta gave him a beating. And that was a no-no.

Tony despised him. Cullotta claims in his book, "I was his right-hand man." Bullshit. They had so much hatred for this guy. Mike Sausage Fingers had a fight with Cullotta, and he don't fight with nobody. They were rolling in the street on Chicago and Damen. They couldn't even fight.

30

INTERNAL AFFAIRS

Hoagie's Pub, Michael Spilotro's joint, was on North Avenue just east of Harlem. Great spot. Every time Tony came to town he told his brother to get in touch with me. "Get ahold of Inspector Clouseau"—that was my nickname. (Bill's nickname was Scrambled Eggs, because he had the braids on his hat.) And Michael would call me. As soon as he would say Clouseau, I'd say, "All right, what time?" and that was it. I knew Tony was in town and I went by his brother's to see him.

Tony just loved to see me, for the fun. And he wouldn't let me go. So one night we eat, and now we're drinking. We're just reminiscing, now we're pitching quarters in front of Hoagie's Pub.

I says, "Tone, I gotta work tomorrow. It's getting late."

"You ain't going nowhere."

We go back inside. He says, "Freddy, I got problems. There's four cars outside full of FBI agents. I don't want them to see where I'm going. You think you can get me over there?"

"Whatever you want." I didn't give a shit. Hanhardt always called me reckless. "You've got guts," he said, "but you're reckless. You shouldn't do that stuff."

Tony took Poopsie Ruggierio's coat, Poopsie's hat, and his car. Poopsie had a Buick convertible. We jumped in the car, I'm driving. And they're following. One car. We know they're behind us. Tony says, "Go this way, go that way. Get on the toll road." We can't shake them. Now we're going north on the toll road, toward Milwaukee. Tony says, "Get off at the oasis, we're gonna go have an ice cream." We get off, they come right with us. We park and go in the oasis, over the highway. They have an ice cream joint in there. Tony gives me the ice cream, he says, "I'll see you later."

I says, "Where you going?"

"I got a car waiting for me over there." He points to the other side, the parking lot on the southbound side.

"Good move. They can't come through." And I walked out.

The FBI guys jump out of the car. "Where's that other guy?"

"In there. I gave him a lift over here. What am I gonna tell you?"

So we got away with it. He had it planned.

The next day I get the call from Hanhardt. "Get over here." He throws some pictures on the desk. "Laugh about this." I see my picture, me and Tony. We're pitching quarters in front of Hoagie's.

I says, "Did I win? I don't remember if I won or not."

Bill says, "Fuck the jokes. Now you got a big beef with the FBI and the IAD."

"Well, how do you know he's not my informant?"

"Informant?"

"That's right. How the fuck do they know? I'm a policeman, you know."

"Well, you got a beef. And the movies are even better than the pictures."

251

So I get charged for consorting with a known felon. And the felon is Tony Spilotro. We got caught pitching the quarters. I got a hearing coming up, I'm gonna get sixty days suspension and maybe fired. I got a lawyer provided by the police union, the Fraternal Order of Police.

Even with all this shit against me, the other policemen that knew me loved me. So the night before I'm going to the hearing, a policeman I know shows up at my house. He says, "Freddy, good luck. But I want you to read this. You're gonna walk out of there tomorrow. And nothing's gonna happen to you. But read this. And don't tell nobody. The first person you tell is the hearing officer."

"OK." I open it up. "On March fourth at this time, Alderman Thomas Keane, ex-alderman of the Thirty-First Ward, a felon who did his time in jail, was picked up at this hour by two policemen in uniform, squad number this, and driven to his law office. At fourteen hours, this Keane was picked up by the same officers and driven to lunch. At this hour, Keane was taken home by the same policemen, on duty." And he's got a whole roster, a list, of weeks and months of all this activity by uniformed, on-duty policemen. Now, this guy had been in jail.

Whoa, I says. This is dynamite.

✑

Thomas Keane was a member of the Irish ethnocracy that ran Chicago. He had inherited his Northwest Side Thirty-First Ward fiefdom from his father and risen on the coattails of Richard J. Daley, whom he had helped get elected in 1955. By 1973 he was the second most powerful man in Chicago, head of the city council's finance committee and chief string-puller, fixer, and enforcer of the Democratic Machine. He was also increasingly criticized for using his clout for his own gain and that of his associates. In December 1973 he was indicted by a Cook

County grand jury on charges of conflict of interest but was acquitted in a bench trial before a Democratic judge, a fellow Irishman.

Keane's clout didn't work so well with the feds the following year, when a rising US attorney named James Thompson, fresh from bagging former Illinois governor Otto Kerner on tax evasion charges, indicted Keane for mail fraud and conspiracy in connection with a nice little racket he had been running through secret land trusts, buying up tax-delinquent properties and reselling them to city agencies at considerable profit. Keane was convicted in October 1974 and served twenty-two months in federal prison before being paroled. (Thompson went on to serve as governor of Illinois from 1977 to 1991 and, as a mark of true distinction for a former holder of that office, has never been indicted on state or federal criminal charges.)

Following his release, Keane regained his law license and devoted most of his energy to fending off a Better Government Association lawsuit to recover the money his scheme had earned and attempting to have his record expunged following a Supreme Court decision invalidating part of the mail fraud statute. He died at ninety, still protesting his innocence.

⌒

I go to the hearing, sit through it. At the end the hearing officer says, "You have anything to say, Pascente?"

I says, "I sure do." I got this memorized. "I want to make a statement. What am I charged with? What is my official charge?"

"Consorting with a known felon."

"All right, well, I think it's this. I think it's consorting with an Italian felon. Is there a charge, 'Italian felons'?"

The lawyer's looking at me: What the fuck are you talking about?

I says, "I got this in print. 'On this date, Alderman Keane, a felon of Irish background, was picked up by Officer . . .'"

"Recess!"

Recess? What the fuck is this, recess? Now I could see them scrambling. There's three exempt-rank officers and one patrolman. Here's the patrolman: "Yeah! Fuck them." They go out. The lawyer's going, "What the fuck?"

I says, "Don't worry about a thing."

Now the hearing officer comes out. He says, "Will you accept 'unfounded' and all back pay?"

"No, I won't accept that. I want, 'It never happened.' You have a category, 'It never happened'? That's what I want."

The guy says, "What? 'Unfounded,' that's the best thing."

"No."

He wanted to give me exoneration.

I says, "No. It never happened."

I got it. Never happened.

That's because the guys loved me. They brought it to me.

⌇

John Hinchy was Bill Hanhardt's old partner. He hated me. Hinchy didn't want anything to happen to the boss, because they had been partners. After I got in that beef with the department because of the Spilotro boys, Hinchy calls me downtown. Bill is out of town, and Hinchy is the deputy chief of detectives. He's pointing his finger, and he's going, "I'm sick of you getting your boss in trouble," referring to Bill. "You get him in trouble once more, I'll kill you." Just like that.

That was it. I jump up. I says, "See these things?" Making my hand like a gun, like he did. "They don't make 'em one at a time, cocksucker."

And guess what? I get a call from out of town. "Did you threaten the chief?"

So I'm a bad guy now. But Hinchy forced the issue.

31

DORFMAN

When Allen Dorfman took a half-dozen shots to the head in the parking lot of the Lincolnwood, Illinois, Hyatt on January 21, 1983, it was front-page news in Chicago. Dorfman might not have had the high-profile gangster glamour of a Spilotro or a Giancana, but mob aficionados knew who he was: he was the money guy. Dorfman was a natty dresser with a distinguished head of gray hair and thick black eyebrows who owned Amalgamated Insurance Services Inc. This agency was in the fortunate position of handling health insurance claims for the mighty International Brotherhood of Teamsters, with a membership of over a million.

The insurance business had made Dorfman rich. But his true source of clout was his position as a "consultant" to the board of trustees of the Teamsters' Central States Pension Fund. Dorfman was, in essence, the Outfit's banker. Pension funds have lots of money to invest; they are always looking for ways to make the money grow so they can pay off the retirees years down the road. Meanwhile, certain types of people find their attention irresistibly drawn to large pools of money. The two do not always make good counterparties. Wise fund managers look for safe, boring, reliable assets. If you have little in the way of safety and reliability to offer but want a pension fund to entrust its money to you, you need to find a way to exert some serious influence on the people who hold the purse strings.

The Outfit's influence went back to a Detroit union organizer named Jimmy Hoffa, who while engineering his rise to the top of the union in the late 1940s had met a Chicago racketeer named Paul Dorfman, nick-named "Red" for the color of his hair. Red Dorfman brokered a deal swinging the Chicago Teamsters behind Hoffa in exchange for Hoffa giving Red's stepson Allen the union's insurance contract and making him the power behind the throne at the Central States Pension Fund.

Allen Dorfman had not, at that point, been Allen Dorfman for very long. He had been raised as Allen Melnick, and it was under this name that he had attended the University of Illinois and served with the US Marines in World War II. When his mother married Red Dorfman, he took her new husband's name. This unusual move for a grown man was most likely done to open doors in his newly chosen profession. At the time of his elevation to the union brain trust he was teaching physical education at the university he had graduated from, credentials enough if your father is Red Dorfman.

Allen was acquitted on jury tampering charges in 1963 and nailed in 1970 for embezzlement; he did a year in federal prison. He had hardly readjusted to life on the outside when he was indicted in 1974 in connection with a Teamster loan that had gone to a phantom plastics factory in New Mexico that produced nothing but phony orders for molds that were sent along with large checks to a suburban Chicago fiberglass business owned by Joe Lombardo's ill-fated friend Danny Seifert. The case against Dorfman and his co-indictees Lombardo, Anthony Spilotro, and Irwin "Irv" Weiner died with Seifert.

DORFMAN

The feds nailed Allen Dorfman again, in 1981, when an FBI bug caught him conspiring with Lombardo to bribe Senator Howard Cannon of Nevada to hobble some legislation making its way through Congress that would have hurt settled Teamster interests. The defendants were convicted in December 1982. Dorfman remained free on bail awaiting sentencing. There is no more dangerous position to be in for a man with lots to say and lots of jail time ahead of him.

∽

I was close with Dorfman, because of Hanhardt and Tony. I used to go to parties at his house. He had a house in Eagle River, Wisconsin, the most beautiful place. You never seen parties like this. Everybody had their own cabin, and we'd meet at dinner in the main house. And he put on a spread. He's got boats, he's got everything you want. And he was a good guy. "You need anything, you come and see me. You don't have to go through Bill Hanhardt."

Dorfman was in charge of the Teamsters loans to the Las Vegas clubs. There was a loan made by Dorfman himself, through the Teamsters, that he gave to Tony and Irv Weiner and another crew, where they gave them three million dollars for a plastic pail company in New Mexico. And they torched it. There was not one pail in the joint. They just melted the place. And they got the insurance back, and they paid their loan, they made a score. It turned out to be a big profit for them. And this was Dorfman. Most of the Teamsters' loans in Las Vegas were a success. The Teamsters got their money back. But Dorfman was the key. He was in charge of the Central States Pension Fund.

And Irv Weiner set him up. I hate to say it; I like Irv Weiner. I was very good friends with him. But he brought Dorfman there. Irv Weiner was a brilliant guy. And he was a scrappy, tough little guy. Irv Weiner didn't take no shit. One day I was out with him in

Hy's of Canada on Walton Street. Beautiful place, good food. This guy we knew who was a drunk, he's harassing the piano player girl, and that was Irv Weiner's girlfriend. And Irv hit the guy, cracked him with a full bottle of booze. They had to take him to the hospital. But the guy, to his credit, didn't say a word. "I don't know who the guy was."

I saw Dorfman with Irv Weiner just before he was murdered, on the same day. It was at a video store on Cicero. I would go there every day, because the owner was my friend Warren. He was a bookmaker, Jewish fellow, nice guy. So I go there to pick up some movies. Now, we're talking, then I see Dorfman. You can't miss him, he stood out, handsome guy, well dressed, he's with Irv Weiner. It's a little before noon. I said hello to Irv, I said this and that, and they said, "We gotta make a stop, we gotta go, good to see you."

I went home from the video store, and on the TV it hit: *badda-boom*, bulletin. "Allen Dorfman, he got murdered."

I says, "I just saw this guy."

Now, the FBI and everybody is there, the Lincolnwood police, they come for me. When they were at the door, they said, "We want to speak to him about the death of Allen Dorfman." My wife, she knows I wouldn't do anything like that. She knew I really liked the guy. And she says, "Oh, you must want him to help you with the investigation."

"No. We want to talk to him."

What the fuck are they bothering me for? Well, the clerk at the video store, when I took the movies out, she recorded my name. So when the police went there, because Irv Weiner told them, "We stopped there," they want to know who I am.

I had a green Dodge squad car, detective car. The hit car was a green Dodge. I knew Lombardo, Spilotro, I knew Irv Weiner, I knew all of them. So bingo. They pegged me, and I got a notice for the grand jury under the US attorney, Douglas Roller, as a potential suspect.

I was nervous. I says, "Motherfucker, they got circumstantial evidence here. The car, same car. Did I see him? Damn right, I was talking to him, right before he died. I knew him, I knew his whole crew." Commander Wodnicki took me off the street, made me work inside. No more squad car, no more police duties, I just did office work. I was in big trouble. I was a suspect.

Tony Onesto was my lawyer. I told him, "Tone, I got nothing to do with this."

He says, "You're a target." So I dummied up, I didn't say a word. I refused to answer any questions.

Months later, they call me again. Now I'm no longer a target. I'm going as a potential witness. So Tony Onesto says, "Now you don't want to refuse to testify. Just answer the questions." And up pops two guys that they feel did it. The FBI buys anything they think could clear something up. And the guys that they had in their head for that murder were Ray Spencer and Lenny Yaras.

Lenny Yaras was a Jewish guy, a bookmaker. Ray Spencer was a big fat guy. Spencer died in Florida of a heart attack. And Lenny Yaras got killed on Division Street in 1985. They wanted these guys. I don't know why. They showed me their pictures, I says, "No, this guy wasn't there at the video store. And neither was this guy." They were trying to tout them guys. And they showed me other names. The showed me the German, they showed me this guy, they showed me that guy. I says, "I didn't see none of these guys there."

And that was it. They never charged anybody.

Joe Lombardo was assigned to Dorfman to make sure he was under control, because they had a lot of things going on with Dorfman. Lombardo had the most to lose. He was afraid of Dorfman beefing. They killed him just to make sure. I don't buy it—he wasn't going to say anything. Dorfman didn't beef on nobody. The guy was a marine war hero.

32

POLITICS

The spring of 1983 witnessed a miracle in Chicago: the instant resurrection of the moribund Republican Party and a surge in support for the Republican candidate in the mayoral election scheduled for April. Overnight, entire families who had voted Democratic for generations discovered an unsuspected fervor for the GOP. In a city where the Democratic primary had essentially been the mayoral election for decades, the Republican candidate was now nipping at the Democrat's heels in the polls.

What had the canny Republicans done to engineer this turnaround? They had sat and watched as Jane Byrne, the incumbent, and Richard M. Daley, son of the former mayor, split the white vote in the Democratic primary, allowing Harold Washington to take the nomination. Washington was the US representative for the South Side's First Congressional District, but he saw a chance to come home from DC and wield some real power by becoming the city's first black mayor.

The general election was contentious. The Republican candidate was a Hyde Park lawyer named Bernard Epton, who had expected merely to make the usual pro forma appearance on the ballot. The color of the Democratic candidate's skin, however, made Epton instantly competitive. White Democrats flocked to his banner in droves, their support more or less openly organized by Alderman Edward "Fast Eddie" Vrdolyak, who also happened to be the chairman of the Cook County Democratic Party. Epton, who had never been identified with racial politics, declared his intention to run a clean, nonpolarizing campaign but found it difficult to ignore the racial theme and became, whether he liked it or not, the symbol of white resistance to the threat of advancing black political power.

Washington won a close election. He presided over a fractious city council, with Vrdolyak leading opposition to an array of reform proposals, until 1987, when the mayor dropped dead at his desk of a heart attack. An appointed interim mayor held the office until Richard M. Daley was elected in 1989, beginning his twenty-two-year reign.

⟲

In 1983 I got into politics. I worked for Eddie Vrdolyak, who was the Tenth Ward alderman. Vrdolyak organized the New Republican Party. We were Democrats who turned Republican for Bernie Epton. We went against Harold Washington. We had all been for Jane Byrne, because she was good to us. The primary was a three-person race. It was her and Washington and Daley, and Daley wouldn't drop out. She's the mayor, why should she drop out? This guy, Richie, he was just a punk. And he spoiled it.

Now you got Washington. Where are you going? You ain't gonna win. Washington would be in forever once he won.

The organization was formed quickly. We had an office in every ward. We got backing from all the Democratic committeemen, but nobody knew. They gave us their manpower, they gave us money, they gave us everything.

Once Byrne lost the primary, now everyone's scrambling. Vrdolyak is in charge. He's the one we answered to. We were trying to get Epton to back off and have Jane Byrne take his spot. Then it would have been Jane Byrne against Washington. And Epton wouldn't go for it. So he's the guy we're stuck with. But we were in good shape with Epton, because we called the shots.

It was a war. It was black and white, and we didn't want Washington. Vrdolyak couldn't go in the forefront, because he's a Democrat. So we got Jimmy Cozzo. He's a kinky guy, but he's pretty strong with politics and unions. So we used his building and his office; that was our headquarters. We needed a person to represent the New Republicans in each ward. We got black wards, South Side wards. I was the Thirty-Ninth Ward.

My brother Billy took several precincts. I should have never used him—he's cuckoo. He goes to this house, and there's six votes. Polish, classy people. The woman was so nice. He goes there just to say, "We need your votes. We're in this war . . ."

"Oh, no, sir. Thank you for coming here, but we're Democrats and we're sticking with the Democratic candidate."

"Lady . . ." Now, he don't know this woman's values. Street idiot that he is, he says, "Lady, this is no election. This is a war! That fuckin' . . ."

"What?"

"I'm telling you. You're gonna vote, and your daughters . . ." She had five daughters. Here's him, when he left: "I hope they all marry fuckin' niggers!" These exact words.

She came into my office to beef about him. I'm in the office, and here comes this classy woman, dressed up, in a nice suit, and she comes in, she says, "This is your office?"

"Yes, ma'am. Can I help you?" Now, I'm the hundred-percent opposite of Billy.

She says, "Well, I know he came from this office. He wanted our vote, and the words he used . . . This man should go to jail."

I know who it is. I says, "Really."

"And he resembled you, by the way."

Let me tell you something, buddy, we almost won that election. We lost by thirty-five thousand votes. How good was that?

33

THE SUN SETS IN THE WEST

When I would go to Vegas Tony loved to hang with me, because of the fun. I was with him constantly. The book *Casino* says Lefty Rosenthal ran the hotel. Oh, yeah. He ran the hotel. But he didn't run them guys. They ran him. Lefty was there to run the joint. He was there as a gambling impresario. He knew gambling better than anybody. But he didn't tell these guys nothing. Tony told him. He was scared of Tony, believe me.

Tony went in there to the Stardust often. He went in there and gambled. But he was not supposed to be in there. He's in the Black Book.

He'd say, "Meet me in the coffee shop."

"Tony, are you supposed to be over there?"

"Nah, don't worry about it."

He'd think that nobody knows. He's got sunglasses on. Come on, Tony. I says, "You got a hundred other casinos. Let's go over there."

"This is my joint."

"OK, Tone."

~

Tony blew his money gambling. There wasn't enough for him, because of the gambling. And he had showgirls, and money is a problem there, too—you gotta keep them going. He had a girl, a Japanese girl. Beautiful girl. She had a lounge, and next door they had a restaurant. They used to hang in the joint, but he used to go by her, and he started a romance with her. And she wasn't the only one.

You could say what you want, you're a friend and you want to make excuses, but he screwed up. He really did. Tony was carrying on with Lefty's wife. He was crazy for that woman. Poor Lefty. I felt bad for him. Tony was laying his wife. That's for sure.

Now the word came down. Louie the Mooch came to me and said, "The old man wants to know. Is that Tony fuckin' that Jew's wife?" Just like that.

I says, "That's absolutely not true. No way."

Now Tony starts to lose favor with everybody. Phil's gone, Tony don't have that guy anymore. Now there's Lombardo and Schweihs and Tony. Now they had to answer to Louie the Mooch, who they didn't want. Aiuppa named Louie the Mooch as the boss of that crew, the Grand Avenue crew. Louie the Mooch was not a crook per se, like Tony was a lifelong crook, Lombardo, a lifelong crook, Schweihs. These guys actually went on scores. This guy never did that. Louie the Mooch was in the jukebox business. He was not a muscle man. But they had to answer to him now.

Now Joe Lombardo and Joey Aiuppa went to jail with that big Kansas City case, when they tried to bribe the senator, Howard Cannon. So the Outfit needs a new overall boss. And Joe Ferriola is the guy, with his crew. That means big Rocky Infelice, Sol DeLaurentis. So Ferriola wants to meet with Tony, Tony don't want to meet with him. "Fuck him." And that's the way it was. There was bitterness.

The reason? Tony's stiffing everybody. The money used to go to Aiuppa, what they skimmed from Vegas. Before him it used to go to the other guys. He was stiffing them all.

So that started the move to off Tony.

～

Tony Spilotro spent a lot of time with lawyers in the last few years of his life. In January 1983, he was indicted back in Chicago for a twenty-one-year-old crime, the so-called M&M murders. This was the affair that saw him put Billy McCarthy's head in a vise to get him to give up his partner, Jimmy Miraglia. The indictment rested largely on the testimony of Frank Cullotta, who was working overtime to justify his transactional immunity. Cullotta was well informed on the matter because back in 1962 he had helped set Miraglia up after McCarthy gave up his name to the man cranking the vise.

～

The story of the M&M murders is this. The only reason they got killed was money. That was a fight in a tavern. The Scalvo brothers ran the tavern. McCarthy is the guy that caused everything. He had a fight with these brothers and he caught a shellackin'. So he got his guy, Jimmy Miraglia. He brought Jimmy Miraglia there, confrontation, *boom, boom, boom.* These Scalvo guys beat the shit out of them.

So they laid for these brothers. Now remember, these brothers are no Outfit guys, nothing. The Scalvo boys were just tough kids. And the sad thing of that story is that the night that they got killed, they brought a girl with them. So Miraglia and McCarthy chased them from this place on Mannheim, Andre's, and they wind up in Elmwood Park. They crashed into a house in Elmwood Park. And Miraglia and McCarthy get out, and they kill all three people.

Now, everybody in the city knew that these two guys had a fight with the Scalvos. And the story around town was that Miraglia and McCarthy got killed because they killed these guys in Elmwood Park—they're not supposed to do nothing in Elmwood Park. But the real story was, Tony and Milwaukee Phil got a big stack of money to do it. When the Scalvos got killed, it broke their father's heart. The father was gonna give his whole life, his house, a hundred thousand dollars. "I want them, they killed my boys." So he got ahold of somebody, because he knew people, and he came up with the money. That was all for money. The first approach Tony got was not directly from the family of the boys, it was from somebody else, who wouldn't do it. Because that's not priority. Priority is business.

Anyway, the Scalvos got killed. With a poor innocent girl. For a fight, you're gonna get killed? And then the M&M boys got killed. By Tony.

〜

Spilotro's luck held, however, as his bench trial was conducted by Cook County circuit judge Thomas J. Maloney, who would later star in the federal investigation of judicial corruption in Chicago known as Operation Greylord, under which he was convicted of taking Outfit bribes to fix murder cases. Arousing only moderate surprise, Maloney found Cullotta's testimony to be unconvincing and acquitted Spilotro.

Tony had barely caught his breath when he was smacked with another indictment on September 30, 1983, this time resulting from the FBI's Strawman II investigation. Convictions from Strawman I for the long-running skim of the Tropicana Casino in Las Vegas had decapitated the Kansas City mob. Now Strawman II went after the Chicago guys for their cash siphon at the Fremont and the Stardust. Spilotro was only one of fifteen indictees; the list included Joey Aiuppa, Jackie Cerone, Angelo LaPietra, and Joe Lombardo.

Spilotro by this time was suffering the consequences of years of high living, with heart trouble increasingly limiting his activity. Under treatment for coronary heart disease, he managed to get his trial severed from the main proceedings so that he could undergo bypass surgery. He would not set foot in a courtroom again until early 1986.

New Year's Eve was out by Tony. That's an order. He says, "You're coming here." So what I'd do, my wife and me, with the kids, Christmas we'd stay home, and the day after Christmas we'd go out there and we'd spend the whole week. I took my vacation in that time period. Sammy was still out there at the time, and we'd go by Tony's house. He had the most beautiful parties. He had big people there. But I was the fuckin' guy. "My friend Freddy . . ."

Tony couldn't have children. He adopted his son, Vincent. And that took a lot of doing. Tony was a special guy. You gotta know. He was a heart of gold. I'm not condoning everything he did, because he did more bad than good. But he was a good guy. He was thrilled when he got that kid, Vincent. And he named him after his oldest brother.

They got the baby, now he's raising him. He goes everywhere with the kid. Now, one day I'm there at his house. And his wife,

Nancy, says, "Look at this." And her words were like a truck driver. "That motherfuckin' . . ." She was tough.

And here's Tony: "She gets too emotional, this woman." And he's going about his business. What do you think he's doing? The kid wanted a jukebox, Tony can't get the thing through the door, so he's breaking the wall. Just to get a jukebox in the house, he's breaking the wall down. For his kid.

Nancy was on this "Save the Whales" stuff. She saved eleven dogs. In this beautiful home. So now Tony's showing me all these dogs. One's got three legs. He says, "Look at this. The fuckin' dog don't even have all his parts." Tony says, "She saved the whales. Why don't she save her husband? I'm in trouble, save me."

Tony was the best guy you want to know. The best, bar none. Good guy, lot of fun. Scary guy, but he was just a good guy. If a guy wants money, he'd give it to him. He'd open his pocket. I was broke in Las Vegas, he said, "Here. Take any part of this."

Tony wanted me in Vegas. And I thank God that I didn't go there.

34

CRIME STORY

The chief put me in charge of the Bruce Springsteen concert, the security. "You're in charge. You go see the rep from Jam Productions. You'll do good, you'll make some money." This was 1985, at Soldier Field. Seventy thousand people. They had five groups prior to him coming on.

So we got uniform officers on every gate. The Park District didn't approve of booze. Anybody bringing booze in, you confiscate it, or you allow them to take it to their car. That's the rule. So I'm in charge. I got ten dicks. "You take care of these five gates, you take care of these five gates, you make sure, because the chief give me the job. I don't want to fuck him." And it was covered.

Well, by the time the concert was getting ready to go, you could fill three of these rooms, up to the ceiling, with beer we had confiscated. Beer, beer, beer! Well, now my head is going, my criminal mind is going. . . .

I'm waiting until it gets dark. So now they're all happy, the dicks: "We're gonna take this home, we're gonna split it up."

I says, "You're thinking too small." I had the plan already. I get all the dicks, not the uniform guys. I says, "Soon as it gets dark, we're gonna use these uniforms here, and the hats. And you got these strap-on things, you put the beer, you throw the ice in, we're gonna sell it out there."

"What?"

"We're gonna sell the fuckin' beer."

"Are you crazy?"

"Three dollars a beer. We're selling it. You want in? If not, this is my beer. You want in?"

We're all inside the stadium, selling the fuckin' beer. "Beer, beer, beer!"

"Didn't you take this from me?"

"Nah, I didn't . . ."

We sold every beer. Bruce Springsteen didn't even come on yet. And it's dark.

I go, "Who's got a van? Go buy some more. Here, take this." I give him the money. We bought more beer. And we sold it all.

How much money do you think we made? Eighty thousand dollars. Eighty thousand, cash. I got the money. I give the ten guys some, I didn't give them a full end. They were tickled.

I didn't see Hanhardt yet. But I got a call. He woke me up. "You motherfucker. I want to see you before I go to the office. Got it?" And this guy's a scary guy.

I met him. I says, "What's wrong, Bill?"

"I got a call. What did you do with this fuckin' beer?"

I says, "Hey, boss. A couple of guys . . ."

"A couple of guys? It was wall-to-wall, cans all over the place."

I says, "Maybe a couple were weak at the gates."

"Weak your ass, you motherfucker. You got me into . . ."

I gave him twenty thousand. Well, that changed his tune. He says, "You schemer. I'm gonna call you fuckin' Freddy Swindell."

The wheels were turning. *Madonn'*.

⸎

Joe Hansen was a bad, bad guy. He got arrested by Eighteenth District for drunk and disorderly, fought the whole district. I mean, they couldn't print him, they couldn't picture him. That's how bad this guy was. They threw him in the cell; he was lumped up.

So I get the call from a guy that was close to Frank Schweihs. He says, "Somebody wants to see you." He wouldn't even say his name. But he told me to come to Schweihs's apartment. It was on LaSalle Street, I would say maybe the ten hundred block.

So I go there. I says, "What's up?"

The German says, "You gotta get this guy out of jail." He didn't ask. He told you. "You're gonna go to the Eighteenth District. And you're gonna get our friend Joe Hansen out of there. He's refusing to let them print him, and he's fighting them. Just get him out. And you tell him that I told you. This is the order. OK? Any way. If he has to get printed, you make him get printed."

I says, "OK." I had no obligations to this guy.

He said, "You know him?"

"Sure, I know him."

"Well, he ain't gonna listen to you. So we got a note here. And you go get him, you tell him, 'Read the note.' And that's it."

And the note that they had written to Hansen says, "Hook or crook, you give them your name, you let them print you, let them picture you, and we're getting you out of here. And they'll set up a date for the disorderly."

So I go into the Eighteenth District lockup. I knew all the Eighteenth District guys. The lockup keeper, he's a nice guy. I walk in there, I says, "I want to see this guy you got."

He looks at me, he says, "You know, we had a bet. And the bet was, if anybody's gonna come and get this guy, it's gonna be you."

So I go back there, here he is. Like a caged bear, growling. And he's walking back and forth. Now, if you don't know him, I don't care if you're a cop, if you got a bazooka, you ain't gonna go near this guy. So I says, "Hey."

He turned around. "Yeah, what do you want?"

I says, "Come here." Just like that. So he gets close, I says, "Read this note and give it back to me." I gave him the card, and I took it back. I says, "All right. Now here's what you do. Don't be a stubborn mule. You get printed, you get pictured, and I'm getting you the fuck out of here. And the Nazi told me to tell you this."

He says, "OK."

So I go picture him. The guy says, "How the fuck . . ."

I says, "Picture him, print him, and if you're gonna make a bond, I got the bond." It was a hundred-dollar bond. It was disorderly conduct. And we got him out. I don't know the reason that they wanted him out of there, but they did.

So we got him out on a signature bond. They all knew I worked for Hanhardt. Remember, it's no big case. They couldn't secure him, that's all. And he put up a fight. He caught the shellackin'. But he must have fought the whole district.

I don't know why, I don't know what, I got him out. That was it.

⁓

With the bounce back in his step after bypass surgery performed by star surgeon Michael DeBakey, Tony Spilotro showed up in Las Vegas in February 1986 for his trial on the 1981 racketeering indictment resulting from the Bertha's bust.

A surprise witness for the defense was William Hanhardt. Questioned as to his qualifications with regard to knowledge of the underworld, Hanhardt is recorded as saying, modestly, "During this period of time I developed—or, I should say—I had a forte for the development of informants." Hanhardt testified that he had known both Spilotro and Cullotta since they were young hoodlums on the West Side. Cullotta, he said, was "unreliable as a witness."

The proceedings ended in a mistrial when an attempt to bribe a juror was detected.

By most accounts William Hanhardt had been an effective chief of detectives who did real police work and ran a tight Detective Division. But there had always been skeptics, and Hanhardt's role in Spilotro's trial seemed to strengthen their case. A persistent murmur tagged Hanhardt as the source of a leak to Kansas City mob boss Nick Civella back in 1979 about a secret meeting between the FBI and police in his city. But nobody was saying it very loudly.

Hanhardt retired from the Chicago Police Department in March 1986. His first gig in retirement was as a technical advisor for a TV series being filmed in Chicago, a gritty police drama called Crime Story in which former Chicago cop Dennis Farina, who hailed from Hanhardt's North Avenue neighborhood, played the head of a thinly fictionalized version of the CIU: the "MCU," or Major Crimes Unit. The series was coproduced and partly written by Charles Adamson, a retired CPD sergeant who had worked with Hanhardt before being mentored in the film business by producer Michael Mann, another Chicago guy.

⌇

Charlie Adamson got me on the show. He says, "Listen, you're not gonna be no movie star. But I want you in there. You're my friends. So he took about eight of us. And we're all in suits, black suits, hats. They gave us the stuff. He says, "You're gonna be in a hostage situation." It was filmed on Bryn Mawr and Broadway. Guys were upstairs, we were down on the street. And we had the heavy-duty equipment. One of us had a line: "Hold your fire!" That was Mike Malone. And I just wanted to get him. So he says, "Hold your fire!" I let one go. *Boom!*

The director goes, "I said hold your fire."

I said, "Listen, we never listen to that little motherfucker, and we're not gonna listen to him today."

~

The series makes fascinating watching for anyone familiar with Hanhardt's career. The story arc eerily shadows real-life events, presenting the fictional Mike Torello (Farina) as a tough street cop unfairly suspected of being corrupt and pursued by a vindictive and unscrupulous US attorney. In one episode Torello is compelled by a defense attorney's stratagem to appear as a witness for Ray Luca, a character clearly based on Tony Spilotro. If a few insiders picked up on the references and were impressed by the clout of the Hanhardt lobby, the general public saw only a quirky and stylish crime drama that made Farina a star.

Crime Story would premiere on NBC in September 1986. But by that time real-life events had left fiction far behind. While awaiting retrial in June, Tony Spilotro flew back to Chicago. He and his brother Michael were last seen on June 14. Their bodies were found buried in an Indiana cornfield on June 23.

35

GONE

The week before he went missing, we were all together. We had a big party, for my son Joey and my daughter. One graduated high school, one graduated grammar school. So Michael says, "You're gonna have it here," at Hoagie's. We had the whole restaurant. Michael and Tony's mother was there. We were having so much fun. This was the week before, one Saturday before.

And Tony's leaving. I says, "I'll see you when I come to Vegas."

"Ah, I'm gonna stay another week." I'll never forget, it was the last thing he said: "I'm gonna stay another week—I gotta straighten something out for Michael."

A week later, early Sunday morning, the phone wakes me up. It was like between four-thirty and five o'clock. It's Sam DeStefano, nephew of the famous Sam DeStefano. His father was Tony's old partner, Mario DeStefano. "You see the boys?"

"What boys?"

"Tony and Michael."

"Last time I saw them was last Saturday, at the party for my kids. What's up?"

"They left at two o'clock in the afternoon. They haven't shown up."

I was sick when I heard that. I says, "Listen. They're gone. You'll never see them again. I'm giving you my professional advice: they're gone."

I called Hanhardt. I says, "Bill . . ."

He says, "Freddy, they're gone."

Sure enough. I knew.

⚬

Among the family secrets spilled in the course of the federal trial of that name in the summer of 2007 were the circumstances surrounding the deaths of Michael and Tony Spilotro. Until then it was more or less accepted that the vivid depiction of the killing in the movie Casino *was accurate, the brothers being beaten to death with baseball bats in the cornfield where they were later found.*

That image was relegated to the category of fiction when the government's star witness, Nicholas Calabrese, took the stand on July 18, 2007. Calabrese described how Michael and Tony Spilotro were lured to a house in Bensenville, Illinois, where they were set upon by a group of men lying in wait in the basement. According to Calabrese, he, John Fecarotta, and Jimmy LaPietra were driven to the house by James Marcello and greeted there by Outfit bosses Joseph Ferriola, John DiFronzo, and Sam Carlisi. In the basement of the house were five more men, all wearing gloves. Calabrese named two of the men but said he did not know the other three. He testified that he and the others waited in the basement for half an hour before the Spilotros arrived and were ushered down the basement steps, Michael leading. Calabrese said that he tackled Michael Spilotro and held him while

Louie "the Mooch" Eboli strangled him with a rope; he was unable to see what happened to Tony. Calabrese did say that he heard Tony Spilotro ask, as he realized that he had walked into an ambush, "Can I say a prayer?"

～

The head of Tony's crew at the time was Louie the Mooch. Louie was afraid of Tony. But he still had to work with him. And Louie was the last word. He had to put the word out to kill Tony. You couldn't do it without going through his superior, who was Louie the Mooch.

The FBI says this is the way it went. Thirteen guys killed these brothers? Don't believe it. I don't believe it, because I don't believe thirteen people are gonna show up at a murder. And that's what were there, according to Calabrese. I don't believe that those guys were the ones that did it. Because they weren't capable of that stuff.

Frank Schweihs? Absolutely. I'll always say this, because I was witness to it: The day they went missing was a Saturday. Saturday night I was out with my wife and another couple. We go to a joint on LaSalle, just down the street from Frank Schweihs's apartment. Who's there? Schweihs, Joe Hansen, Paulie Schiro. These were Tony's three main guys. This is the night Tony went missing. And they were celebrating, drinking their asses off. I didn't think nothing of it, because I didn't know at the time.

Sunday morning, when I get the phone call, five o'clock . . . "Missing?" Well, that was it. I said, "They're not missing, they're gone. Forget about it." Soon after, they were found.

Michael Spilotro told his wife, "If I don't come back by a certain time, it's over." He put his stuff aside, he told her where all kinds of stuff was, personal. So he knew it was serious. Now, when you go to see a guy, whoever is representing him, you go with your guys and he comes with his guys. And you talk it out, air out your differences, and that's what happens, a sit-down meeting to square away problems. That's what it was supposed to be.

When they met, it was all arranged—all sides turned on the two brothers. His guys and their other guys. It was these guys. Frankie Schweihs, Joe Hansen. I don't have no proof. But if you're somebody that's in the know or has any kind of knowledge, that's what happened. Before this happens, Joe Hansen's in California. Paulie Schiro's in Arizona. Now all of a sudden they're here, and Tony is dead? Come on. And those are two guys who could have done that kind of damage.

Those guys Calabrese said did it—no way. With all the testimony, they still didn't get convicted on that. I have the right story. His friends got him.

There's ways to get killed. And there's always a message. You get shot here, behind the ear, that's it. That means, 'You were a good guy, but you had to go.' For whatever reason. Like Dorfman. They killed him, but they didn't destroy his face, like in the case of Butch Petrocelli. Butch Petrocelli, they burned him because he was a no-good rat. They got the messages. One guy was laying a woman that he shouldn't have. They cut his dick off. And Sam Cesario they did in front of his house, in front of his family, they blasted him. Because he was nailing Phil's girl. There's different ways.

In Tony's case, they just wanted him. They were all mad at him. There was a lot of jealousy. Michael and Tony were fucking guys out of their end, Michael was muscling guys that he shouldn't have. And Michael was a jet-setter, he was going all over the country spending money; Tony was gambling, huge money. And then, everybody gets convicted, and he got a new trial. But he was no threat to beef on anybody else. Tony had a good chance of skating.

And if he survived, he would have been the boss. But they were all going away forever, and they were pissed, and they ordered him dead.

And what a brutal way they got him. They didn't have to kill them like that. Shoot them and get it over with. To me, the reason was pure jealousy and fear. Because this guy was gonna be the boss. That was it.

∽

My mother loved Tony so much. She didn't believe he was this kind of a guy. My mother made me take her to the priest who wouldn't bury Michael and Tony. The priest wouldn't give a Mass. And she went and gave him a piece of her mind. She says, "When these guys gave you the money every week, it was OK. Now, because of some newspaper people, you don't want to bury them? This is for the parents, this is for the family. They're gone." She says, "I go to church four times a week. I'm the most devout Catholic you ever seen. But that's a sin, what you're doing." My mother told him.

And that funeral? Caskets closed, both, side by side. I went, I didn't give a fuck. Hanhardt told me, "Don't you . . ."

I says, "Fuck them, I'm going. I don't give a fuck. I'm going to the fuckin' funeral."

36

GYPSIES

On June 29, 1995, the New York Times *reported the sentencing of David Ballog, age forty-nine, to twenty months in federal prison for an insurance fraud scheme that had scored $758,000 from several insurance companies. The brief report cited gambling debts as a motive for the scheme and quoted Ballog as saying, "I blame nobody but myself."*

This was the government's second try at sentencing Ballog; three weeks earlier US district judge Charles Kocoras had, much to everyone's surprise, rejected a previous plea deal worked out by Ballog's lawyer with federal prosecutors, saying the sentence did not "do justice" to what was "essentially a lifetime of crime." The chastened lawyers huddled again and came up with a new number. The second deal still fell short of the forty-one months Ballog could have drawn according to federal sentencing guidelines. While awaiting sentencing, Ballog had traveled around the country lecturing on fraud at insurance company seminars, a guest expert if there ever was one.

Ballog had turned himself in in April 1993 after the FBI busted the Las Vegas–based Kallao family for running a similar scheme, involving a series of staged accidents designed to extract quick payoffs from insurance companies. Ballog was related to the Kallaos by marriage and apparently judged that cutting a preemptive deal was a better bet than trusting to family solidarity to keep his name out of the discussion.

∽

The Gypsies have all the reading rooms, where you come in and they read your hands, and they predict your future. Ballog explained this to me. They tell people, "Your money, it's cursed. Here's what you do. You bring your money to me, we're gonna bless it." Some of them come up with a hundred thousand dollars. How blessed is that? And then they pack up, they're gone.

Then they have guys that are repairmen. I don't know how they get their information. But they'll go to your house. Generally it's old, retired people. And they go in there: "We're gonna do your driveway. We're gonna tar it, we're gonna clean up your eaves, we're gonna do everything."

"OK." And while they're in there, they're searching the house. They come up with jewelry, come up with cash. It's done every day. This is their scam.

But Ballog made more money than them guys, all on these slip and falls, all insurance claims. And he loved my insurance company, Fireman's Fund, because they pay fast. So he came up with an idea for me. He had a young kid, a friend's son, sixteen or seventeen. "We're gonna claim it on your homeowner's. Here's the scam. These kids are playing football. You, as a spectator, you walked over from Kelvyn Park, you wanted to show the guy how to play the game. So you tackled him, and that's where he got his injury." It never happened.

Now he's got my name, he made a claim on my house. They got the insurance company for it. Hundred twenty thousand. And of course, I'm his partner.

We used my mother-in-law one time. She didn't even know it. The story was, she was going to Las Vegas, and she had jewelry on her person that her mother had left her, and she set her purse down and someone nailed her jewelry. It never happened. We used her name, her numbers. And they settled for forty-four thousand. My mother-in-law finds out about it later through the FBI, she says, "What?"

Then I got the guy with the broken back. He was in my van, and it was bullshit. We made a police report that I made a sudden stop, and swerved to avoid something, and he fell and broke his back. And he made a claim against my auto insurance.

In '92, Matt Raimondi asked me to do his girlfriend a favor. The Gypsy was handling her case. It was stolen jewelry. Matt says, "If you would call her insurance agent, the adjustor—he's balking on this here." The Gypsy is the one that set it up for her, he did all the legwork. He got her the policy. He's got the adjustor, he's got the person who makes the appraisals in the jewelry store, he's got everybody. If you need a check cashed, he's got the currency exchange. He's got every end locked up. He knows what insurance companies have been hit—stay away from them—he knows the ones that aren't hit. I don't know how he's got that network, but he does. That's his job.

Now, if you want to do jewelry, you don't just get an insurance policy. You gotta get a rider for it. A rider for this piece of jewelry, that piece of jewelry. The insurance man tells you, "We need appraisals for all these items." So the Gypsy goes and gets the appraisals. The items never existed. But he brought the appraisals to them. Now she's got her policy. Six months later they make a claim. Sixty thousand, seventy thousand, it's ridiculous.

So now, I made that call. That was the one thing they got me with. I called the adjuster on Matt Raimondi's request. I shouldn't have done that. I says, "You got this case?"

He says, "Oh, yeah, this one?" He gives her name. "Yeah."

"Well, I'm the detective on the case. I got the case. I feel bad for the woman. The woman lost this and that . . ."

He says, "Yeah, I don't know, there's something a little . . . What's your opinion?"

"Well, to me, she lost it. And that's that."

I shouldn't have listened to Matt. Because where does a policeman call the adjuster? Never. That was a mistake. Then they had heat on Davey. Another guy beefed to the FBI, he says that Davey works with a policeman, a Chicago policeman. They grabbed Davey, and everything started falling.

37

CRAZY HORSE

In '92, around the holidays, Perry Mandera calls me. This was a guy with money—he built an empire with his trucking company. His father had two trucks; Perry's got 130 drivers. Perry Mandera was a well-educated kid. I knew his father, helped him with a personal thing one time, and I knew Perry when he was a baby.

Perry says, "I want to meet you. I want you to give me advice. There's an offer on the table." And he explained the whole scenario. He had a chance to buy into a new strip joint called Thee Dollhouse, owned by a guy named Michael Peter. Michael Peter was a Cornell University graduate, very sharp. And he had joints all up and down the East Coast. He had Dollhouse, he had Solid Gold, he had Pure Platinum, he had Stringfellows. Perry says, "This guy Jimmy Levin, I want to buy the license and I want to go partners with him. What would you do?"

I says, "You're gonna be the license holder?"

"Yeah, he can't get the license."

"You got the only game in town, Perry. You gotta take it, and that's that."

"Ah, it's a little too much money."

"Give him extra. When you get a strip joint, it's a matter of weeks where you're gonna make up that difference. Take the fuckin' joint. Perry, you know trucking but you don't know this. You gotta take it. You won't believe it."

So he took my advice, and he did it. He says, "You're working here. Quit your job. You're gonna be here."

We opened Thee Dollhouse in February of '93. The owner was Perry Mandera. I was the main guy. I was contemplating quitting the police department like Perry told me to, but I didn't want to do that yet.

I got my son Joey to be the assistant manager. He was a young kid, but he was sharp. The joint took off from day one. You couldn't get in the door. But we were employing people from Dollhouse, Michael Peter's big chain all over the country.

Thee Dollhouse was at 1500 Kingsbury Street, where it runs along the river. That's at like Sheffield and North Avenue. And there's rats running all over the place, because it's all abandoned warehouses. You never seen rats like this—you could saddle these fuckin' things. So I said, "What am I gonna do with these fuckin' rats?"

I told my brother. Billy comes one day with a truck and this guy who had cats. Billy says, "My guy, he goes in warehouses, he cleans out the rats. You don't need poison, you don't need nothing. Just sic these cats." And I'm telling you, when you see these cats, they were no little kitty-kitty cats, they were striped cats, and they let them loose, by the river.

Two days. We saw a bunch of fat cats, their stomachs were hanging, no more rats. And they would patrol these parking lots right by the river. You wouldn't see a rat for nothing.

So anyway, we got it going. Now, a few months into the job, I see a lot of shenanigans. I see one of the Dollhouse guys taking cash and writing slips out. We were doing twenty-two, twenty-four thousand a night. That's huge money. We're doing over nine million dollars a year. And I catch this guy stealing.

I told Perry, "You gotta get rid of the Dollhouse people. This guy's stealing, they have dope parties here . . ."

He says, "OK, we'll get rid of them. But we're under contract."

So he puts me in touch with his lawyer, a sharp guy, Mike Abramson. He knows the rules. He's got the contract. So he says, "Well, there's only a few things that we could beat them on. We're giving them 6 percent of the joint for using their name, but they guarantee, by contract, they have to provide thirty of their girls every night. Whoever we add, it's our business. But they must have thirty Dollhouse girls a night. That's the easiest way to do it."

So I got to be friendly with one of the Dollhouse guys, because I'm working with them every day. I see the roster. He says, "Well, I got eight girls."

You got what you got. I made a note: January 8, eight girls.

And another time: "Fred, I got twenty-two girls." Eight girls short. Put that date. I'm not intelligent, but I'm smart, buddy. I get not one date, two dates, three dates. I got many dates. So the payroll shows it. I had a roster. I get Abramson, I says, "Hey."

And bing, they were out. I got rid of the Dollhouse people and we brought in the guys from Vegas. We changed the name to Crazy Horse, and we brought Rick Rizzolo in.

◡◠

The Crazy Horse Too in Las Vegas was flying high when Rick Rizzolo and the guys from Vegas were brought into the Chicago operation. There was a long-forgotten original Crazy Horse in Vegas, but it was the second joint on Industrial Road, with the "Too" in the name, that Rizzolo took over in 1984 and propelled to the top of the Vegas strip club business. By the early 1990s the Crazy Horse Too ruled the roost, boasting hundreds of strippers, streams of celebrity customers, and a gross reputed to be as much as twenty million dollars a year. Rizzolo himself was a celebrity, enjoying the friendship and patronage of Vegas establishment figures like future mayor Oscar Goodman and spreading the wealth with lavish benefits and contributions to charity.

The generosity, along with the campaign contributions to local officials, made it easier to ignore the murmurs about the rough side of the business: the allegations of prostitution and drug trafficking on the premises, the parking lot beatings of patrons outraged by inflated bar bills. In 1985 Rizzolo, defended by Goodman, pleaded no contest to a misdemeanor battery charge after personally taking a baseball bat to a patron out behind the club. Mostly, though, he left the heavy work to his bouncers. One unsatisfied customer wound up a quadriplegic after disputing his tab with the staff, and in 1995 another was found beaten to death behind the club.

Amazingly, no criminal prosecutions resulted.

Rick wound up getting thirty thousand a month from Perry. He shows up twice a month, every month, to see what the problems are, to correct them, show his face. And he ran a good show. Now he gets an apartment here, on Lake Shore Drive. He's hanging with Lombardo. I said, "This ain't the guy to hang with." He'd go by Lombardo's warehouse on Racine. He'd play cards with him.

Lombardo is the Babe Ruth of gin. You don't beat Lombardo. Rick never played gin in his life. He'd go in there and lose ten thousand, twelve thousand. Just give him money.

Perry was happy with it. The joint was thriving, we were doing over nine and a half million a year, which ain't bad. Put it on paper, that's 65 percent profit. There's no business that you could think of that's profitable like that.

I ran everything. I was listed just the way they listed Lefty Rosenthal at the Stardust: food and beverage. I was not the manager. My son Joey was the manager. But they all listened to me. May worked in there, on the front desk—she took care of the coatroom. She made a ton of money.

All we paid for was booze, and the payroll was almost zero. We gave everybody minimum wage, five dollars an hour. They all worked on the tips. They all thrived from the girls' tips. And the girls, the entertainment, we don't pay them at all—they pay us. When they come in, the girls pay us to work. Tuesday, Wednesday, Thursday, they paid sixty dollars a night. Sunday, Monday, they paid forty dollars a night. Slower nights. Weekends they paid a hundred dollars. A hundred dollars a night. You got forty girls, put the math there. That's all you need every night. Four thousand dollars a night. Is that good? That was me. I set that all up.

Now, that was the revenue from the girls. We also had funny money. That's where the profit was. The other guys wanted to put ATM machines in. I says, "No. We don't want ATM machines." If there's an ATM, you're a customer, you go to the machine, get your money, use your credit card, you get a thousand dollars. You only have to pay 1 or 2 percent on the transaction. Instead, we have our own money—we have it printed out. Similar to dollars, but it's with the Crazy Horse logo, funny money. We sell it at our front desk. Only thing is, you pay a thousand dollars, cost you a hundred dollars. Ten points you pay for that money. And you can't purchase anything with it. You can use it for dances and your tips. So the girls wind up with most of it.

And at the end of the night, when the girls accumulate this funny money, we put a charge on them. We charge them 10 percent. So that's 20 percent. Now, put the math together. We averaged two hundred thousand a week in funny money. We got 20 percent of that, every freakin' week. So now, I didn't finish there. Every six months, we changed the color of the money. Now it's black, and the next time it's red, and the next time it's yellow, and the next time it's white. You know what that means? There's like 30 percent isn't turned in. And most of them are out-of-towners. If they don't turn it in, it's no good. We made a fortune with that stuff. That was all me. The whole thing was me.

And the cash. I used to give Perry twenty-five thousand a week. I controlled the money. Every night I counted the money. So I know, *badda-bing*. And the tips, everything was turned in to me, I would divide up the tips. Which was good, because that stopped the guys from hustling over other floor men. They had to turn their tips in. They get caught, they know it's the job. They don't want to lose that job, because they were making five to seven hundred a night. The bartenders we put in the pool, and they turned their tips in, too. So I'd get all the money, and I'd have it all spread out, and I'd divide it up.

There's eighteen, nineteen ends, whatever it was. We got six bartenders, twelve floor men, doorman. And I'd have all the envelopes, they'd be waiting around, and I'd cut it up for them. Bartenders, floor men, doormen, they all figured in. The only ones that didn't turn in their tips were the cocktail waitresses. They kept their own. That was the fair way. Why should one waitress who's a hustler, or doing it on charm, why should she have to share with one who's a lazy broad? So that was it.

Now these are my rules, to protect ourselves. Louise, let's give her a name. "Louise, how'd you get to work?"

"Well, I took a cab."

"OK." Louise, cab. "Mary, how'd you get to work?"

"I drove my yellow Corvette."

"OK. How'd you get here?"

"My husband dropped me off."

"OK." So, sixty girls working, I got every one down.

At the end of the night, the place is closed. I kept the girls fifteen minutes for a bullshit meeting. There is no meeting. It's for all the customers to get out of sight. Because this way there's no prostitution, because that's how you get closed down. Now, I give every floor man a copy of this roster. And they got it, and they walk the girls to their cars. My rule. "Louise. You took a cab. Get in the cab." If she gets in another car, that means she made a deal with a customer.

Now, if they do anything off the premises, fine, go ahead. We don't care. But you ain't doing nothing here. So we made sure every night that they got in their car that they stated they came in. That's my rule. And then I'd have drug-sniffing dogs come in. At random. They'd go into the locker room, sniff out the shit. If she was dirty, I'd sit her down and have a talk with her. "You can't do this. They come in here, bust you, you lose your job, everybody else loses their job." I watched that pretty close.

And I'd sit in the back of the room and make notes. This one didn't put her money in the garter. That's the rules. Because if a liquor commissioner guy sees it, you got problems, because they're not supposed to take it from the hand, hand to hand. That was the rule. The customer had to put it in her garter. So I watched things like that. If I see a waitress not bringing the drinks with a tray, make a note. If they come with the drinks in the hands, no, that don't go. On the tray. Stuff like that. We had spotters to watch the bartenders. I didn't have to watch that.

But the money, *madonn'*. I had a drug guy come in, he wanted me to sit with him. I despise them guys. He wanted to prove a point that he's gonna get me to sit with him. So finally he tells my son, "Joey, you tell your dad that I'll give him ten thousand dollars."

I says, "I'll be there in a couple of minutes." I went right over there.

So the guy told his runner, he says, "Pull out a package, ten thousand." He handed the money to me. "Here." I put it in my pocket. I stayed with him an hour, broads were dancing for him. After he left, I gave Joey five thousand. I says, "Put this in the tip pool for all the boys."

38

TROUBLE

When everything went down with me, with the investigation, Joey was a probationary policeman. Went through school, passed everything, now he's in the squad car, he's learning, he's with his training officer, and the FBI calls him in.

So he says, "Dad, what am I going to do?"

I says, "Here's what you're gonna do. Any question they ask you, you tell them the truth. Don't worry about me. You cannot hurt me. But you could hurt yourself. You answer every question. 'Did you ever see Dave Ballog here, the Gypsy?' 'Yes.' 'Did you ever meet . . . ?' 'Yes.' Don't lie. Do not lie, because you're not involved with me. You're not involved with me one iota."

So he says, "OK." And he answered everything. And they fired him. As a probationary policeman, they could fire you on the littlest thing.

I said, "Why are they firing you?"

"Because I failed to notify my immediate supervisor that I was being investigated."

The lawyer went in, he says, "He wasn't being investigated. They were investigating his father. They just wanted to talk to him."

Even his probationary officer who broke him in, he said, "I'm his immediate supervisor. He told me."

They said when he was investigated by the FBI he didn't notify his immediate supervisor. But he did. He told his training officer. But they stuck with it. They just wanted him, for me. So Joey got fired. It was a sin. I was sick. It's all because of me. That was horrible, what they did to him. But he got on. He got on with his life.

I paid the price. Am I bitter? Absolutely not. I know what I did. I was the bad guy.

⌇

There was a beef with me and another cop because of this Ballog. He had nailed this guy's friend, a currency exchange. Beat him for a lot of money. And the guy comes to me, the other policeman. He says, "You go to bat for this guy."

I says, "I don't know what the guy does. I'm sorry for your friend, but what am I gonna do?"

So he was a heavy-duty guy, and he went in and saw his commander, who was Callaghan, the boss of Six at the time, and he had me transferred. He says, "I don't want no conflicts with you guys." So I went to Area Five at Grand and Central.

Now it's the middle of 1993. I was on the job. The FBI called me down to their office, ninth floor of the Dirksen Building downtown. They lured me down there on something to do with the Dorfman case that they needed me to put the final touches on. The Dorfman killing was in '83, but they said they had it open. I get down there, and they say, "We just want to end this thing."

I says, "Dorfman? I went to two grand juries on that. I felt horrible about it, because he was a good man."

He said, "Well that's it. By the way, somebody else wants to talk to you." And the agent they brought in was this guy for insurance fraud. And this and that, he's telling me about certain things. And he goes, "Do you know Dave Ballog?"

Here's me: "*Whoaaa.* This is what you want to talk about. You don't want to talk about Dorfman." Then I know they got him. I says, "I can't talk to you no more. That's it."

I went to see Davey, I wanted to talk to him. I couldn't find him. I still trusted this guy. But then things started to unravel. Now they come officially, probably a week after the first meeting. And they come to the office. I used the commander's office. There's three of them. I says, "Oh, this is trouble here." I had introduced Davey to a girl. And he took her for a hundred thousand. And this girl killed herself. I didn't know that. And they brought that up. I says, "What? Well, I'm sorry to hear that." Now I'm thinking, they got Davey on murder or manslaughter or something. I said to myself, "Wow. They got me. I'm in trouble." I says, "You go see my lawyer. We'll be talking to you."

My lawyer was a guy by the name of Vince Connelly, who was a former US attorney. He knew his way around the office and he was a good attorney. I went to see him. He says, "Well, I don't know nothing yet." So then they called me in, and I went downtown with Vince. And he said, "You're gonna get indicted, because of the paper trail. There's no escape." They got my mother-in-law—they know she didn't make the claim for the stolen jewelry. "They got this Ziga"—Tony Ziga, the guy with the broken back—"he's talking on you. Ballog, he's talking on you." The kid we said I tackled, everybody. "You got thirty-one witnesses against you."

"OK." So when the indictment came, I said, "No disrespect to you, you're my lawyer, but I'm gonna go see another lawyer."

He says, "Absolutely."

So I went to see Oscar Goodman in Vegas. Before he was the mayor, he was a practicing attorney, and an excellent one. He was Tony's lawyer. And I got to be friendly with the guy. So he says, "Fred, I'm gonna look at the papers. I'll take the case home with me. You'll have my answer before you leave town. Spend a couple of days, let me read it through. But in the meantime we'll go to dinner. Piero's, on me." So we went and ate. The next day he called me, he says, "You're a loser. You're dead. You'll never win this case."

"What a fuckin' vacation this is."

"But I will tell you this. I know the sentencing guidelines better than anybody. They're gonna threaten you with a hundred years, whatever they tell you. But they can't give you more than thirty months. So if they're buffaloing you, like you're gonna get more, they can't."

And sure enough, was he right. When they come with the subpoena, that's when they told me. "You're gonna get ninety months. You're gonna lose your pension, you're gonna do time." I had come back and told Connelly what Goodman told me, and he agreed. So we knew they were lying, for their reasons.

Now they says, "You know, it don't have to go this way. You want to help out? You'll go home. You'll walk out of here. You'll get your pension."

I says, "What do you want?"

"We want you to tell us about Bill Hanhardt."

⌇

The FBI had a long and ambivalent relationship with William Hanhardt. When the Bureau started going after major jewel thieves in the 1960s, it worked closely with the CPD's burglary unit and the Criminal Intelligence Unit, both of which were headed by Hanhardt at different times. Surveillance was carried out, phone records examined, informants pumped. FBI memos from the early '70s cite close CPD cooperation in the effort; J. Edgar Hoover went so far as to write a letter of commendation to Hanhardt thanking him for his work.

A major target of the effort was James D'Antonio, a Grand Avenue guy who had made a name for himself as a big-time jewel thief. In 1980 a federal informant named Gerald Shallow made an interesting allegation. Shallow himself had a long and intriguing history: he had been Richard Cain's partner on the police department, accused of a variety of misdeeds, including murder, before flipping when caught by the feds for securities theft and going into the Witness Protection Program. Now Shallow told the Bureau that as a patrolman back in the 1950s he had seen William Hanhardt taking money from D'Antonio.

More dirt got thrown when Ken Eto, Joe the Jap, miraculously survived three shots to the head in a bungled hit and scurried for the shelter of the Program. When it was his turn to testify in 1985, he claimed among many interesting tidbits to have paid Hanhardt for protection of his gambling rackets.

That was at the height of Hanhardt's power and prestige in the CPD. Anybody who wanted to take on Hanhardt would need a lot more than stray allegations from federal snitches. But the Bureau started getting even more careful than usual in their dealings with the CPD.

The relationship between the FBI and the local department is historically uneasy; coppers consider the G-men to be prima donnas who share nothing, and the feds think the local flatfeet are all in the mob's pocket. Those caricatures still occasionally disrupt an essential working relationship that goes through periodic highs and lows. The two agencies have different missions and different cultures, and

*a common enemy is not always enough to reconcile them. The rela-
tionship was cooling in the mid-1980s as the Bureau started looking
into the links between Hanhardt and James D'Antonio. By the time
Jimmy D. died of injuries sustained when his car slammed into an
abutment on the Edens Expressway in 1993, the Bureau had a pretty
good idea that the heist crew he left behind included a certain retired
Chicago police heavyweight.*

⌇

The FBI tried to get me to beef on Bill. They said, "Here's what
we're gonna do for you. You'll keep your pension, you ain't going
to jail, and you stay where you want. We just want him."

In other words, beef on Bill Hanhardt and your problems are
over.

Look at the deal they offered me. My pension. That's forty-
eight hundred dollars a month. No jail time. My son keeps his job.
How good was that?

It ain't in me. I couldn't do that.

It's not out of fear. I don't beef because it's not in me. If, God
forbid, a man raped my mother, I wouldn't say he did it. I'd bond
him out. And then I'd show you what I'd do with this guy. I don't
need you. I'll take care of him. Different rules.

I says, "Bill Hanhardt? The greatest guy I know. I don't know
a better man."

He says, "Well, we want him. And we know you know about
him. You want your pension?"

That was it. I could have had no jail, no conviction, my pension. That's how strongly they wanted him.

I says, "I can't do nothing for you, buddy. I can't tell you nothing but good things about that man."

"Your case will go away, your pension will stay."
"But if you want me to lie, and make up something, I'll do it."
"No, no, no."
I says, "That's all I can do for you."
That was it. That was the end.

39

DEMISE

Vince told me to quit before the indictment, because it's not as strong an impact on the papers. "If I'm you, I resign. Because you're gonna get indicted. But the indictment isn't as strong if you're off the job—it says '*former* policeman.' If it says 'policeman,' that hits the front page." And he was right.

I retired in November 1993. My retirement party was in December. They had the Christmas decorations in the place. It was in Schiller Park, Illinois, at the Starlight Inn on Lawrence and Mannheim, top of the building. Beautiful place. The police parties were held there. I got deals like you never seen. The ticket sellers were Bill Hanhardt and my brother Dicky. And we ran out of tickets. We had to print forty more tickets. I wanted five hundred, they had five hundred and forty people. Full house.

Tom Dreesen the comedian was host—this guy toured with Sinatra. Dreesen's from Chicago; I met him through Dennis Farina, when he asked me to get some guys and be the security for a big fundraiser, a charity thing Dreesen did for multiple sclerosis. And we just laughed, and we had more fuckin' fun. Dreesen was so good. He had everybody bow their heads like he was gonna give the invocation, and he says, "We're here in a room filled with half cops and half robbers, and we're here to honor a man who was both a cop and a robber." Guys were laughing their asses off.

When I got off the job I bought this big house in Skokie and we moved there. My daughter was married and she had her own place. She could have come with us; we had a big enough house. Rocky stayed with us, Joey stayed, then Joey moved out, so it was Rocky and us.

At the Crazy Horse we were making, between us, half a million a year. Perry gave me a check, three thousand a week. With deductions, of course. Then I included myself with the tips, because I made the tip envelopes for all the guys, and I gave myself one, too. So there would be six, seven hundred a night. And May was doing twelve hundred, fifteen hundred a week. I kept the cash. We could have paid for the house with that, but no. I made the payments from the police check, every month.

And then the indictment came in May of '94. And I was a dead goner.

At my arraignment in the Dirksen Building, the US marshal in charge of things was Joe DiLeonardi, the old acting superintendent of the CPD under Mayor Byrne. He didn't like Hanhardt, and Hanhardt hated him too. Bill, in front of me, says to him, "You're a two-bit no good motherfucker. I should break your fuckin' nose." And DiLeonardi left.

I said, "Sure, *you* could tell him that. But you know who he's gonna remember. Me, not you."

And sure enough, at the arraignment, DiLeonardi made me sit there all night. Everybody got out but me. He just fucked with me. This is when you're making your bond, after you're read the charges. You go to the room. And then you sit there. They print you, they take your picture, and you sit. No handcuffs, but it's a locked room. And they got holding cells in the back. And then if you don't make bond, they transport you to the MCC—the Metropolitan Correctional Center, the federal jail on Van Buren. And that's your final destination. You're gonna sit there until your court hearing, which is what I thought I was gonna do, because I seen what DiLeonardi was up to. Everybody made their bonds but me. They kept me sitting there till the last minute. And the guard, who was a retired policeman, told me, "DiLeonardi's keeping you here." I just sat there for maybe fourteen hours. Just sitting there, like a fuckin' mope. Finally, "You're ready to go. Signature bond, we want you to sign here." So I didn't have to come up with money for a bond, and I didn't have to go to MCC.

↬

Vince started looking at the case, which he told me was grim, because of the paper trail. He says, "We gotta work on the length of time."

The trial was in March 1995. Thirty-one witnesses testified who were all indictees. They got out by testifying against me. I decided during the trial I had better take Vince's advice and plead guilty. I said, "You know, you're right. We can't win this."

The day I was sentenced there was no snow, but it was cold. My wife, I didn't want her there. I didn't want the kids there—I didn't want nobody there. Well, as it turned out, friends came. My mother was there. I didn't want her to be there, but Dicky brought her. Billy didn't come, but his oldest son came. And we were in the hall, and this older black lady gets off the elevator. She's got a print dress and a dress hat, and she's made up nice. And she got close and I know her. I said, "Look at this woman." She came right up to me and gave me a big hug. She says, "They told me you was here. I'm gonna talk to the judge."

It was Mrs. Chester, the woman from the Ida B. Wells projects. That was like repayment. Vince put her on the stand as a character witness and she proceeded to tell the judge what a wonderful human being I was, all the help, the groceries and the cash gifts. I had tears in my eyes. She said, in her own words, I'm a good guy. What a mistake that was—I'm a good guy? My mom sat with her holding her hand and thanked her and told her how much it meant to me.

The judge sentenced me to two years for one count of mail fraud and a small fine. I got lucky with the fine. When the US attorney says, "What about the $250,000 fine?" the judge says, "He's been punished enough. The time, the loss of his pension, the loss of his job, everything. He's punished enough."

And the guy screamed. "Your Honor!"

The judge told him: "You don't scream at me. You address the court in a proper way. I'm the judge. By law I must sentence him for the guidelines. But the fine, that's up to me. And he's not getting fined." So we got saved $250,000. The judge gave me a couple of months to get my business in order, and then I had to turn in.

Bill Hanhardt, the day I was sentenced, he says, "I'm gonna be east. Call me when you're done, I'll meet you by Gene & Georgetti's, we'll have lunch."

"What, to celebrate me going to jail?"

So I go see him, just him and me. We're in Gene & Georgetti's, he says, "Well, what did you get?"

"Two years."

He says, "What the fuck you hot about? You owe them twenty years."

When I was going to jail, I grabbed all my kids, one at a time. "Nicole, I gotta talk to you. I did something bad. I'll never do it again, because I'm gonna pay for it."

And she cried. "Are you sure you did it? You're not taking it for nobody else?"

"No. It's me."

Rocky, I know he holds grudges. I said, "Don't get mad at the FBI. Get mad at me. I'm no good."

"Don't say that."

"Well, what I did was no good. This is my fault. What I did was wrong. I don't want you to be mad at the FBI. Because they did their job. Those people are good for our country. They're here to protect us. It's my fault. Be mad at me. I made a mistake; it ain't gonna happen again."

I let them know. I don't want them to be like me.

I did wrong. And I knew it. That was greed. When everything was going good, when I was making money, it was OK. But I got caught. My demise was my own ways, my recklessness and greed.

40

AN OXFORD MAN

To me, prison was bad; it was part of the downfall. But it wasn't the worst thing. It's the ramifications. They fired my son, took my pension, put me in the crime book, put me in the Black Book in Nevada. I'm in every book there is. Give me five years and forget about this nonsense.

The pension board was a whitewash. The whole eight- or nine-person panel voted against me. So that's rigged. So now we go to court, we sue the city. We based our case on Kenneth Cullen's. He was a patrolman from the Thirteenth District, and he murdered a guy in a traffic violation. He got in an argument, road rage, and a twenty-two-year-old kid lost his life, because Cullen blew his brains out. He got twenty-five years for that, first-degree murder. And they tried to take his pension. He said, "I was off-duty." And he got his pension.

In my case, Lester Foreman was the judge, and he says, "No way. He gets his pension." The law was on my side. If you use your badge or your office as a policeman to help the crime, that means you lose your pension. With me it was insurance fraud. So how was I a policeman? I was off when it happened.

So now the city appealed it on the twenty-ninth day. You have thirty days to appeal. They waited till the last day, they appealed it. There was a three-man board. One guy recused himself. I knew his brother, so he didn't want to make the decision. The other two stayed, and they replaced him with a black woman. I says, "I'm roasted."

Guess what? She voted for me, the two white guys voted against me. They said, "This guy Cullen had one incident of passion. Pascente's life was crime."

And I jumped up. "OK, so we could murder a fuckin' . . ." Just like that I told them. "This is a roast if I ever seen it." But that was it.

And then the Illinois Supreme Court. Eddie Vrdolyak was trying to help me with this. He knew the chief justice, Charles Freeman. He wouldn't touch it. He says, "I won't hear it, but that'll give him the opportunity to go forward."

OK, so you know what my next step is? US Supreme Court. Who's got a million dollars to go and fight that? That's how they got me.

⏤

I was supposed to turn in in April 1995. Then I says, "How about in May?"

"OK. Yeah, that's fair." They continued the bond. I went in the next month.

The day I turned in, May didn't sleep all night. I slept like a baby. I get up, I shower; she's doing this, she's doing that. "I got you this, you could eat on the way. I got you Gene & Jude hot dogs, you could eat on the way." All my favorites. "I got you the Fannie May turtles. Eat on the way."

I said, "How much am I gonna fuckin' eat on the way?"

Nicole came. She stayed at the house. Joey came. They were all there. Billy's wife came. She says here, take some money."

I says, "I don't need no money, Phyllis. I don't need it."

Bill Hanhardt shows up. Skippy from the Crazy Horse shows up, Perry shows up. My brother Dicky. Mickey Caplan, the lawyer. How many guys we got? We got one car.

May was a wreck. I says, "May, don't worry."

Dicky says, "I'm here. Whatever you want, I'll get it. You need the kids disciplined, whatever. I'll do anything you want." And he was good.

I says, "I'll see you." And they're all crying. I says, "Look at this. You make me feel worse. Come on, make me feel I'll be fine over there. They ain't gonna torture me, they ain't gonna whip me. This is just another place to live. That's it."

I said good-bye. "I'll be home in no time. Don't worry about it."

Saying good-bye to my kids killed me.

ᔆ

Bill Hanhardt, Mickey Caplan, and my brother Dicky drove me up there to Oxford. It was a rural area. You're going on Route 51, and it's all dairy farms—you're in Wisconsin. It was a nice day. In fact I told Hanhardt, "Slow down. I got a lot of time to be up here. I want to enjoy the scenery." You got up until the end of the workday, five o'clock, to report. We got there in time. It's not fenced in, because this was the minimum security camp. You drive up to a brick building, all one story. They had four wings—that's where all the rooms were.

I said good-bye; they couldn't come in. I shook hands, hugged them, kissed them, and they're on their way. And I was on my way. You go in through the door, and there is a guard. I told him,

"I'm coming in to turn in. My name is . . ." Gentleman as I am, I always was. They know you're coming. They got the big folder.

"Go sit in there." All cold. I had a little bag, which they took away. I had shaving things and a toothbrush and stuff like that. The first thing I did was sign in and answer questions, go through a bunch of rules. Then he took me to the supply room. He says, "All right, tell this guy what you need."

The guy in the supply room was real stern. "Yes, sir. I'll get you your size . . ." This and that.

The guard leaves. Now the supply room guy says, "I'm gonna put you in with Dvorak and Fred Roti, they said you were coming." I had a dozen guys waiting for me. He says, "You're gonna be in a good wing, don't worry about a thing. What size clothes?" I told him. It made you feel a little more comfortable.

He says, "You're gonna be in a temporary room until you get through with your physicals and everything." I didn't get the physical for two weeks. I put the bedding in the room. There was another guy in the room. I put the bedding in there, and I went back to the guard, sat with him, and he starts giving me rules.

He says, "You're gonna be doing a temporary job. Eventually you're gonna have a regular job. But for now you're gonna be doing A wing, and you're gonna mop with the guys."

So now I'm all set, I got the room. He says, "You gotta stand for count. You gotta be in your room and at attention when the guards come and count."

But before that I see Roti. He tells me he got me in their wing. Then I see Dvorak, and I see Blackie Pesoli, and I see all the guys. They're all coming, and I feel good. Roti says, "You eat by our side. Now, tomorrow morning, we have the count, and then we walk. Then we go read. Then you do your job."

In Chicago just as anywhere else, being an Oxford man confers distinction. The medium security Federal Correctional Institution in Oxford, Wisconsin, may not be the most feared federal penitentiary (it generally makes the lists of "country club" federal joints), but it has to be near the top for distinguished alumni. When former Illinois governor George Ryan was convicted on federal bribery charges in 2006, it was to Oxford that he reported, the latest in a procession of Land of Lincoln miscreants caught with their hands in the cookie jar.

Former alderman Fred Roti may actually have been more powerful than an Illinois governor until his RICO indictment in 1992 sent him to Oxford, where he pined for the comforts of Booth One at Counsellors Row while eating prison food off plastic trays. Roti did three years at Oxford and then toiled in a work release program with the Salvation Army before expiring in 1999.

Blackie Pesoli was a jack-of-all-trades, a policeman whose nominal job was to oversee security at the old Greyhound bus station on Randolph Street in the Loop but who spent most of his time brokering fixes in traffic court, running dice games and sports books, and managing fighters (including the tragic Jumbo Cummings, who got as far as fighting Joe Frazier to a draw before going away to prison for life on a three-strikes robbery conviction). Pesoli was KO'd on federal perjury charges when he lied to a federal grand jury about bribes he had taken to fix a divorce case in Chicago. His influence in the court system, astounding for a mere CPD patrolman, earned him a year in rural Wisconsin.

James Dvorak was a CPD homicide dick who took a leave of absence from the department to help his friend Jim O'Grady run for Cook County sheriff as a Republican in 1986. O'Grady surprised everyone by winning, and he made Dvorak the undersheriff, giving him power over patronage and contracts. Dvorak went down in 1993 when he pleaded guilty to taking bribes and hiding money from the

IRS. He avoided conviction, however, on a charge that had dogged him since a tape surfaced in 1989 on which Cicero Outfit boss Rocky Infelice could be heard indiscreetly murmuring about payoffs to Dvorak to shield gambling operations from harassment by the Sheriff's Department. The judge ruled that the government had failed to prove the allegation, and Dvorak was relieved to draw only forty-one months at Oxford.

ᗡᗡ

The fun we had in the prison.

There was a mailman who was in there for not delivering the mail. He didn't steal it, he just threw it away, he hid it. He was just lazy. I called him Rockhead.

We had mail call every night. So Rockhead, he's in the front. I'm in the back with my guys. So they call me, I got a letter. "Pascente!"

So here's Rockhead: "I'll get it for you, Fred."

"Fuck you, you never delivered the mail." The guard was laughing.

I'm in there a while, I know everybody. I got along with the black guys. I prevented a big riot once. You have two TV rooms. One is movies, one is sports. Playoffs—Bulls, Michael Jordan. I want to watch the Bulls. So I go, "We're gonna watch the Bulls." Well, these white guys, no. They want to fuck the black guys. "We're watching car racing." And they got the votes.

I said, "Are you guys crazy? I want to watch the Bulls. I get a headache from watching these races."

Well, they stood their ground. The blacks are up in arms. So I see this guy Archie. Big guy. He loved me. He said, "Fred, this ain't right. These motherfuckers . . ."

I says, "Give me five minutes. I'll get this thing square."

I know Father Kelly, the chaplain. I go see him. I says, "Father, I got a dilemma here. You got a TV in there. In the chapel. Is it possible you could let us watch the basketball game in there?" And I told him the story.

He says, "I'll let them watch the movie in here. You guys will be screaming, and the visitors will be hearing all that. The movies, they ain't gonna be screaming."

I go see the guys. "You guys in the movie room. You want to go in the chapel? It's more comfortable. Nicer chairs."

"Yeah." So the movie guys moved in, we go into the movie room, we watch the basketball game. Guess what? The white guys, they didn't want to watch the races no more. You believe it? They did it for spite.

Archie said, "Man, you got it done, Fred."

Yeah, I got it done, buddy. I got it done.

~

I had to tell May to stop coming to visit me. I loved to see her. She'd come every week or every other week, and she'd come with my mother, and she'd come with the kids. And she'd cry. And I'd say, "Listen. I don't want you coming here. Because it upsets you. I could talk to you on the phone. I don't want you here. It bothers me. Forget about it." And when they came, they saw how good I was. I was working out every day. I was in the weight program. I was benching 225, which is a lot for me. I was cut.

That was it. I did two years. It wasn't hard. It was nothing.

When I left, they changed the rules because of me. They gave you six hours to get from Oxford to the halfway house. Rick Rizzolo and Perry Mandera said, "We're gonna get you so you can spend some time with your wife before you go there. If you drive you're not gonna have any time."

So Rick and Perry picked me up in a helicopter. It was across the way; they landed it, they got the permission of the farmer over there, they worked it out. Now, you sign how you're getting to the halfway house. I says "by private vehicle." I didn't lie. It was a private vehicle. After me they changed it. Car, no helicopter. I changed the rule.

These guys were laughing. "Look at this guy in the helicopter." They rented it. I don't know what it cost. That was nice.

41

THE END

I went back to the Crazy Horse after I got out of prison. I was doing real good there. Everything was on all cylinders. I had the big house in Skokie. Everybody was living good, my family. And then they took it away from me. Out of jealousy.

I'm running the place as usual, and Joe Lombardo wanted me to put his brother Rocco to work. And Perry says no. "Can't do it. I got enough trouble with you. You don't know the trouble I have keeping this license."

The brother was not a convicted felon at this point. He'd been convicted of a misdemeanor. But it's Lombardo's brother, and he was arrested with Michael Spilotro on a couple of things. So I don't want him. I says, "Hey, Rocky. You can't work here. It's not me. Perry don't want you. I cannot do it." And he went and squawked.

Now Joe is pissed. So they come up with this coup.

They had tried to put the arm on me before I was in prison. They wanted to muscle Perry. I know their game, and I told them,

313

"You can't mess with this guy. Number one, it's not my place, so I'm not the one to say, 'Well, here, you get so much.' It's not mine. It's his place, Perry's. So you guys want to do it, do it on your own. You can't use me, because this is a friend, he gave me the job. And number two, Vrdolyak is part of it"—Perry would give money to a lot of politicians. So I told them, "Listen. Do yourself a favor. Don't mess with this guy."

So now, because I didn't help them, the focus is on me. And Lombardo put the bad word to get me out of there. Vrdolyak found out, and he went to Perry and told him that there's problems with Freddy. He says, "Lombardo is squawking like hell. You don't want trouble with Lombardo. So if he don't want Fred there, get rid of him."

They did it real slick. One morning I'm at work, at the Crazy Horse, like I'm always there, five in the morning. I'd get all the money, and I'd do the accounts. The phone rings. It's Rick Rizzolo, in Vegas. He says, "You're a candidate for the Black Book in Nevada."

I says, "What? How the fuck could I be a candidate?"

"Freddy. I'm not kidding you. It was in the paper, the *Las Vegas Review-Journal*."

He sent me a copy of the newspaper. And there it is. I'm a candidate for entry into the book. I call him back, I says, "What are we gonna do?"

"Don't worry about it. I got John Momot. A real good lawyer. He'll take care of it."

"OK. Just tell me when I gotta come there, tell me what I gotta do."

That was it. They had many hearings, and there's a lot of newspaper clippings on that. But in the end, I went in the Black Book. There's only fifty guys ever hit it. And I'm one of them?

THE END

That was the end of '97. And they used that as the premise. Lombardo had his lawyers write a letter on behalf of Rick, about me. The letter says, "I have to disassociate myself from Freddy because Freddy's in the Black Book. I have this license in Vegas to protect." Rick never signed it. They just had his name printed on the bottom. Up until today he denies it. "I never wrote that letter."

But Perry got the letter. Now, he knows the scenario with Vrdolyak and Lombardo. He says to Rick, "You stay. I'll find something else for Freddy." Which he never did. So eventually they got rid of my wife, my son, anybody connected to me. That was all Lombardo's doing.

Rick has made statements to other people saying, "They really waylaid that Freddy." It's all Lombardo, because I didn't give his brother a job. And I couldn't. I couldn't give it to him. The owner didn't want him. What am I supposed to do? And he couldn't accept that. He thought that I could do magic, just like when I got Milwaukee Phil's son out of the army. That's magic. He thought I could continue the magic. I can't do it.

These guys were always good to me. Until the end, when you can't do nothing for them. I mean, they do an about-face that's second to none.

༄

On October 19, 2000, the US attorney in Chicago announced the indictment of six defendants on charges of racketeering conspiracy and conspiracy to transport stolen property in interstate commerce in connection with the theft of more than five million dollars' worth of jewelry over a period of several years. The indictment named William Hanhardt as the "leader of the criminal enterprise." According to the feds, Hanhardt had directed his coconspirators in the surveillance of potential victims, using police department resources to gather information about jewelry salesmen and their movements, as well as participating in some of the thefts himself.

The indictment polarized observers of the police scene in Chicago. A chorus of I-told-you-so's rose on one side and attempts to explain, mitigate, and excuse on the other. Hanhardt had grown bored in retirement; he had finally succumbed to fatal temptation after long association with the underworld; he had been set up by the feds. Supporters, including many police officers with spotless reputations, pointed to his ruthless effectiveness as a division chief and claimed that outweighed any wrongdoing.

A long-serving and highly respected retired officer says, "Bill was a tough cop who was not afraid to make Outfit guys informants. He saw the clout that these people had and tried to trade with them, which eventually got him involved with the First Ward. Why he went on the jewelry scores is another story, but he has paid for that. He had a good heart and helped a lot of honest policemen. He was the classic stand-up guy. He even helped those who shouldn't be helped. Aside from his alleged Outfit problems he was a policeman's policeman. Unmatched in our generation.

"There was an incident when an Outfit guy broke a straight [non-Outfit] guy's jaw over a woman. Hanhardt knew that the guy would end up in a trunk if he beefed, so Hanhardt made the Outfit guy pay the guy's medical bills and promise not to mess with him. It may not have been kosher, but was it wrong in Chicago the way things were? The police department was filled with empty-holster guys. You can say what you want about Bill, but he was not one of them."

Whatever the case, William Hanhardt pleaded guilty in October 2001 to charges of racketeering conspiracy and interstate theft. At the plea hearing one of his daughters confronted an assistant US attorney, accusing him of carrying out a vendetta against her father. Hanhardt's plea came a week after he took twenty OxyContin tablets *in the middle of the night in a suicide attempt, which was thwarted by his wife's timely 911 call. In January 2002 he was sentenced to sixteen years in federal prison; the sentence was later reduced on appeal. During his prison term Hanhardt contended with multiple medical issues, including testicular cancer and congestive heart failure. He was released from prison in January 2012.*

To this day many people believe that William Hanhardt was the victim of a federal smear job.

∾

Bill Hanhardt knew Milwaukee Phil. I got that from Phil. And when I told Hanhardt about what I did for Phil in the army, he says, "You know, he's a very good friend of mine." There you go. It wasn't widely known that he was tight with him.

I never saw Bill do anything other than good police work, and insisting on us doing good police work. He stressed it at meetings— he wanted certain things done, and we did it. He was admired; we looked up to him. That was the way it was done. He was a solid investigator. Nobody could put it together like him. He was good. Because he knew the names. He knew who worked in this crew, who worked in that set, who worked there, who worked here. Bill was good, buddy.

∾

On February 21, 2003, Chicago Tribune columnist John Kass reported that Nicholas Calabrese had gone into the Federal Witness Protection Program and was talking to the FBI. Nicholas had been in jail since 1997 along with his brother Frank Sr. and his nephews Frank Jr. and Kurt Calabrese. The family had run an extensive juice loan operation for the Outfit's Chinatown crew until the FBI bagged them with a RICO indictment in 1995. Over the next two years tantalizing hints emerged that an Outfit snitch was doing real damage by talking to the feds. On April 25, 2005, the Justice Department announced the indictment of fourteen defendants in a case they called Family Secrets. Unlike previous federal cases against individual Outfit members, this one treated the Outfit as a criminal enterprise under the RICO statute, applying the law's broad powers to bring racketeering charges against the leaders of the enterprise. The indicted included Joe Lombardo and Frank Schweihs, both of whom disappeared before federal agents could arrest them.

Schweihs had gone to prison for extortion in 1989, after he bragged obliquely about the killings of two porno theater owners on an FBI tape. But he was out of jail and living in Dania Beach, Florida, in April 2005 when he slipped Bureau surveillance and went underground after his indictment in the Family Secrets trial. He was finally tracked down in Berea, Kentucky, in December and brought back to Chicago. Severed from the main Family Secrets trial because of his ill health, he would die in a Chicago hospital in July 2008, escaping conviction one final time.

Lombardo, meanwhile, remained on the run until January 2006, when he was nabbed after a visit to his dentist, Pat Spilotro, brother of Tony and Michael.

The trial riveted Chicago mob watchers in the summer of 2007. All but five defendants pleaded guilty, leaving Joe Lombardo, Frank Calabrese Sr., James Marcello, Paul Schiro, and ex-cop Anthony Doyle to face the jury. The parade of witnesses included law enforcement figures, informants testifying after receiving immunity, and victims, including Danny Seifert's widow and son. Nick Calabrese took the stand in July and admitted to a series of murders, expressing regret. Lombardo, Calabrese, and Doyle took the stand in their own defense, to no good effect. On September 10 the jury handed down guilty verdicts for the racketeering charges; two weeks later they

*assigned responsibility for ten of the murders involved in the indict-
ment, including the killing of Seifert, which was attributed to Joe
Lombardo. James Marcello was convicted of the murders of Anthony
and Michael Spilotro. Calabrese, Lombardo, and Marcello were sent
away with multiple life sentences; the other defendants received sentences of between six months and twenty years.*

*Some observers called it the end of the Outfit. Others said that
was overly optimistic, considering how deeply rooted the culture of
corruption is in the Chicago power structure. The consensus seemed
to be that federal power had, at least, finally ended the assumption of
impunity with which Outfit bosses had operated for so long.*

*A mark of the feds' success is that in the second decade of the
twenty-first century nobody can say who the top boss of the Outfit is.*

⌇⌇

The Outfit that we knew is dead. I credit the FBI. That's the truth.
It took a lot of time, but they knocked them down. They knocked
them out of the box. At one time, my God, who wanted to mess
with these guys?

It used to be they had five or six groups that ran the whole
Chicagoland area. It's probably only one today. Years back, they
were into gambling, but the gambling has waned, because you can
gamble over the Internet now. Now they work on drugs, and they
work on criminal activity. If you're a crook, a burglar, you gotta
come in and pay your dues. You make a score, you gotta bring it
to them.

So they don't have a handle on things. The last of the old-time
guys don't want to hear nothing from nobody. One of them put
his grandson to work running his business in Melrose Park, and
he goes to his farm. He's got a big farm, he's got animals, he goes
to the lake, that's it. If you see him, he says hi. He don't want to

know nothing. Another guy owns restaurants. And that's all he does. He goes to the restaurant. I say, "Hey, what's going on?" He says, "Absolutely nothing."

Today, there's outlaw guys. There's a guy who answers to nobody. Oh, *madonn'*, this is a bad-ass guy. All the burglars in his area gotta pay him. They make a score, they gotta bring it to him. If he finds out about it some other way, they got a problem. Because he knows all the burglars, and they're all afraid of him. And he don't give nothing to nobody. He's all for himself. And that's the way it is. The Outfit as we knew it is dead.

The CPD changed, too. It weeded out a lot of the guys like me. The job of a policeman is to serve the public and protect them. To protect the citizens and their property. From criminals—like me. I was there to protect people. That was my job, and I did my job. I crossed the line by favoring people that I knew or favoring people that came up with money. That was a mistake, but that was the way it was. There is no justification for taking money. It's criminal.

I have regrets about the stealing. Especially from a person that's in need. I regret that more than anything. The little guys. I took from them, and I'm sorry for it. I really am truly sorry. Now, a bank, an insurance company, no. I have no regrets. Because they don't miss it.

I never felt regret about doing what I did. But I wound up in jail. I didn't feel it until then. I felt terrible. "Motherfucker, I should have been bigger than this." Because I'm smarter than that. But I'm not going to blame the environment, because I was part of it, too. I knew what I was doing.

We grew up and we saw these guys who had everything. I was in a neighborhood with all criminals, and I jumped right in. I wanted to be part of them—I saw the money. They had power, and whatever they said by the snap of a finger they got. They made decisions, and they helped people, but they hurt people, too. And that's who I looked up to, and it brought me down.

～

I got on my feet after Crazy Horse. My cousin Nick LaCalamita, Uncle Nick's grandson, wanted someone to run a nightclub in Florida, South Beach. He was a guy with money. "There's a place, and we'll buy it." It was called the Living Room.

I go to Florida, and it was a loser. It went down. I lost everything. My house was taken. All my good friends who gave me money. Everybody who helped me went down. My brothers, my wife's mother, they all helped me with it. It was my fault. I should have never tackled it. That wasn't my game. My game was the strip club. This was just glamour, this and that, the topless beaches. But two years, and it went down. Lost everything.

～

And there you go. That's how you wind up at age seventy-two broke with no pension, watching the interstate reel past in the middle of the night. The money's just a memory, like the guys. Chuckie Nicoletti, dispatched by three shots to the back of the head in his idling Cadillac, fifty years after he pulled the trigger on his old man and thirty after he bought a bunch of neighborhood kids some bats and balls. Dinger Carusiello, bleeding out in the gangway between two houses, shot to seal his lips about the Judas kisses he had planted on his friends. Allen Dorfman, an impeccably dressed corpse cooling in a motel parking lot. Herbie Blitzstein, ambushed by minor-league mobsters from Buffalo looking to grab rackets that didn't amount to much. Tony Spilotro, perhaps getting religion as the gloved hands clap onto him, watching his brother go down with a rope around his neck.

Not all of them are dead. Joe Lombardo sits staring at cinder block walls in a federal prison in North Carolina, six hundred miles from the Ohio Street apartment he will never see again, just across the street from the Mitchell School playground. Bill Hanhardt, an old, sick ex-con, contemplates the ruin of his reputation from his home in the northern Chicago suburbs. There aren't a lot of happy endings in a life of crime.

Not for the criminals, and not for the victims. The victims of organized crime, of course, are not the tough guys who get whacked for breaking the rules. The real victims are the minimum-wage toilers in hock for life to the loan sharks, the small business owners muscled out of the fruits of their labors, the insurers taking a hit for a warehouse cleaned out by thieves, the public that pays a little more for everything because of pervasive corruption. Crime does bad things to cities; it does bad things to people.

All things considered, Fred Pascente came out OK.

ᔕ

My wife and kids are my whole life. I'm married to May all these years—this is still my girlfriend. I joke with her, I have fun. She stood with me one hundred percent, through everything. They took my pension; they put me in every book there is. There was never nothing, no problem, between me and her.

My kids are great. Joey does promotions for nightclubs, he fills up the joint, he gets an end of the take. Joey's very sharp. He's in sports, he plays softball, plays basketball. Works out, takes care of himself. Nicole, my daughter, she's great, a hard worker. She's in the medical field, medical billing. She works two jobs, that girl. She's got two kids. And Rocky, that's my heart. Rocky runs the produce department at Whole Foods. Rocky was a great basketball player. You never seen a guy in shape like this. He's iron. He runs from where he lives to Foster Avenue Beach and back. But he's a sweet kid. He's really a good kid.

Regrets? I'd have did it different, buddy. I never would have got caught. But the guys I knew, I loved them guys. I wouldn't change that for nothing.

⌒

In one respect you have to term Fred Pascente's life a success: he grew up to be one of the guys he admired. Or close, anyway; if he didn't attain full gangster status like his friend Tony Spilotro, you have to say that's to his credit. Fred didn't have that last measure of ruthlessness, that complete suppression of conscience that you need to rise to the top of the profession. Maybe he would have if things had gone a little differently here or there, if the temptation had been great enough. Who's to say? For that matter, maybe he would never have been a criminal at all if things had gone differently—if his father had lived, if he hadn't dropped out of school, if he had fallen in with different guys . . .

People are complicated, even if the rules are simple. We're allowed to judge; we have to, in fact. We have to teach our children right and wrong and insist they follow the rules. But we should judge with humility.

Fred Pascente got out of the rackets. He may have had his regrets, but he didn't do remorse. It could have gone a lot worse. He may not have had his pension, but he had his family and he had his health, and that's more than a lot of guys wound up with. At seventy-two years old he was still a working man, but that meant he was still a man.

Maybe more of a man than ever before.

⌒

One time a few years ago Joe Lombardo was sitting in Rosebud restaurant on Taylor Street, and I walked in there with Mikey Swiatek and Danny the Greek. Danny's a neighborhood guy, a big-time burglar. He did twenty calendar years. This guy never would beef, nothing. He's just a stand-up guy.

Lombardo was sitting there with a couple of guys, and Mikey went up to him and said hello. And they're talking, and Lombardo says, "There ain't many tough guys left in our neighborhood, huh?"

And Mikey says, "There's only three of us. Danny, me, and Freddy." And he walked away.

AFTERWORD

On September 22, 2014, while this book was in production, Fred Pascente passed away following a severe stroke suffered nearly a month before. He was seventy-two years old.

When an acquaintance of mine, a retired police officer, e-mailed me in August of 2011 asking if I would be interested in sitting down with an Outfit-connected ex-policeman who was looking for a writer to help him do a book, I said yes, with some trepidation. I was a novelist; I'd never done nonfiction and I knew there would be a learning curve. Further, in doing research for my crime novels I had always relied on law enforcement sources. I had never met an actual professional criminal and wasn't entirely sure I wanted to.

The last line of the e-mail read: "He's a nice guy." That piqued my curiosity; we were talking about a hoodlum, weren't we? I gave it a little thought and decided I had to at least meet him.

A couple of weeks later Fred and I and our mutual friend met for breakfast at a north suburban pancake house, and after the handshakes and the chit-chat and the sounding each other out, Fred got down to talking about his life. I was immediately hooked by his story. This was a man who had rubbed elbows with the Outfit his whole life, been close to some of its most notorious figures, and protected its interests as a serving police officer. It was the story of a Chicago that appalls us and fascinates us at the same time.

Fred told it all with his characteristic self-deprecating humor, stopping at intervals to banter and flirt with the waitresses or shake hands with friends passing by the table. Of course, he picked up the check. I still wasn't quite sure what to make of him, but I knew that there was an interesting project here that I would be foolish to pass up. We agreed to begin work as soon as I had spoken to my agent about preparing a collaboration agreement.

Over the succeeding months we met every Saturday and Fred talked for a couple of hours into a digital recorder. At our first meeting he said, "Sam, I'm going to tell you everything. We'll worry about what we can and can't say later." Ultimately we decided that we could and should just tell the truth, regarding just about everybody. There were some names and some incidents that Fred insisted on leaving out, often to spare the feelings of family members who were not criminals. He was frank about his own misdeeds; he was frank about the culture of corruption that he participated in with enthusiasm. He did not wallow in remorse but neither did he make excuses.

Aware that I was talking to a career criminal, I took everything with a grain of salt. I fact-checked and cross-checked what I could. I don't think Fred ever lied to me; on a couple of occasions I caught him out in memory lapses, and on a couple of others I got him to expand a little on things he obviously wasn't proud of. Of course, I had to take a lot of it on trust. Subsequently a very competent editor and fact-checker at Chicago Review Press turned up mistakes and inconsistencies I had missed. If there are untruths left in these pages, I welcome the efforts of others to expose them.

AFTERWORD

Fred Pascente was generous, funny, courteous, and good-humored, if a little rough around the edges sometimes. He was a loved and loving husband and father. He was, indeed, a nice guy. That's not the same as being a good man. But it counts for something that Fred made an effort to come clean and let other people pass judgment.

ACKNOWLEDGMENTS

Sam Reaves would like to acknowledge the generous contributions of Arthur Bilek and Bruce Clorfene in the preparation of this book.

The blog *Second City Cop* at http://secondcitycop.blogspot.com provided useful background material, as did the following books:

Coen, Jeff. *Family Secrets: The Case That Crippled the Chicago Mob.* Chicago: Chicago Review Press, 2009.

Demaris, Ovid. *Captive City: Chicago in Chains.* New York: Lyle Stuart, 1969.

Lindberg, Richard C. *To Serve and Collect: Chicago Politics and Police Corruption from the Lager Beer Riot to the Summerdale Scandal, 1855–1960.* Carbondale: Southern Illinois University Press, 1998.